D0906172

French Dive

French Dive

Living More with Less in the South of France

ERIC FREEZE

SLANT

FRENCH DIVE
Living More with Less in the South of France

Copyright © 2020 Eric Freeze. All rights reserved. Except for brief quotations in critical publications or reviews, no part of this book may be reproduced in any manner without prior written permission from the publisher. Write: Permissions, Wipf and Stock Publishers, 199 W. 8th Ave., Suite 3, Eugene, OR 97401.

Slant
An Imprint of Wipf and Stock Publishers
199 W. 8th Ave., Suite 3
Eugene, OR 97401

www.wipfandstock.com

HARDCOVER ISBN: 978-1-7252-6615-5
PAPERBACK ISBN: 978-1-7252-6614-8
EBOOK ISBN: 978-1-7252-6616-2

Cataloguing-in-Publication data:

Names: Freeze, Eric.

Title: French dive : living more with less in the south of France. / Eric Freeze.

Description: Eugene, OR: Slant, 2020.

Identifiers: ISBN 978-1-7252-6615-5 (hardcover) | ISBN 978-1-7252-6614-8 (paperback) | ISBN 978-1-7252-6616-2 (ebook)

Subjects: LCSH: Nice (France) -- Description and travel. | France -- Nice. | France -- Social life and customs. | Travelers' writings, Canadian -- France. | Spear fishing.

Classification: PR9199.4.F7375 F71 2020 (print) | PR9199.4.F7375 (ebook)

Manufactured in the U.S.A.   JULY 27, 2020

For Freeze FC

Contents

PART III: SURFACING

Part I

TAKEOFF

Once on the board, do not form the habit of hesitation.
—GERALD BARNES, *SWIMMING AND DIVING* (1922)

Chapter 1

Arrival

FOUR KIDS, AGES ONE TO SEVEN, two years apart—lines on a height chart like marks on a graph—arrived with Rixa and me at Indianapolis International Airport. We extracted ourselves from our friend's minivan, each child carrying one of four thrift store backpacks: army-green canvas, black with white stenciled basketballs, a red Speedo pack, partly waterproof. The last a clamshell brown with pink accents, the size of a hand purse. Our one-year-old Ivy toddled like an awkward Ninja Turtle. She would be in my hiking backpack for most of the trip but still it seemed important for her to have her own bag. Inside each bag were four sets of socks, four pairs of underwear, four individual toys for the two-day trip to Nice.

In the check-in line, we learned of a delay. Tornado warning. Potential flash flooding nearby. The gate agent said, "You're all on a flight for tomorrow." Our ride was already halfway back to Crawfordsville so we booked a hotel. What was one extra day when we'd be there a year? We checked our bags and now the individual backpacks seemed pure genius for our foresight.

The next morning, we had clear skies to Chicago, then on to Frankfurt. An immigration officer scrutinized our American and Canadian passports, our year-long French visas. I will be on sabbatical, I said. He nodded.

What I didn't say: we bought an apartment. We were potential immigrants. This year was our testing ground, to see if we could renovate a tiny apartment and live in it with our family of six. I didn't tell him that our apartment was the most expensive thing we had ever purchased, that in order to get a mortgage we had provided a document to the bank stating my full salary and not the half-salary we'd actually be living on. I didn't tell him that up until the day before our departure, the bank still hadn't finalized the processing of our loan. The notary wanted to delay the closing till the middle of August, leaving us homeless for a couple weeks. I didn't tell him about the emails between our bank, the notary, our real estate agent, and our mortgage broker that whizzed back and forth. Would it be possible for us to move in before closing? Unlikely, since we would have squatter's rights and could remain in the apartment for years without paying a cent. Would the notary accept a scanned PDF of the completed loan? No, the French government required the originals with your signatures and handwriting, *s'il vous plait*. And lots of complicated stamps.

I didn't tell him how then magically it was done; overnight express mail and emails reconvened closing and our coffers emptied into a French bank account. A scanned document declared us owners of a 700-square-foot apartment across from the Palais Lascaris in Old Nice. Our optimism regarding this singular feat eclipsed our financial fears. Where would the money come from? We didn't know and he didn't ask.

In Nice, the tempo slowed. The airstrip was like landing on the water. Palms swayed. It was the second of August, and the heat sapped energy from the crowds. We rolled our bags out to the curb, one by one. A Mercedes van pulled up. A man shook my hand. We were thinking of taking the bus, I said. "With all these bags? Non, non, monsieur." The pneumatic hatch shushed when it opened and the taxi driver piled our bags inside. Our kids clicked their seatbelts. No car seats or boosters marred the black leather. Till now, my children had rarely heard another adult besides Rixa and me speak French. It was an intimate language, the language of bedtime stories and family meals. To have this burly man with his knitted black t-shirt, his hipster jeans and leather shoes, suddenly parlez-vous-ing felt invasive. How did this guy know the same language as Papa? We closed the doors. Air blew through the vents.

"Where to?"

"Old Nice," I said. "We just bought an apartment."

"You bought an apartment in Old Nice?" Silence. He pulled out into traffic: the famed Promenade des Anglais, the walkway of the English. Now the taxi driver played tour guide. We passed the Lenval hospital where year earlier Angelina Jolie gave birth to twins. "Imagine running into Brad Pitt at the bakery," he said. We passed the Negresco, where Isadora Duncan died, her scarf caught in the wheels of her car. Affectations can be dangerous.

Soon we turned up along the Place Masséna, skirting Old Nice. The driver tapped his hands on the steering wheel, more and more irritated the closer we got. "Old Nice, Old Nice. You know, couldn't pay me to live in Old Nice. Why would you ever buy there? You can't get in and out, the place is packed with tourists all day. I never can find parking."

Till now, everyone we knew had approved of our decision. His disdain took me aback. I explained: it was a different way of living. We wouldn't have a car. We would walk everywhere. The kids' school was right around the corner. A small grocery store was across the street. We would live more with less. All the exasperating logistics of buying our apartment and the precariousness of our finances were still forefront in my mind. It wasn't like we hadn't given this a lot of thought.

"A grocery in the Old Town? Maybe if you won the lottery you could afford it."

"There are two discount groceries within walking distance, cheap as you can find anywhere."

"And the noise. Have you thought about that? Just a few years ago, the place was dangerous—knife fights, prostitution. Not at all the kind of place for a family."

"But now there's the *coulée verte*, all the playgrounds, the *miroir d'eau*. Families go there all the time."

"You do what you want but you're going to regret it. Why didn't you buy in the Port neighborhood? That's the only truly Niçois neighborhood anymore. The only place where you can get real *socca*."

"We looked at the Port but it was further from the amenities we liked."

"Four kids in Old Nice." He held a hand to his head like a migraine was coming on.

He dropped us off at the Place Centrale. No way he was driving his Mercedes any further. Every car in Old Nice had a ding on its bumper, scrapes down the sides. "I have to back us up or I'll never get out of here," he said. The Place Centrale connected a grocery store, Lou Pilha Leva, a popular socca place, two other restaurants, and a realtor's office. It was 9 p.m.

and every bench and table and café was full. He inched his way through the crowds. Parked. Clicked his hazard lights on and flung open the doors. Our children clambered over the seats. The taxi driver piled our maximum ten allotted bags on the street. Passersby dodged them like they were dog poop.

"Good luck," he said. "Four kids in Old Nice. You guys have got to be crazy."

No worries. We were here. Our realtor Bart was supposed to meet us with the keys. The kids were whining, hungry after two days of sleep deprivation and airplane food. We trucked our bags in segments to the awning of a clothing store advertising blue-tinted beach dresses on sale. An Italian couple offered to help: where were we going? Thanks for asking but we didn't really know. We were nearer to our apartment than we thought, having deferred to the taxi driver's knowledge of Old Nice more than our own. Our kids munched on rolled-up portions of socca: the pancake-like Niçois street snack made out of chickpeas. We perched on our suitcases. Across the street diners sat on café chairs or wooden benches.

A Frenchman with a close-cropped beard power-walked his way through the crowds. Bart had the bearing and dexterity of a soccer player; at any moment he could cut down an alley or sprint after a fallen coin. We shook hands and he *bised* Rixa and patted our son Dio on the head. "The apartment's just up the street. Turn at the cannon ball." We slid Ivy into the baby backpack. Bart grabbed two of our suitcases. Our three-year-old Inga rolled a clacking carry-on across stone tiles. Bart pointed to the cannon ball. "Catherine Ségurane," he said. "Most powerful woman in Nice. Beat the Turks in the late 1500s. The cannon ball is from the siege." Three iron prongs attached it to the corner of the Rue Droite: the straight street that ironically wasn't straight. Soon we passed the Palais Lascaris, the aristocratic residence that now housed a museum of musical instruments. Now we stopped in front of a gray door: 18 Rue Droite. We were home.

Bart flipped through his keys. "Use the tiny key here," he said. "The fancy one is for the apartment. You should really go to the *syndic* to get a magnetic key."

The hallway and stairs were dingier than I remembered. A line of concrete about a foot wide extended all the way to the back wall, covering up a waste pipe. The yellow plaster walls were cracked and peeling. I carried two 50-lb suitcases and Ivy in the baby backpack. When we got to the fourth floor, I was winded. Bart opened the apartment and we all filed in. The kids careened around the empty living room in circles. Bart and I dropped bags and trudged back down the stairs for more.

The last bags up, Bart and I downed glasses of water. Rixa stood with her arms folded, looking up at the fourteen-foot ceilings and examining the white walls like she was in either the Sistine chapel or a maximum-security prison.

"It's smaller than I thought it would be," she said.

Till now, I was the only one who had physically seen the apartment. I had brought back video footage and a SIM card full of pictures but the only one who'd been here was me. The foyer led into a living room/kitchen bisected by a half-wall partition. To the left was a bedroom with a sink and a shower. A tiny hallway separated the front and back halves of the apartment. The back bedroom had lower ceilings. A wooden range hood from when it used to be a kitchen dangled over a bare mattress. Above the bedroom and cave-like back bathroom was an attic and storage space that qualified as another bedroom. But the bedrooms still had beds and dressers and linens from the apartment's time as a student rental. We could finally put our exhausted children to bed.

Outside the front window, a guitarist sang Johnny Cash's "Ring of Fire." The children were already upstairs in the attic, laying claim to their sleeping arrangements. Dio and Zari would fit nicely on the double mattress, Inga would be in the back bedroom and Ivy would sleep with Rixa and me in the front. It was only 700-square feet but everyone fit.

Bart said goodbye and wished us luck. We had business that could wait till next week. Get settled. Enjoy your new home.

Rixa started to put Ivy down and Inga was already zonked. Our two oldest were still energetic and I proposed taking them for a walk to give Rixa and Ivy some peace. "Make it quick," she said. She wanted to get to sleep too. Soon we were bounding down the stairs and out the front door.

It was past eleven and the streets were full. The Place Rosetti was lit up with crowds of tourists waiting for ice cream at Fennochio's. When I visited in March the façade of the Cathédrale St. Réparate was under renovation but now it was finished and the yellows and greens were day-glow bright.

Where the Rue Benoit Bunico met the Rue de la Préfecture, a street performer stretched a string with two batons. A bubble emerged. Zari and Dio stared and giggled. The man handed the batons to Zari and the string drooped like a smiling mouth. He showed her how to open it, to pull the batons through the air till a gigantic bubble built and then separated. We walked through the arcades. Soon we were on the Promenade des Anglais. The boardwalk was a necklace of light.

We climbed down the stone steps onto the rocky beach. Waves raked the pebbles. Circles of college kids passed around bottles of wine. *It's the ocean!* my children said and I didn't correct them. They picked up rocks the size of their fists and tossed them into the water. I wanted to tell them to remember this day, this first meeting of the sea, but I knew that the memory would blur with so many others over the next year.

We would come to this spot, following almost exactly our same route, carrying beach toys and snorkels and bottles of sunscreen and mats to lie out in the sun. The sea would change from a milky fluorescent blue to the gray of an overcast sky. Storms would bring water from the mountains and churn the water tan or brown. *You're going to regret it. Four kids in old Nice.*

As tourists emptied the beach of their sunburned bodies, we'd gradually become more visible, the residents who shouldn't be residents, the Nordic-looking family with their blond braids and smiling faces. Neighbors would register surprise—you're still here? We thought you were tourists! Our children would start school, wearing their secondhand clothes and talking French in the accent that they had inherited from me. We were academics in the humanities and this was the first time that we had moved somewhere deliberately, uprooted our family from everything familiar to come to this place with its narrow pedestrian streets and proximity to the mountains and sea. We couldn't know what would come: the challenges in school, the home renovations, the friends and visitors who would change the trajectory of our lives. But today? Today my kids laughed and squealed at each tiny wave lapping near their feet. This was the beginning. Each rock they tossed was like a wish or a promise, falling to the bottom of the sea.

Chapter 2

Nissa la Bella

NICE IS ONE OF THE OLDEST inhabited places in the world. Its first settlers, primitive hominids in search of the essentials for survival, found here a stream-fed plain, a sea abundant with fish, and grazing aurochs and rhinoceros. They built huts and used fire to cook their food. Paleolithic remains show that it was home to people on and off for thousands of years between 400,000 to 250,000 BC. A primitive paradise with all the trappings of civilization. It's no surprise that sixteenth-century frescoes in Old Nice depict it as the garden of Eden.

I imagine early ancestors arriving in the valley and plain that constitutes the Port, now full of luxury yachts. Where the shore met the sea, they found rocks and pebbles already shaped into forms that were useful for hunting. Chip a corner or break off an end and the fragments created tips for spears or blades for hatchets. The sun—endless sun—warmed their bodies as they cut bountiful saplings and arranged them into A-frame huts. And the fire. A fire burned in the middle of several dwellings, the first one of its kind ever found in continental Europe. A fire signified gathering and community. It meant an increase in hygiene, a group of people who weren't on the brink of starvation. A fire signified leisure, the prehistoric equivalent of having it all.

Nearby, the Lazaret cave tells of more recent inhabitants, cave dwellers who sheltered there from 170,000 to 90,000 years ago. The dates for both of these periods is immense. How much was the cave really used during that time? Archaeologists estimate that early hominids used it anywhere from a few days to seasons but never continually. In between intermittent habitation, giant carnivores fed in its hollow caverns, feasting on the same prey that the cave dwellers stalked and killed. During these many years, they were nomadic, the cave a place to return to. It was a summer hunting home that remained cool even in the long hot months.

The first permanent modern human civilizations in Nice were the Greeks and the Romans. The name "Nice" comes from Nikaia, the Greek word for victory. The name may commemorate a military success in the region. Or perhaps it's named after the Greek goddess of victory, Nike. Yet another theory believes it's because of a nearby freshwater spring called Nissé. Whatever the origin, the name has evolved during the years, from the Italian "Nizza" to the Nissart "Nissa" to the French "Nice," a designation that stuck after France's acquisition of the city in 1860.

The English word "nice" has an interesting corresponding evolution, beginning with its roots in the old French word "nice," meaning "foolish" or "ignorant." The connotation of the word carried into English, gradually morphing to "finicky" till about the mid-1700s when it started to mean pleasing or pleasant. The mid-1700s also signified the first interest in Nice by English aristocracy for winter vacations. It's impossible to know whether the English travel guides of the mid-to-late 1700s influenced the word's connotation but it's hard not to imagine that the bucolic representations of this sleepy medieval town had some effect. The following centuries in Nice saw an increase in tourism, first as a destination for English aristocracy and wealthy to now one of the most visited cities in the world. Nice is nice and it has been for a very long time.

When I tell people that I live in Nice, it provokes different reactions. They have an idea of the south of France that's idealized, an image that's lodged itself in our collective consciousness. On Facebook a while ago, a friend posted "29 Reasons You Should Never Go to the South of France," an internet meme employing a healthy dose of verbal irony. Each contrary description was accompanied by a postcard-worthy photo of southern France: fields of lavender, blue waters of the Mediterranean, the tiny perched villages of Provence. The level of detail reveals an author who likely doesn't know France that well, who is perhaps meme-ing the photos for some high school project or pay-per-post meme site. Several of the photos don't even come from the south of France. The photos of Cannes and St. Tropez aren't of Cannes or St. Tropez, and "Côte d'Azure" is misspelled, but the message is clear: the south of France is a beautiful destination and you are crazy if you do not try to go there. "Cannes? How Can U Not?"

Those Americans who have been to France often have a different impression of the Côte d'Azur. They have traveled over and over to Paris and think of Nice the way that New Yorkers think of Coney Island. Or Florida. It's a place with palm trees and boardwalks and ugly apartment buildings with views of the beach, a place where retirees go to warm their ossified joints, to soak up some vitamin D before they die.

Parisians come to Nice with a sense of entitlement. Nice, and all the azure coast, will never be Paris. It will never be the center of industry and culture. It is where you go when you want to escape the dreary weather, the endless *bouchons*—the corks or bottlenecks of cars. Parisians swoop down for Carnaval or during school vacations and complain that the sun is too strong, the pace of life too slow, the people too relaxed or *decontracté* and oblivious to their presence. They're not acknowledged by the Niçois, who, although friendly, are proud too, and that irritates the already irritated Parisians all the more. Most would switch jobs and move here in a second but it's not Paris, this Nice where it's sunny all the time. It's unnatural. And besides, down here their jobs don't exist.

Talk to the French who have made the move and they'll tell you why: the moderate climate, the combined proximity of mountains and the sea, the large urban center with its eclectic mix of nationalities. Soon we would meet our neighbors Sam and Vincent two floors down who moved from Paris to open a restaurant. Across the street, owners of a small organic food store also saw an opportunity for business and lifestyle that didn't exist back in the City of Lights. "We were always coming here for vacation," Sylvia said. "We bought the grocery with an apartment over top. I quit my job as a lawyer and moved seven years ago now."

Expats' stories are even more transformative. For them, Nice existed as a concept, an ideal. Maybe they had visited or studied in Nice for a period of time or came to Nice temporarily for an internship or a job. One family we met did a home exchange for a year and didn't want to leave. So they bought a home and started a business. He was a Stanford MBA grad and could have made millions through his connections in the states. "You can't find a place with a better quality of life," he said. Another family bought an apartment on the Cours Saleya a block from the beach. They moved from the overheated market in San Francisco. The money left over from the sale of their condo allowed them to buy their apartment outright. After that, friends came to visit and liked what they saw. So they helped another family move, then another. Now their building is full of expats and they manage the properties full time. Story after story of finding a dream and then pursuing it.

Today, Nice welcomes people both permanently and intermittently. For every year-round homeowner or long-term renter, there is a vacation rental around the corner. It's a different kind of a place depending on who takes a mind to it. Rixa and I first came to Nice during the summer as educators for a study abroad program almost twenty years ago. It was the final destination on a month-long Paris-based homestay program, a travel portion that took our twenty-thirty students to the famed Côte d'Azur. Several summers later, we directed a program housed in Nice's famous Lycée Masséna, one of France's preparatory high schools for the Grandes Écoles, the French equivalent of the Ivy Leagues. The city had just begun construction of their first tramway line and much of the center of the city was dug up. Temporary metal barriers all around the high school separated it from the Old Town. After the construction, fountains and parks, the tramway, the beach, shopping, restaurants, and the Cours Saleya market, would all be within a few blocks of each other. We were young and had just started our family. We thought: this would be the perfect place to live once it was finished.

But the primary impetus for our move was to find a way for our children to have a regular French immersion experience. I am a bilingual Canadian and I speak only French to my children. Every morning I tell my kids to *se brosser les dents* and *aller aux toilettes*. If I ever slip up, my kids look at me like I've lost my mind.

The forces that brought me to this point are complex. In Canada, bilingualism is available for anyone who wishes it, even in Anglophone-dominated areas of the country. It was an education that I took for granted. In the US, French immersion schools are either competitive charters or expensive private schools often catering to a privileged demographic. The nearest French immersion school to us was forty-five minutes away in Indianapolis and it cost almost half my salary as a professor. Plus our commitment to public schooling went beyond financial convenience. The threshold for belonging excluded too many people.

So I decided to speak only French at home. Switching to French with my children was a struggle at first. At the time, our oldest Zari was three and our son Dio was one. It wasn't always clear that they understood me and sometimes saying the words felt futile, like I was speaking them into a void. But after a while Zari seemed to understand—*manger* means to eat! *Jouer* is to play! Of course I will play with you! For a while, Zari would reply only in English but her comprehension improved every day. Some words merged into her vocabulary with eternally French designations: *bateau* for boat, *pastèque* for watermelon. I spoke French exclusively to my children for over a year while they spoke muddied franglais back. Sometimes I worried that my French-only policy would alienate them, victims of some bizarre linguistic experiment. But the opposite seemed to be happening; French became a language that bound us, a language associated with all the positive elements of my parenting: bedtime stories and horsey rides, family meals and games. My children's French increased in complexity and frequency. Then one day, Zari started speaking only French back to me, like someone had flipped the linguistic master switch.

We were upstairs in our attic, playing games. Dio had just inadvertently hit Zari and she said, "Dio tu dois me donner un calin MAINTEN-ANT!" You have to give me a hug NOW! I calmed her, asked why she was upset. She responded in French. Very good! Now what did she want to do? She responded in French. Good! And how are you doing today?

When Rixa got home, I could barely conceal my excitement. We had a bilingual four-year-old! The exigency of finding an immersion environment for our children now was stronger than ever. From that moment on, Zari used English with me only when she needed to ask how to say something—comment dit-on *hairy* en francais? But there were limitations to what I could teach her. One of Rixa's friends growing up was raised by bilingual parents. Although he spoke excellent French, he never adequately learned to read and write till he was an adult and there were huge gaps in his vocabulary and comprehension. Short of quitting my job and turning into a full-time home schooler, I'd unlikely be able to give her language skills beyond my own.

Our kids needed an immersion experience. French schools. French teachers. French kids to play with on the playground. That, combined with my constant reinforcement at home, should be enough to secure some level of native bilingualism. And the French school system continued till the first week in July. We finished teaching university the end of April or the first week of May. But if we came over on a tourist visa, our children weren't eligible to enroll for those couple months. We weren't residents. Residency required a permanent address.

And so, the plan.

Back when we worked for the study abroad company, I'd sometimes stop in and talk with realtors to see what buying a property in France would entail. I'd ask how much money down we needed to have or whether or not it was easy to get a loan, as though I were a potential client with a coffer full of euros and not some broke educator. In the states, I'd browse online listings and read books like *A Year in Provence* and speculate. At the time, the dollar was at an all-time high and buying an apartment in France seemed within the realm of possibility, even as we struggled to pay back student loans and scraped our way through graduate school. But most narratives of expatriation were outside our experience. They were stories of moneyed executives or people in the twilight of their careers who wanted to get away from it all, very rarely educators with a young family. Who in our situation could afford it?

But once it became clear to us that buying a property could be the key to our children's bilingualism, we felt compelled to try, even as the numbers put us on a razor's edge for what we wanted to do. Over the years we had invested and worked and saved for this. Zari was seven now, Dio was five, and Inga and Ivy were three and one, perfect ages for linguistic immersion. I had an upcoming sabbatical, a year where we could tackle renovations and enroll our three oldest in public schools. After that, we could come back year after year for as long as we were able, putting our kids back into French public school for as many months as we could, hopefully reconnecting with the same friends and teachers, making the mid-year transition to their second language less difficult. Now all we needed to do was find a place we could return to, a place that would welcome our family the way it had since humans first came to its shores, took shelter in its caves, and lit fires to celebrate their abundance.

Chapter 3

Umbrella Bed

THE DAY AFTER OUR ARRIVAL, we took stock of what we had. A white camp table with four maple folding chairs. Three bowls and some mismatched cutlery. Two plates, one with an enigmatic kanji on the rim. Glass tumblers that once held Nutella or Dijon mustard. A wok. An empty under-the-counter fridge the size of a suitcase. Our children were still conked out, sleeping the sleep of the dead.

"We should probably get something for breakfast."

"Probably."

It was almost noon. Outside, tourists carried beach mats and folded umbrellas down the Rue Droite. An old woman wheeled a plaid grocery cart full of produce from the market. I wound my way through the pedestrian streets to the Fougasserie bakery. A line stretched out either door. I wanted some *pains au chocolat*, the pastry that I craved every time I stepped foot into France, the two lines of dark chocolate down the middle of a croissant-like flaky crust, about the size and shape of an overstuffed wallet. *Six*, I said when I got to the counter, *et une baguette s'il vous plait*. The teller placed the pastries in a paper bag and passed me the baguette, poking halfway out of a paper sheath. I stopped by the small grocery across the street to get some milk and cereal. *Maybe if you had won the lottery*, the taxi driver had said. Now I had an idea of what he was talking about.

Back in the apartment, Inga and Ivy, our two youngest, were up.

"I got some pains au chocolat," I said. "And some cereal."

"Where'd you go?"

"Just the *épicerie* downstairs," I said.

"How much?"

"Umm," I said.

The apartment was already starting to take on some semblance of order. Rixa had opened up all the suitcases and several now stood empty against the wall. On the counter, she had started an inexhaustible "to do" list. My brother was going to be visiting us in less than a week with his wife and two children. A week to transform our apartment from feeling like a bare-bones dorm room to a home that could accommodate guests.

"We need a Pack and Play for Ivy," Rixa said. "And groceries."

We were starting from scratch, so we went to the one place where we knew we could find everything: Carrefour, France's most successful *grande surface* store. After a few months in France, we very rarely went to Carrefour, often because we could find things priced lower closer to home and we were familiar with all the tiny shops nearby selling everything from padlocks to spices in bulk. But finding all these places required being in the neighborhood and living for a while among the artisans and restaurateurs and educators and plumbers who relied on these same stores and services. Still, the rampant success of these Walmart-style chains in France is astonishing. While France never experienced the kind of desertification of some of US cities' downtown areas, the chain stores are always busy, making the tourist crowds buying cheese and olives at the open-air Cours Saleya market seem like leisure strolls on an empty beach in comparison. Certain periods in the late afternoon in Carrefour are like Black Friday specials or looters grabbing everything before the onslaught of a zombie attack. We probably knew this, must have, had we not been still jet-lagged and thinking ahead to dinner time and the empty shelves of our tiny fridge, but that didn't stop us from getting all the kids dressed for a big shopping trip at three in the afternoon.

On our way into the store, we briefed all the children: keep close to us, don't run in the aisles, no crying or screaming or we'll leave. For a moment, all of them complied, and the glass doors slid open and the waft of dry air-conditioned air lifted our hair away from our faces and ruffled our cottony summer clothes. A woman walking toward us exclaimed, "*Quelle belle famille!*" She touched her hand to her chest like she'd just had a shock and was about to fall down.

"Merci," we said.

She asked where we were from. "Le Canada," we said, not wanting to get into the confusing explanation of our multinational family. "We just moved to France last night."

"You're not serious?" she said.

You could see her trying to compute: this golden family abandoned their home for *this*? We were in the entrance of a boxy supermarket constructed in the 80s. Outside, old chains hung around poles where motorbikes had been stolen. Cigarette butts littered the ground. Splotches of chewing gum were smashed into the concrete, turned black from years of foot traffic and dirt. Before we parted ways, the woman said, "Canada is such a beautiful country. I hope you don't regret your move."

In less than twenty-four hours, two random strangers had warned us against our decision. It would not be the last time people saw something in our family that was praiseworthy, nor the last time that we would be the recipients of curious gazes. We were foreigners, blonde and tall, very unlike the olive-skinned Mediterranean-looking Niçois. Everywhere we felt on display: in the central business district, on the Promenade des Anglais, even on the street in front of our apartment.

We fished through our change and found a euro to unlock a cart. We corralled our children through the mall-like interior to the main store. A row of thirty blue tills beeped and shoppers raced to stuff their reusable grocery bags. We walked through the chrome entrance gates, past the security guards and into Carrefour.

Shoppers crowded the aisles. Teenagers carried cartons of table wine like footballs in the crooks of their arms. Sunburned tourists wheeled suitcases full of food. Vendors and shelf-stockers wound their way among us, fast, while we examined cans of *cassoulet* or weighed bags of fresh fruit. We swung our cart around till we were facing an aisle of cheese.

"This is how we know we're in France."

We picked through a few of our favorites: Pont de l'Eveque, Lou Pérac, St. Marcellin, Crotins de Chavignol, Comté. We cradled wheels of camembert, pressed our fingers into their soft centers, brought them to our noses. We looked for "lait cru," a sign that the cheese hadn't been pasteurized, killing the cultures that gave the best cheeses their powerful flavors. All thought of the woman's warning and our crotchety taxi driver were behind us now. This was variety and taste, the reasons we had committed ourselves to France.

"Now we just need to find a Pack-n-Play."

I said bonjour to a passing vendor and she stopped long enough for me to say "excusez-moi." I asked if she knew where we could find baby beds.

"Baby beds? Check Conforama," she said.

"Not big beds," I said. "Small ones." I mimed closing a book. Ones you can fold up—*pliable*.

"Oh," she said, her face brightening. "A *lit parapluie!*"

So that was it. "Yes, yes, show us the umbrella beds."

The vendor took us to the baby clothing section and there they were in rectangular boxes. It was our last purchase, but probably the most important. Last night Ivy our youngest had slept only off and on between us, which meant we were barely holding up better than our kids. Rixa especially suffered since nursing was the only thing that seemed to calm Ivy down. Rixa was up multiple times, rolling back and forth with our sleep-deprived baby. The umbrella bed signified a transition to coming days of rest.

At home, we unfolded the umbrella bed, pulling the sides taut till they snapped in place. Ivy snored in the baby carrier, her face pushed up against the back of my wife's summer dress till it was wet with sweat. Rixa undid the straps of the carrier and Ivy flopped into my arms. An umbrella bed. Our first new piece of furniture. I laid Ivy down and smoothed a lick of her hair away from her face.

Chapter 4

Surface Dive

THE NEXT MORNING, SUN LIT UP the streets. Outside our window, the sun cut diagonally along the facades. The stone balconies of the Palais Lascaris cast elongated shadows. The salmon-colored building across from us brightened to a ruddy orange. Every chink in the plaster produced pits of brown or black. The sky was a liquid blue.

"Let's go to the beach," I said.

"If you can get the kids ready."

Everyone except Rixa and I were still asleep. Ivy had been a little restless but for the most part the umbrella bed had done its job. The second time Rixa nursed her, Ivy fell asleep snoring. I was reluctant to force everyone up but yesterday we had spent the whole day either grocery shopping, unpacking, or going through the odd contents of our attic. We found a tile saw, putty knives, a pool noodle, rolls of old wallpaper, and a fishing pole. But since the first night, we had yet to go to the beach.

Before we had children, the sea was always a vacation destination, someplace synonymous with relaxation and calm. We'd slip on our sandals, grab a book, and lie out on Nice's smooth rocks till our bodies baked. We swam and snorkeled to cool off, only coming home when we were tired or hungry.

Now going to the beach was a big production. Kids shimmied into swimsuits, rolling around on our empty floors. Where were the water wings? After a night sweating in bed, Zari's almost waist-long hair was a blond tangled bird's nest. Inga and Dio fought over the pool noodle we'd found in our attic. Ivy sat cross-legged, rubbing her eyes and whimpering.

Once out the door, everyone's mood improved. We found a beach umbrella and a pair of fins in the downstairs closet, more gifts left by the previous owners. Inga had triumphed over the pool noodle and now wielded it like a light sabre. Zari and Dio slalomed between tourists. We yelled at them to slow down, *attention!*, and took turns shouldering bags and holding hands with Ivy. Soon we made it down the couple blocks till the Rue Droite opened up to the Cours Saleya and the sun hit us in full force.

Finally we were at the beach.

Before our move, I bought Dio a mask and snorkel to help him learn how to swim. The snorkel helped him to stretch out and remain afloat. In the pool he brought his arms out of the water and slapped them down again, pulling himself forward in an awkward front crawl. Now he had garnered enough courage to try it out in the Mediterranean. I hovered near him, watchful.

"Keep your head straight. Breathe through the tube. Kick your feet," I told him in French.

Dio still liked to be able to stand, so he stayed in the shallows. It wasn't long before he popped his head up.

"I saw a fish!"

I swam beneath him and he showed me. A rockfish. Soon he noticed others: saupe and sar, black goldfish-shaped castagnoles. Under a rock, I found a baby octopus. Its two eyes were obsidian-like slits and it pulled its tentacles back against its body. Dio had never seen an octopus before and didn't know why I was pointing to the rock with such enthusiasm. I surfaced and explained and now he was staring and vocalizing through his snorkel and waving his arms to show Zari. Soon they were both entranced by this tiny hiding cephalopod. I told them not to touch it. This was its home. He needed to be left alone so he could grow and move to deeper water.

After a while their interest waned. Zari's goggles were like knobby agates sucked into her face. Would she like to get a mask and snorkel too? She had never needed them before but maybe it would help her learn to dive. I swam out with Zari, to show her where an underwater mound of rocks peaked in the bay at Castel beach. Castel was the nearest beach to us, with the most diverse underwater fauna. Sometimes I wondered if we subconsciously chose our apartment because of its proximity to this place, as though we were drawn to it like metal filings to a magnet. It was also the beach with the most to offer young children: small pools, rocks jutting into the water, a jumping platform for shallow dives. Crabs scrambled into crevices. Fish darted along the shore. Enough activities to keep our kids amused for hours.

Out in the bay, I pointed to a black labre with a line of fluorescent blue along its caudal fin. A school of almost meter-long mulet nipped among the rocks. I wanted to get closer. I signaled that I was going down. I took a deep breath, and dove.

The mulet were down about twenty feet. I held my nose and pushed out the air to equalize my ears. I had been diving deeper and deeper since I started snorkeling several years ago, every dive a test for how far I could go, how long I could hold my breath. I had learned how to alleviate the pressure in my mask by blowing just a bit of air through my nose so it didn't make my eyes feel like they were popping out. I stayed down for thirty seconds, a minute. This time, I tried to follow the mulet through the rocks. They seemed unaware of me till I was just a foot away. I swiped with my hand and felt the flutter of a fin as one of them whooshed past. I had read about how free divers were often able to get closer to wildlife than scuba divers. No bubbles or noisy equipment. With my flippers and my breath secured in my constricting lungs, I was more like the fish, finning my way among the rocks.

My lungs burned with CO2. Zari treaded water just above me. I surfaced next to her and she said the words that would impact our story in ways that we couldn't yet comprehend. We were educators living on half-salary, having dispensed almost all our income on a property that would require more money than we had to renovate it. Our plan was fraught with risk. Questions about how we would live, how we would pay for basic necessities of food, clothing, and shelter still weren't entirely clear to us. "What kind of fish were those?" Zari asked. And then, hopeful, hesitant: "Can we eat them?"

The next day, I took Dio and Zari to the Place St. François, home to two long-standing Niçois institutions: the first, the Boucherie St. François, a high-volume butcher shop that employs some twenty-odd people and has a gold reputation for quality and price. By ten a.m., lines of people extended back from each of the seven butchers who cut and prepared meat for their customers. Buying meat at the Boucherie St. François was a cultural experience of its own. Butchers cajoled each other and flirted with the clientele. One butcher grabbed a duck by the neck and extended the plucked head to a woman for a kiss. She laughed and directed the butcher to chop it off and he obliged with a resounding thwack.

The second was the daily fish market where local fishmongers plied their wares. Fish and seafood of all sorts lay underneath blue awnings on beds of ice: s-shaped conger eels, schools of dorades, rockfish, and mulet, and kilogram nets of mussels. Early nomads first came to Nice to hunt and fish its abundant fauna. But unlike them, most people now got their meat from places like this, the fish arranged like a smorgasbord on ice. A small retired woman with bow legs and a plaid wheeled grocery bag waited for her turn in line.

"Marguerite!" a fishmonger said, "I didn't see you there."

"If I'd been wearing a mini-skirt you would've noticed me," she said.

I hid behind the woman and avoided eye contact with the fishmonger. We weren't buying. Unlike the Boucherie St. François, the daily fish market was more expensive, the prices per kilo putting local fresh-caught fish beyond our budget. I simply wanted to show Dio and Zari the fish that we saw yesterday. Which ones were edible? How expensive were they?

The cheapest were the labres. They were in a mixed pile of fish labeled "poissons pour la soupe": mostly bony rockfish that were too much of a pain to filet and clean but gave fish soup body and flavor. Ten euros/kilo. I estimated one fish at about five hundred grams. The mulet was fourteen euros/kilo, a little pricier but also much larger and likely easier to clean. The most expensive were the dorades royales, pan-sized game fish with a band of gold between their eyes: twenty euros/kilo. Each fish looked about a kilo each, the same size of fish I saw just yesterday darting into the rocks.

Je peux vous aider? The fishmonger said. He was gray-haired, portly, and he wore a blue t-shirt tucked into his jeans. I said no, thank you, I was just showing my kids the fish I saw snorkeling. You saw a dorade? Yes, I said. Where were you? Out at Castel beach. Ah, he said. One of the best places for fishing. Dorades were hard though. Cunning and *mefiant*. Best way to get them was by spearfishing.

Spearfishing?

In my mind, I pictured spearfishing as a surface-to-water thing, like what I imagined the early nomads who first came to Nice doing: thrusting a barbed stick into the water. Maybe our path toward sustenance wouldn't be so different after all. But no, the fishmonger explained, it was with an *arbalète,* an underwater gun with an elastic-triggered spear. I thought back to all those meter-long mulet so close I could feel the whip of their fins brushing my fingers. The prospect of spearing fish at this range seemed ridiculously easy to me, like plucking fruit from an overhanging bough. How did one get such a spear? I asked. Or learn to spearfish?

"You want to be my competition, eh? Put me out of business."

"Just curious," I said.

"Try one of the dive shops."

I thanked the fishmonger and bought a consolation bag of mussels, the cheapest thing I could find. I couldn't bring myself to buy any fish. It was noon and my children and I were all hungry. We loved fish, we really did, but the exchange rate was not in our favor and we had just blown a pile at Carrefour. We needed to be cautious. I had visions of one of these dorades in a tinfoil *papillotte,* filled with tomatoes and olive oil and tarragon, the flesh flaky and moist. Yesterday we had seen these same fish within hands reach. Did we want any fish? Yes, yes, we did, but I wasn't going to buy them from a fishmonger, no matter how gregarious he may be. Those I would catch myself.

Chapter 5

Les Décroissants

A MOVEMENT IN FRANCE the past several years has been gaining momentum. Adherents call themselves *les décroissants*. A good translation doesn't really exist—the decreasers? The diminishings? The closest philosophy I can find is minimalism, although the American version of this is more extreme, even evangelical, owing in part to the roots of many of its most ardent practitioners. But some essential commonalities remain: don't clutter your life with unnecessary stuff. Simplify. Avoid consumerism in all its forms. And the catchphrase that I'd see in French over and over again: *depenser moins, vivre mieux*: spend less, live better.

Other tenets of les décroissants elaborate what "vivre mieux" actually means. At the center of all the suggestions is time. Time to spend with family. Time for leisure activities or artistic pursuits. Time to eat, to socialize, to exercise. Practical suggestions like buying used clothing or furniture, trying to preserve the life of items, not participating in throw-away culture, also impacted what living better meant. "Vivre mieux" implied living better not only for yourself, but for others around you on a planet with limited resources.

Just coming to France already put us more in line with a décroissant way of life. Europeans consume on average 50 percent less than Americans. We would be living in a small apartment in a pedestrian area of Nice. We would walk everywhere. The conditions of where we lived also put us in contact with people due to their sheer proximity. For socialization or sense of community, it was difficult to leave the apartment every day without

interacting with someone. Bonjour le boucher! Bonjour le florist! No se-
questering ourselves away in a car through our daily transactions.

But the economic realities of our situation also made it so that spending less was imperative and not necessarily a choice. If we wanted to find a
way to make our lives here work, we would have to economize.

One of the first times Rixa and I ever came to France, we directed a
study abroad program for high school students. Before the program started,
we had six weeks of travel planned and very little money. Our budget was
about the equivalent of five euros/day. But the exchange rate at the time
was favorable and with a compact two-person tent, the occasional stay with
friends, street performing and hitchhiking, we survived just fine. Dépenser
moins, vivre mieux.

Living this way sometimes required us to transcend boundaries that
people in our same socioeconomic situation would balk at. Once we hitch-
hiked to Marseille in the back of a windowless electrical van. At markets
we would wait around till the end and ask vendors for the vegetables that
they were about to throw away. Our itinerant travels took us from Paris to
the Loire valley, to southern cities like Carcassonne, Narbonne, or Fréjus.
Once we hitched with a viticulteur who offered us free bottles of wine and
then put us up in his Bandol apartment overlooking the sea. We were never
without and the French seemed eager to share whatever they had with us.
On long walks between stops, our backpacks digging sweaty lines into our
shoulders, we would become tan and lean, our muscles taut and strong. We
were spending less than we ever had before, our perceived penury guiding
every decision. We were healthy and active, living better with less.

I remember seeing a guy once walk up to a restaurant after a couple
had finished eating. They had left most of their salads and part of their piz-
zas to rot there on the table. The French have yet to embrace the concept
of doggy bags and most of the time they simply throw the food away. The
man waited till the couple had paid and left their few centimes tip. He sat
down, grabbed the vinaigrette-covered salad leaves and tomatoes with his
hands and then chased them with bites of pizza. In a cool five minutes he'd
eaten the rest of their food: meals that had been paid for and would've gone
to waste. I thought: now there's a décroissant who has got it all figured out.

Old Nice seems to attract décroissants along with people who want to
be like them but still have some leftover *petit bourgeois* tendencies. I talked
once with Djamel, a parent who lives not far from us on the picturesque

stone walkway up to our children's school. He had curly grey hair fastened into a loose bun and a fu-manchu beard that he stroked reverently when he was deep in thought. He wore poofy Nepalese pants and colorful sweaters. "My partner and I are very committed to not working." He explained: why work away in a capitalist system that continually pushes you to spend more, to make more money? The problem was often work itself, the kind of jobs that were available slotting people into occupations like gears in a complex machine. But not he and his partner. No way they would be duped. Work was for the petit bourgeois. Do it long enough and you start to accumulate or expect things and soon your behavior has changed. You've violated the very principles that brought you to this place to begin with. Going without work was a necessary rebellion, an ideological pursuit, an ideal. A kind of job.

At the beginning of our year-long sojourn we weren't sure where our budgeting would bring us. We had children now and responsibilities. We would pay the taxes that would fund the public schools that our children would attend. We'd scrimp and find ways that the south would share its bounty with us. Although we wouldn't have to busk for money or shovel platefuls of leftover food from finicky diners, some of our earlier survival tendencies would start to assert themselves as we started to make a new life in the crowded streets of Old Nice.

Chapter 6

Antiques

MY BROTHER KENT AND HIS FAMILY would be here in a few days. We had finally emptied all our suitcases and packed them away in the attic. Now, children's clothes teetered in piles in the back bedroom. Our living room was so empty it echoed. We needed couches and dressers and tables, rugs for the fake hardwood floors. Something to make our apartment feel like home and less like a ballet studio. And we needed to do it on the cheap.

In the years we'd been traveling to France as tourists or educators, we marveled at the beauty and variety of antiques: hulking armoires or gilded mirrors that you could find cheaper than new. They fit with our décroissant philosophy by providing a new life to items that besides being beautiful tended to be more durable. No melamine dressers that would end up in a landfill, thank you very much. Now that we had an apartment here, all we needed was to find antique furniture that we could afford on our constricting budget.

We decided to visit the Port, the antique quarter on the other side of the chateau from Old Nice. This was the neighborhood that our taxi driver had claimed was more authentic, more the Nice of days past. All year round, the Port would be full of luxury yachts from around the world: Norway, the UK, the Netherlands, Australia. On the lea side of the chateau, streets paralleled the Port and then spider-webbed in a variety of directions north to Riquier, west to Garibaldi and the Old Town, and east to Villefranche and the lower *corniche*, a picturesque road just above the sea that eventually led to Monaco. Antique and art dealers crowded the Port, from glitzy storefronts with Louis XVI chairs and crystal chandeliers to the humble *brocantes* selling more middle-class wares. We visited the *marché aux puces*, a collection of about thirty stalls right on the Port with the least expensive antiques. With Ivy strapped to my back, Inga in the stroller, and our other two children holding our hands, being hushed repeatedly, told *not to touch that* in French, we attracted attention. Even among the shopkeepers who were used to feigning indifference, we elicited inquiries after our well-being or comments on our children's behavior. *Ils sont si sages*! they said, regardless of how much they were acting up: so well-behaved!

We were looking for a dining room table with seating for six, an impossibly large object for the cramped stalls piled high with vintage linens or model sailboats with masts delicate as toothpicks. Would we be interested in a desk maybe? Or how about a set of chairs? You say you just moved to France? As word got around we felt the buzz of anticipation. Shopkeepers emerged from behind bookcases. People straightened lamps, looked up from their coffee, heard us speaking French and asked, *je peux vous renseigner?* Thank you, we said, just looking for now. In a back stall we found an ornately carved armoire behind a split-leaf table covered with old china and silverware. It was massive, a solid mahogany color, the kind of armoire we would love but likely could not afford.

It's *Breton*, a woman nearby said. She was short with glasses, a bowl of dyed brown hair and olive skin from too many days in the sun.

"Is it for sale?" we asked.

"Undoubtedly," she said. "The shopkeeper, she is never here. *Elle est Italienne*," as though that explained her absence.

"Do you know how to get a hold of her?" As far as we could tell, they had to be stall-mates for the proximity of their wares. "We just want to know how much she wants for it."

"No no," she said. "I've given up on that one a long time ago. You'll have to try back later."

Nothing. Even the least expensive items we found—secretary desks or one-drawer end tables with fluted legs—were still out of our price range. On our way out, we stopped at one of the booths closer to the street. Two oriental *tables de chevet*—knee-high dressers with tiny drawers and compartments—caught our eye. You like these? A man asked. He was an older gentleman, a little overweight, and he wore a toupee. He lifted one of the dressers onto a display table in front of us so we could get a better look.

"They're turn-of-the-century," he said. "Good investment for the kids! You'll need to fix the latch. And the back is splitting here." The second one was also damaged, but the detail was great. Each was a dark wood, almost ebony in appearance. Carved dragons hid among decorative vines. "How much?" we asked.

The low price startled us—made us realize the "investment" bit was a line. We were obviously foreigners who had no idea of their intrinsic value. Pulling out the tables de chevet led to more discoveries: Eric, do you like this rug? And what about this chair thing? The chair thing took a while to uncover. The back half leaned against the booth wall, rising to a triangular point just above my head. Two inch-diameter fluted columns extended down to a flat seat that jutted out. It was like a miniature personal pew or a narrow throne. The dark mahogany wood matched the oriental night-stands.

"What is that?" Rixa asked.

"We don't exactly know. We bought it at an estate auction. But it likely came from a church. The carved dove here signifies calm after death. We call it 'the Throne of Peace.'"

The Throne of Peace. We thought what we could use it for. Maybe like a gothic hall tree? A place we could sit near the entrance to put on our shoes?

"I can give you a deal if you'll take all three," the man said. "I'll even throw in the rug. It has a rip on the side anyway."

We couldn't believe our good fortune. Now if we could just get the armoire that we saw earlier. Rixa ran back while I entertained the kids and talked with the man—Thierry, he said—about what he could do for delivery. For a fee, he had a moving truck with plenty of space if I didn't mind waiting. Soon Rixa was there, flushed and breathless. "The Italian lady is back. And you won't believe the price. I think we should get the armoire."

A couple hours later, I was driving with Thierry in his boxy Renault moving truck, the furniture stacked neatly in the back with flannel blankets between them. The woman had parted with the armoire below what she had paid for it at an estate auction, ten times less than what a similar armoire would have cost in the states. I asked Thierry about his business. Had it been a good year? Oh, the economy you know, he said. Not quite the same as it used to be. But better than last year.

We rounded Rauba Capeu and followed the Promenade till it turned up toward the Place Masséna. He wondered why we moved to France. Everything about us seemed to intrigue him: we were a young family with four kids, buying antiques that had sat in his stall for ages. Usually he sold to octogenarians or bohemian artists. Most families he knew were moving outside the city, to small villages where you could get a house with terraced gardens and some peace and tranquility for the price of an apartment in the city. What was it about France that so appealed to us? I cited the food, the culture, the art, the entertainment. Then I moved on to the strong social net, the health care, and the advantages for families. We pulled alongside the Old Town, looking for the turn. Pedestrians timed crossing in front and behind us. At the stoplight near the Place Centrale, toddlers held parents' hands as they waited to go to the playground on the coulée verte.

"And the antiques," I said. "You couldn't get anything like this back home. Would cost a fortune."

"Really?" he said.

I could see his incredulity—he'd been sitting on inventory for months, barely eking out a living. If only he could get to where people would pay, maybe he could have a different life. He signaled right and turned down the Rue Centrale. It was dinner time and the whole *place* was full of people. They parted as we nosed our way through them. The woman who owned the grocery on the corner wound back her awning to let the truck pass. All around us people stopped and watched the top of the truck and mimed the distance like they were holding something in their hands. Six inches, four. Still we pushed forward. While we drove, Rixa and the kids were back in the apartment eating dinner, waiting for us to buzz up. Soon Thierry would stop and put on his blinkers and we'd haul our antiques up four flights of stairs. We'd be winded and gulp down glasses of water. Sweat would collect around Thierry's toupee. Seeing our family, Thierry would warm to us. He'd give us another rug for free—too much empty space he'd say—and suggest we start shopping on Leboncoin—an online Craigslist-like service that was popular in France. But for now he seemed annoyed, almost bothered by this living experiment in which we seemed determined to engage.

"I can't believe you like it so much here," he said. "Most people I know—most French people—leave if they can. At least all the ones with any brains."

Chapter 7

The Good Corner

THIERRY'S TIP ABOUT LEBONCOIN proved to be invaluable. Unlike many Anglophone countries, Craigslist never took off in France. I had searched for other online classifieds sites like topannonce or vivastreet, but they never seemed very comprehensive. Leboncoin was something else.

"Le bon coin," before the contraction, literally means "the good corner." But "coin" in French has a more familiar connotation than angles meeting at a point, although their website has amply used that double meaning in its icons and advertising. A corner is also a community place, designating insider belonging. "Les gens du coin" is a colloquial way of saying "locals," and the corner connotes security the same way as a favorite bar or speakeasy or church hall or meeting place. It's a good one, this corner, the best, the one with the most products to offer to the most people. Leboncoin has become so big now that even businesses upload their inventory to the site in order to compete. Welcome to a bargain shopper's paradise.

Leboncoin filled a need in France that wasn't being met by other classifieds services. People could divest themselves of their belongings or even supplement their income by buying and selling on the site. As outsiders using the interface, we also gained access to people who we would otherwise unlikely meet. Similarly, it enabled the French to interact with someone like us: a large North American family who was trying to furnish their tiny apartment as tastefully and cheaply as possible. It was a place we would come back to again and again, to buy scooters for our children, ski equipment, and even a car. It's also where we'd go to divest ourselves of everything from old mattresses to broken furniture we'd repair from the garbage depot in an effort to save money.

Leboncoin would lead us further into the stratifications of Niçois society, the underlying tensions in the neighborhoods outside the bohemian bubble of Old Nice. Racist attitudes on Leboncoin revealed themselves in individual advertisements, always shrouded in courteous rhetoric: "Our African friends need not inquire." These were easy to avoid. If they weren't willing to entertain African queries, they weren't going to get our business either. But avoidance became more difficult after we'd already made contact with people and entered into a kind of trust. Leboncoin dissolved boundaries that often took years to traverse. Even in the south, the French can be intensely private people and suddenly we were exchanging phone numbers and meeting in each other's homes.

One of our first experiences with Leboncoin came during my brother's visit. We had added a leather sleeping couch and matching chair to the armoire and the Throne of Peace. We were looking for an antique mirror, something bold and rococo that could open up our living room and give it a feeling of volume. Most antique mirrors we found were out of our price range and too small. The high ceilings of our apartment needed a larger mirror, something that could take advantage of all that blank wall space. During my brother's visit, a mirror came up. It was enormous, over two meters tall, with gold gilding and an elaborate plaster crown with a coat-of-arms at the center. We checked the price: moving sale. Make best offer.

Kent, his wife Melanie, and their two young kids had been at our home for four days now at the end of a whirlwind European tour. We put them all up in our front bedroom with the umbrella bed for their youngest. Their son Isaac would sleep with our three oldest in the attic and Ivy would co-sleep with us in the back bedroom. At first I was apologetic about the accommodations: the spare décor and the cramped quarters. The lack of many familiar amenities would make them feel like they were camping. "This is a nice apartment," my brother assured me. "You should've seen the place we stayed in Rome. It was a total hole."

The next couple days, Kent and their family absorbed as much as they could of this place we now called home. We went to the beach, climbed the wooden marine animals at the coulée verte, and hiked up to the chateau. Even quotidian routines like going grocery shopping or doing laundry had a particular charm to them. So this what it was like to hang wet clothes out your window in France! Fascinating! But didn't they want to do more sightseeing? We had museums they could visit: Matisse, Chagall. They should at least go to the Palais Lascaris across the street.

"Really, it's kind of nice just to relax." He explained: the rest of their trip had been high-octane down-to-the-minute tourism. Kent was the kind of traveler who liked to check sites off his bucket list. At home, a world map with pins punctured every country he'd visited around the world. Now it was refreshing not to be over-scheduled, just to enjoy getting to know this new place where we lived. With cousins to play with, his kids had more fun than during the whole trip. Yesterday, we walked down the Promenade du Paillon, stopping at the miroir d'eau, a kind of giant splash pad that sent jets of water into the air from a black obsidian surface. Children gamboled about, filling the air with screams of delight. Our kids wanted to join in but we didn't really have time to wander all the way back to our apartment to change. Could they just run in the water anyway? Get their clothes wet? I said of course—everyone else was. So Zari and Inga took off their shirts and Dio whipped off all his clothes except his Angry Bird underwear. Kent's son Isaac took some convincing—we were sure it was OK?—but soon he went out and splashed around. Just as long as we were doing the same thing.

So when the mirror came up on Leboncoin, Kent and his family decided to come along. Kent especially was drawn to seeing how actual French people lived. When would he get a chance to otherwise?

We met Bernard at the moving sale the next day, a morning window of time where he hoped to sell off most of his items. The apartment was in an old Hotel Particulier near the Notre Dame cathedral just off Avenue Jean Médecin, the main artery of Nice. It benefitted from full southern exposure with a balcony about half the size of our entire apartment. Huge original windows opened out to a view of a park. Bernard was in the middle of reno-vation with pock-marked walls and new plaster and bundles of electrical cables not yet concealed behind baseboards or encased in plywood boxes. Beneath the thin film of sheetrock dust were wooden buffets, a carved mahogany table, marble-topped side tables and poster beds and dressers. Arriving an hour into the moving sale, we were dismayed to find that he had already sold most items. But the hulking mirror was still there.

It was imposing, filling a wall between two windows. It rested on the baseboards with the top fixed in place by metal spikes plastered directly into the wall. The bulk was impressive, like the hall of mirrors in Versailles. Louis XIV designed the hall to convey economic prosperity. And now I understood a little of what he meant: this mirror would transform our modest living room, make it reflect the space and give it a feeling of luxury.

"Give me your best offer," Bernard said. "Then we can talk."

But when I told him a number, he shook his head. He had a couple other antique mirrors that might be more in our range. He took us around to show us: both were substantial, one with decorative carved rosettes and a thick frame and another with repeating arcing laurel leaves. We liked both of them immensely, but we still wanted the massive gold mirror that presided over the center of the room. Which got us to talking: why was he selling it anyway?

"I had hoped to retire here," he said. "It's my brother's place—he passed away—but the city is forcing me to sell and I don't have any room for all of this back home."

"How could the city force you?"

He began to tell us his story. He was a cop. Over thirty years in the service and he had seen some things. You would have thought that the state would be grateful, take it into account. But no. One politician got in and saw an opportunity to buy votes and he couldn't care less where Bernard lived. Now the city was building a subsidized complex here, probably going to divide his apartment into five shitty studios, this after he'd spent thousands to rewire and update the whole thing. They weren't even paying him market rate. He was a minority interest in the building and now he was forced to sell. "You see all that *racaille* out there? Now they're going to invite them indoors."

I knew the word racaille: a pejorative to describe troublemaking immigrant men who would hang around street corners smoking Gauloises and harass passers-by. A group of them had been outside the building when we came in, sitting on the stone plinths edging the pedestrian area. Kent had followed along much of our conversation to this point but the word racaille had stumped him. I explained briefly and he jumped in:

"Surely the city is responding to a need," Kent said.

"If we don't give it to them, they'll take it anyway. You see that metal box? A security system. I thought the metal-reinforced door, all the locks would deter them. But no, they break in through the transom window and sneak out everything they can. The only things left were what was too big to fit through."

"You mean you had more?"

"They cleaned me out. All the smaller antiques—gone over one weekend."

A West African man came to the door and Bernard excused himself. Bernard gruffly escorted him through the rooms and answered his questions. We were in a side room filled with boxes of books. Like everything, they were covered in a thin layer of dust, dulling the embossed spines.

"That guy is a total racist," Kent said.

"He's just upset because he has to sell his apartment."

Rixa picked up a leather-bound copy of *Madame Bovary* and wiped it clean. The pages were crisp and undamaged. Besides being great literature, they would also look great on our empty shelves. "Do you think he's selling these books?" she asked.

Bernard was at the door again, bidding the African man goodbye. "He came in and gave me a ridiculous price for everything in the apartment. Didn't even look it over. The third one this morning."

Maybe Kent was right. Bernard was a *fonctionnaire*, a government employee who had worked in law enforcement his whole life. He had time to develop his stereotypes to the point where he felt they were backed up by fact.

Rixa held up the copy of *Madame Bovary*.

"You want the books?" he asked, surprised. "You get the mirrors and I'll throw those in for free."

We left Bernard's shattered retirement dream with more than we came for. We discussed and bargained till we settled on a price: 400 euros. For everything. Not only would he give us all three mirrors he would also give us the two marbled-topped end tables and all the leather-bound books. We paid with a check. Bernard started to protest at first, saying how he preferred cash, but then he said, "I'm not worried about you guys."

Not la racaille.

Kent helped me carry the boxes of books home. Bernard gave our children old dolls and antique toys as if they were heirlooms he was passing down to the next generation. Kent and I came back later with Thierry who had become our man with a van. The three of us maneuvered the

it mirror up four flights of stairs, careful not to knock off any of the
delicate molding.

Inside our apartment, we leaned the mirror up against the wall. It
was heavy enough that we'd need to figure out some way of supporting its
weight, a project for another time. I paid Thierry, and he left. All the kids
were playing up in the attic. Soon it was just the adults in the living room.
And our big hulking mirror.

"I feel guilty," I said.

"What are you talking about?" Kent said.

"A gift from a racist. I should return it."

"Don't be ridiculous."

"At least he would know that his attitude was reprehensible to me."

"And what would that accomplish?"

Now Melanie and Rixa offered their opinions. Melanie had recently
finished her PhD in American Political Science. Bernard's attitude was a
classic example of homophily and geographic sorting. He saw characteristics in us that were similar to his own and rewarded us for it. Pointing
out the injustice of preferring us over others would merely insult him and
reinforce the boundaries he had already erected around himself. Direct
confrontation rarely worked. Instead, I should try to share experience that
would speak to his indirectly.

"Like what?"

"I don't know much about French politics," Melanie said. "But it
doesn't sound that different from what's been going on in Minnesota
with Somalis."

She explained. At a dinner party once, a new family who lived in
Faribault said that they wouldn't have moved there if they'd known there
were so many Somalis.

"Yikes," I said.

"I know."

Some people saw Somalis as an invasive species, opportunists who
came to Minnesota to prey upon jobs and resources. What they didn't know
was that most Somalis resisted leaving their communities to begin with and
that coming to Minnesota and integrating into the culture was very difficult
for them. One Somali Mel worked with said that he understood why some
Minnesotans would be upset. It's hard to see an influx of people with a different culture and background. People are drawn to others like themselves.

36

Just look at any suburb in America. Often they were divided along racial, religious, or political lines. It's not often that you find a community where this isn't the case.

"What about people who prefer hanging out with people not like themselves?"

"You're talking about a rare breed. The research is pretty damning. Even liberals who value inclusion as a principle very rarely put it into practice."

So the mirror stayed. I thought about what brought us to Old Nice to begin with: the bohemian atmosphere, the variety of ethnicities, the proximity to amenities. Although we stood out visually, the blonde-haired Nordic-looking family with the passel of kids, we were also likely moving into a neighborhood of people like us who valued diversity. Geographic sorting. But some people, like the taxi driver or the woman at Carrefour, saw our presence as disconcerting. We should be up in some Niçois suburb with other families and not in the city center. The truth was, we still didn't know how we'd fit in. We'd only been here a couple weeks. We were newcomers. Immigrants. How our community would see us wasn't something we could entirely control. For now, we'd furnish our apartment, get our children ready for school, go about the daily exercise of living, and hope to shape our community as it shaped us.

Chapter 8

Nice Diving

A FEW DAYS AFTER KENT AND MELANIE left, the wind picked up and the sea was a milky blue churning with surf. It was the first time since our arrival that we'd seen significant waves along the beach. People still swam but it was too rough for our small children so we walked around the point to the "Navette Lou Passagin," a daily ferry service that cut from one side of the Port to the other. The plan was to walk along the boardwalk past La Reserve restaurant to explore tiny pebbled beaches and coves. Two older women in summer dresses exited the boat, holding tight to the guard-rail descending the gangplank. I asked in French if the ferry was free. The woman laughed and then in strong British-inflected French said, "Well, free for you but those of us who live here are stuck with the taxes." She was gone before I could explain to her that we were tax-paying residents as well.

The skipper's blonde-brown dreads and tanned complexion made him look like he belonged on Hawaii's North Shore, someone used to sun and surf. He wore flip flops and frayed capris and a Bob Marley T-shirt. The kids settled in on the wooden benches and the tiny motor put-putted till we were out in the mouth of the Port. We'd been here almost a month now and we had passed the navette myriad times, never daring to take it for fear of the cost. Now we were in a bee-line for the east side of the Port and I told Rixa another reason I wanted to try the boat: there was a dive shop on the way known for its reasonable prices. They should have good snorkel equipment for Zari. We reached the dock and the skipper thanked us, helping the kids step up onto the gangplank. We filed along till we were at street level and the awnings of Port-side businesses beckoned to us: l'Orée du Port, Iberica, and Corsaire Café. Nice Diving was almost directly across the street, not the first business to pick up on Nice's English meaning, its cartoonish diver mural announcing its wares. We went in and a bell jingled. The store was on two floors with the second open to the first and wooden suspension stairs leading to the middle of the room. Wetsuits, tanks, and vests lined the walls. An assortment of masks and snorkels of all sizes were near the front, partially behind the counter. The shopkeeper, a man in his fifties wearing a tight black t-shirt, showed us several models, popping each mask out of its box so Zari could try it on. A low-volume Cressi mask fit her best, sucking onto her face. It should fit loose, the man said. Too many people pulled them tight. Did we want some fins? A snorkel too? The prices were the same as what we'd pay at Carrefour or Go-Sport for a knock-off set, and we were impressed with the quality. He rang up our items. We were about to leave when I noticed several black tubes of varying sizes hanging on the wall. Spear-guns.

"How much are these?" I asked.

"Depends on the length. The short ones are cheap but they're only good for *chasse au trou*. You can go deeper with the longer guns but they're more expensive."

I had only a vague idea of what "chasse au trou" meant—hunting in the hole? It had to mean searching among the rocks for fish rather than out in the open water. I explained: I was a beginner but I had been getting better at freediving. I could dive down about thirty feet, hold my breath for almost two minutes. I shared these stats like I had something to prove. Did he think that spearfishing was easier than a rod and reel?

"Ah non," he said. "It's much harder."

"But it's more fun, right?"

"I wouldn't recommend it. The season is almost over. Then it's only on the weekends. You'd be better off with a pole."

"We tried fishing with a pole once but we didn't catch anything of size."

"Then you weren't doing it right. Now if you'll excuse me."

I spent the evening looking up Mediterranean spearfishing on the internet, nursing my snub. I was exactly the kind of person the man didn't want in the water: inexperienced, idealistic, impetuous. But every day we went snorkeling, I would get close enough to the fish that I could almost grab them. Spearfishing seemed so much more promising than rod fishing, something we'd tried a couple times with banged-up equipment we'd found in our attic to no success. A good rod and reel, all the lures and gear that I'd need to be effective, all the time that I'd have to spend watching a pole and wondering if anything of size would ever bite the other end, would put me hundreds of euros in the hole in time and money. All I needed for spearfishing was a spear gun. Spearfishing would give me that split-second advantage that I'd need to get something for my family to eat.

I looked up "chasse au trou" on a spearfishing website, and the description came with diagrams and helpful videos. With this technique, the diver located a fish or chased it into a rock. He searched till the fish was in his sights. Each video made the whole process seem effortless. There's a fish! In a hole! So easy. The diver pulled out fish and eels and an octopus, all wriggling on the end of the spear like insects impaled on pins. The only indication of any difficulty was when the diver ran out of breath and had to release the gun to surface for more air. But the gun was still down there, tethered to the spear stuck in the rocks with an enormous fish on the other end. All he had to do now was get his breath back to retrieve it. How hard could it be?

The other two techniques, the website claimed, required more skill. The first was *chasse à l'indienne*. In this one, the spearfisher tracked above the fish so he was out of view, then he dove down just behind it, taking it by surprise. I recognized the technique as one of the many ways that I would get close to fish while snorkeling. While sometimes my dive would alert a fish to my presence, sending it darting into a hole, often I could find a blind spot and sneak up behind it. The website cited the difficulty as being primarily from the physical exertion and stealth it required. But I'd already been doing this almost naturally for the past several years. No problem. Check.

The last, the website claimed, was the most common, the most effective, and the most difficult: *chasse à l'agachon*. In this technique, the diver found a spot on the sea floor near populations of fish. Then he waited. Here, stealth and camouflage were key. The fish couldn't be aware that a spear-wielding predator lurked among the rocks. The diver held his breath for a minute, two. Still no fish. He pivoted slowly from side to side, scanning the sea till a school of dorades emerged from the deep, curious. From the front, their blunt heads looked like silver-and-gold crosses wiggling toward him.

40

A pilot fish led the school. Three minutes. The diver tracked the fish till the largest dorade appeared and he fired.

Chasse à l'agachon. Here was something I could not do. The video seemed to defy the limits of the humanly possible. After the catch, the diver began his ascent. I estimated thirty feet, no forty, sixty. The diver's long fins propelled him upward at an incredible speed but still he had not reached the top. Four minutes. The man broke the surface and he pulled the impaled dorade toward him. He held it up to the camera. It was almost two feet long, full-bodied, a thick game fish in its prime and he had shot it through the head. It barely twitched when he pulled the spear through and attached it to his string of fish.

How could I possibly do this? I was struck by the diver's patience, how he waited even as the fish passed by within range. He could've taken the first fish he saw and been back above water, gulping precious air. But instead he waited. At a minute my lungs would've been bursting. The only thing that felt right when I'd been under that long was to flail and kick my way to the surface. The diver's position and lack of movement were calculated and deliberate. Watching the footage felt eerily predatorial, the perspective of a hunter ready to pounce and kill. And yet still I felt compelled to do this thing. With spearfishing I could get fish, plenty of fish, quickly and efficiently, the bounty of the expensive fish markets now coming to our table, filling my children's bellies. But was this who I wanted to become?

Chapter 9

Neighbors

IT TOOK A MONTH BEFORE we got a magnetic key for our apartment, something Bart had claimed we'd be able to get right away. We'd seen the key fobs: the blue ovals that our neighbors swiped in front of the buzzer outside our building. As per Bart's instructions, we went to the syndic to get it, the apartment management company that took care of our annual expenses. They didn't have any fobs left so had to order new ones. Finally. It was so much easier: no more fishing through purses or wrangling the key into a lock. Now we could just hold the key or even a purse up to the knob and the door would click as the latch released. Voila. In.

One day, we swiped the magnetic key just as our neighbors were leaving the building. The blue oval still dangled from Rixa's hand. "Oh," our neighbors said. "You're not tourists?"

No, we explained. *Propriétaires*. We bought the apartment on the third floor, the old student rental.

"We didn't even know it was for sale!"

We started talking while their son Jessy greeted our children shyly from behind his parents' legs. They were both tall and lithe and they had something of a movie star quality about them. Vincent had George-Clooney gray hair and wore a fitted t-shirt and jeans. Samira's dark hair hung to her olive-skinned shoulders. Their three-year old son Jessy, with his square toddler-sized glasses and his polo shirt and shorts looked like he just walked out of a Lacoste commercial. Samira—Sam for short—had seen us many times before but because of our key had just assumed that we were here temporarily. Now she was curious: where were we from exactly? And how long were we staying?

We have to get together, she said.

The next week they invited us over. The kids all dutifully air-kissed Jessy when they came in and soon they were off down their hallway to play in his room, the layout almost exactly the same as ours. They had installed dark hardwood floors and took down the wall in front to form a large "cuisine Américaine," a kitchen that was open to the living room. Their granite counters, square leather couches, and wall-sized TV was like a preview of what our apartment could look like after renovations.

"I can't understand why you would ever want to move here," Vincent said. Energized from a recent visit to New York, he thought it incredible that a family like ours would prefer France to the US.

He explained. For the past five years, he had struggled with his restaurant Chez Palmyre, a critically-renowned restaurant with a stellar reputation and that especially sweet spot of "bonne rapport qualité/prix." Now Chez Palmyre was always full, with long waiting lists for reservations, even during the winter. For eighteen euros, diners got a three-course meal with a menu of fresh local ingredients that changed every three weeks. He had a growing regular clientele. Tourists from Australia to Japan called months in advance of their vacations to ensure that they would get one of the five tables in his cozy restaurant. Everything was made in-house that day by Vincent himself.

But his success came at a cost. He left at six a.m. to prepare and he often didn't get home till midnight. Then there was the bureaucracy and expense of operating a business in France. Even on occasion when Samira would help cut vegetables before the lunchtime rush, he had to declare her as an employee and give her a salary and benefits. He negotiated a partnership with one full-time waiter instead of hiring someone because of the entitlements that protected workers. If the waiter had a stake in the business, Vincent was convinced that he would work more efficiently and at a higher level.

"A waiter in the states is at least motivated to do good work because of the tips," he said. "When we were in NY, they were always so polite and asking how we were doing."

In some sense, he was right. But the kind of restaurant that he was running in Nice would be almost impossible in the US. The benefits that he so decried paying could be just as substantial if he wanted full-time employees. Most US waiters weren't entitled to these benefits so they would be more transient, less experienced. And it was unlikely that Vincent would be able to have a restaurant with five tables that could support himself as comfortably as in Nice.

We all sat around their granite-topped island on white stools with chrome bases that looked like they belonged in a hair salon. We munched on Belin crackers and pistachios for the aperitif—nothing fancy—the beginning of what we knew would be a long evening of food and discussion. We were *invités*, meaning that the adults would spend every moment till around midnight either eating or talking and generally ignoring our collective children. Our opinions would have to surface eventually.

"I find waiters in the states annoying. They ask you how you're doing because someone's waiting for their table and your time is up," I said.

"But you have to admit that French waiters are rude. Everyone knows this," Vincent said.

"They're not rude, they just feel like they're on the same social plane."

In France, waiters had to have a diploma and were trained at schools to leave the customer in peace. We had the table for as long as we wanted it. Our glasses would be filled without us noticing. If we had questions, waiters would answer them but they weren't there to chit-chat or otherwise interrupt our dining experience. A good waiter was invisible. Vincent liked a system where the customer was king. I liked one where the relationship was more egalitarian, even if that meant that the waiter was an entitled jerk every now and then. I much preferred it to the cloying passive-aggressiveness of the part-time waiter working for tips, suffering in a market economy. As a waiter in France, you could make a decent wage and have a high standard of living; in the US, you were often a waiter as a stop-gap job for something else, sometimes just a step away from indentured servitude, symptomatic of a broken system.

The children raced into the front room, kicking a size-one soccer ball, Jessy leading the way. "Ah non, ça suffit!" Sam yanked the ball from near his feet and picked up the TV remote. She scrolled through to find a movie that the kids could watch. Her scolding stung, like an indictment of our francophone tastes. Now Vincent was placing an hors d'oeuvre in front of us, individual prawns on tiny square plates ladled with a brownish-red sauce.

"Just the other day we were talking about trying to move to the US. The culture here—if you don't belong, the system grinds you down."

I took a bite of the shrimp. It was tender, glazed with the sauce. I could taste lemon and garlic, and then something else—a fresh tangy kick.

"This is delicious," I said.

"Guess what's in the sauce."

"I have no idea but it's divine."

Vincent placed another shrimp on my plate. "Ketchup," he said.

Chapter 10

A Place to Write

FALL ON THE CÔTE D'AZUR has a feeling of urgency to it. *La Rentrée* punctuates September, the beginning of studies for French public schools and universities signaling that the fun is over. Locals return to the playgrounds. The tourists who remain are eager to maximize their time; they are the foreign budget travelers, staying in Airbnbs and discount hotels. There is also an influx of new blood like us, people moving to the area for the first time—new job, new life, new possibilities. It's a period of transition. People move, settle in, stretch their crisp reusable shopping bags full of produce from grocery stores with exotic-sounding names: Carrefour, Intermarche, Lidl, Casino.

Like anything even mildly bureaucratic in France, enrolling our children in school was a chore. Although we had translated our children's birth certificates, we had done it ourselves instead of hiring an official translator. "You could write whatever you wanted on there," the woman at the mayor's office said.

"You could look it up on Google translate right now," I told her. "'Born' means 'né.' 'City' is 'ville.' It's really not that hard."

She didn't like my tone. Next!

The school itself proved much more positive. Since Old Nice is comprised of apartment buildings and relatively densely populated, it housed the two best elementary schools in the city. Our kids would be attending the "École du Château" or "Castle School," a large salmon-colored building with lofty archways and balconies that sat carved into the rock on the way up to ruins of a medieval fortress. Both Inga and Dio would be in kindergarten, Inga in "petite section" which started at age three, and Dio in "grande section" which started at age five. Zari would be in the adjacent "École Primaire" starting CE2, the equivalent of third grade.

The first day, I went with Inga and Dio to kindergarten while Rixa strapped Ivy to her back and left with Zari to go to the École Primaire. The kindergarten director led the new parents and children through the school, showing them where students would put their coats and bags, where they would go for meals and recess. The director wore jean shorts and a polo shirt. He loved the first day of school, he said, all the kids with their new clothes and their hair done. He mimed combing his hair flat against his head. "Impeccable." He ended the tour with a flourish of his arm indicating the horizon. "And this is our humble *cours*." The cours was a small playground area with a million-dollar view of the Old Town and the sea. The rooftops formed a complex terra-cotta tableau and the promenade framed the sea in a long crescent past the famed Hotel Negresco up to the airport. At the railing, I started talking with parents of Bastien, a boy in Dio's class, while we admired the view. They lived outside Old Nice and had petitioned to get Bastien enrolled in the school because of its reputation. "So are you from here?" I asked.

"Je suis Niçoise."

I was cautious. The taxi driver, Thierry, the woman that we met at Carrefour, Bernard—all the Niçois I had met so far seemed to have a negative view of Nice, especially the Old Town. Further interactions with people on Leboncoin reinforced their viewpoint: Nice was no place to raise a family. "Do you like it here? I'm always surprised to meet Niçois who can't wait to move away."

"Ah non," she said. "I'm proud of my town." She gestured to the shimmering sea. "We have everything—the sun, the mountains, the sea, culture, and dining. What more could you possibly want?"

So there *were* Niçois who loved Nice!

The father was also from Nice, an ex-soccer player who was intent on enrolling Bastien in soccer starting next week. I mentioned that we were wanting to do the same.

"Be careful what club," he said. "Some of them are pretty rough."

A couple weeks earlier I had seen a flyer for Cavigal Football. They were starting a dedicated girls team. Did he know if it had a good reputation?

"It's a competitive club so your kids will have to try out. But outside of OGC Nice, it's the best club around and not too far from here."

I left brimming with optimism about our children's future.

I met Rixa back at the school entrance. Zari's school wasn't quite as accommodating. Rixa was able to meet Zari's teacher and talk about the school year but she hadn't realized that CE2 was a year ahead of where Zari should be. Her October birthday put her in the equivalent of grade 2 in the states. She'd be one of the youngest in her class studying a more rigid curriculum. We hoped that she'd be able to keep up.

But for now, time to be patient. I was buoyed by the enthusiasm of Bastien's parents for this place and for their endorsement of the school our children would be attending. It would be challenging at first but they would adapt. Our children would make friends. They would play soccer and learn to read and write in their second language. Their linguistic abilities would continue to improve. I had just turned my children over to a foreign public school system with benchmarks and tests that demanded a high level of conformity. But I was ecstatic when we got home. Our plan was working. Rixa decided to take Ivy to the park and I finally found myself alone in our apartment for yet another reason to be content.

It was time to write.

Since our arrival, I had only written intermittently. Every day we had some new set of challenges: getting furniture, hooking up the internet, paying our utilities and property taxes. Then there was Kent and Melanie's visit. The other recreational activities: the beach, the coulée verte, the miroir d'eau, and the nearby hikes made it so writing just didn't happen with any kind of regularity. It was still summer after all. Plus finding a quiet place in our apartment was difficult—even if I closed the door to one of the rooms and tried to sequester myself away, it wasn't long before someone wandered in needing a band-aid or clothes to get dressed or help resolving some sibling conflict.

The only space that provided any modicum of privacy was our attic, the highest point of the apartment, a third bedroom that was separate from the main floor. It was the size of a toddler on one end, growing to a height of about five feet. A ladder-like staircase led up to it through a hole in the middle of the room. Windows opened to the stairwell so you could see everyone who came to our front door from above. It felt like being in a tree house. It had other qualities: an exposed stone wall with all the variation and texture you'd expect in a medieval-era home, and the original half-timbered ceiling, now flecked with peeling paint. I had found a dresser drawer at the garbage depot that I turned on its side as a makeshift desk and a plastic stacking chair that I set up facing the exposed stone wall. Sitting down, I had about a foot before my head hit the ceiling. Now I climbed up to this sanctuary to get to work.

It's hard to know how a given location or environment can affect a person's artistic output. Countless artists and writers chose residency on the Côte d'Azur. Matisse famously came here for the light. He threw open his windows at the Hotel Beau Rivage after a storm to a sea so blue it seemed lit from within and decided that he couldn't leave. Renoir described the play of light on the olive trees outside Cagnes sur Mer as being like diamonds. Fitzgerald penned *The Great Gatsby* in the Murphy's Villa America in Antibes. James Baldwin lived the last decade and a half of his life in nearby St. Paul de Vence. Frederick Nietzsche wrote two books and started a third in Nice, his famous *Thus Spake Zarathustra*, only a couple blocks from our apartment. Other writers: Ernest Hemingway, Thomas Jefferson (does the *Declaration of Independence* count?), James Joyce, Vladimir Nabokov, and James Thurber all worked in Nice for periods of time. Writers at the beginning of their careers, the middle, or the end—they all saw something in the palms and cedars, the glistening sea, the markets and culture, like an inexhaustible muse.

The writer Anton Chekhov wrote that Nice was a good place to read but a terrible place to write. The statement isn't without some irony given that he completed the second half of the play *Three Sisters* here in a frenzy while actors in Moscow were already practicing the first two acts. Nice is known for its climate, for its indefatigable sun, for its leisurely pace of life. Perhaps this is why writing in Nice was difficult for Chekhov. Though he completed his work, he could have been—should have been—outside enjoying the balmy weather, reading a book on the beach. If he had been cooped up inside during a dreary Russian winter, Chekhov would've happily penned his stories. What else was there to do? But Nice was a place for leisure, for reading, for nightlife, for soaking up the sun and not worrying about commitments and deadlines. "I could never live in Nice," a writer friend from Iowa City once told me. A place like that and he'd never write again.

Old Nice especially, with its numerous bars, restaurants, and boutique shops, is like a generous lover, inviting you to sit down and stay awhile. In August of our arrival, Nice was in the last throes of its summer glamour, wanting its residents to maximize their enjoyment. Musicians played jazz sets to full crowds on the Cours Saleya. Breakdancers gyrated on the checkered paving stones of the Place Masséna. Night markets, concerts, festivals, and fireworks were regular occurrences. With so much going on, it was a miracle every time I got pen to paper, fingers to keyboard.

But now Nice had to be productive. Like Chekhov, I was operating under the constraints of time and purpose. This year I was on a research sabbatical, meaning that I needed to produce something of merit during my year-long sojourn. I was just finishing my third book, a collection of short stories, still searching for a title. I had an idea for another book that had been percolating: a young adult novel about a girl who discovers a race of telepathic dragons during an archaeological dig. It was the kind of frivolous writing that I had been dying to do for years. Now I could while away my morning following my precocious protagonist as she flew up into the air on the backs of one of these magnificent creatures. They were endangered, their breeding grounds affected by oil interests in the Alberta tar sands. As their only link to the human world, she alone could ensure their survival.

I didn't even notice when Rixa came back with Ivy and put her down for a nap. I stopped when I heard the hammering.

"Mold," Rixa said when I wandered down from the attic. She held up a white subway tile she had ripped from the shower to confirm. With Ivy asleep in the back bedroom and me tucked away in the attic, Rixa had got out a hammer and chisel and started chipping away at the ceramic shower.

Blooms of mold blotched the back of the tile, webbed through the grout. I knew what the tile meant. It signaled a commitment: the shower that we had assumed would require only some minor maintenance now needed to come down.

"Are you sure?"

"It's all through the wall and on the floor," Rixa said. "We couldn't see because the bed was pushed up against it."

"But the whole shower?"

"It has to go."

"My parents are coming in less than a month."

Rixa pointed to the corners where the tile met the shower pan. "Who-ever built this was supposed to set the tiles in further. These are *outside* the shower pan. They just caulked it and tried to cover it up. I keep smelling sewer gas and this morning I had a headache."

A couple days earlier we bought a dinky tool set from Carrefour. The previous owners had left some interesting tools—a wet tile saw, knee pads, files—but no basics like screwdrivers or hammers or wrenches. We only bought the set to do things like nail up pictures or tighten loose screws. One of the perks of the apartment, we kept telling ourselves, was that it needed only cosmetic work. Sure we *could* open up the front room and knock down that small dividing wall, but nothing was absolutely necessary. All we needed were some paint and decorations. I looked at the hole where Rixa had removed the tile.

"I could easily re-glue this."

But Rixa was already hammering the chisel under another tile at the top of the wall. I recognized the look: if you don't help me I'm going to do it myself.

A rectangular white tile fell to the shower pan, breaking at her feet. "That wasn't so hard," she said.

"You don't want to re-use the shower pan?"

"We should just buy a stand-alone shower. It would take up a lot less room. Then we don't have to re-tile the whole thing."

Tiles continued to fall, clacking and breaking like dishes tossed in a fireplace. "I think I saw another chisel in the attic," I said.

I took over demolition and Rixa unscrewed the shower door and set it aside. We were always at our best like this, working together on a project. Rixa got some reusable garbage bags to collect all the refuse. I wedged the chisel under tiles and pried them off. They had been glued to the sheet-rock—glued!—and the tiles fell off in sheets. A couple minutes and I was yanking off the sheetrock, exposing the poorly framed shower wall: just a couple two-by fours blackened by mold and braced in the middle. I shoved the wall like a linebacker hitting a sled till I heard the satisfying crack of splitting wood.

The rest of demolition sped along. Ivy was up from her nap and the kids would be home from school soon. I stuffed heavy-duty reusable bags full of broken tiles, sheetrock, plaster and moldy caulk. Half the wood frame was rotted. Just down the street was a local dump drop where I'd seen people leave flimsy armoires or busted lamps, even crumbling sheetrock. I hauled the bags down the stairs and piled them in front of the garbage bins. I opened the windows of our apartment and swept up the dirt and plaster dust. In a couple hours, the glass door leaning against the wall was all that was left of our leaky shower.

The intercom buzzed. Rixa and the kids were home. Zari, Dio, and Inga's voices filled the stairwell. Soon they stood in the entryway, looking at the empty room with the shower door and our bed leaning up against the wall: rectangles of blank concrete, exposed plumbing, an old sock stuffed in the shower drain. Rixa folded her arms, Ivy bouncing on her back in the baby carrier.

"How was the first day of school?"

"Looks like we've got a lot of work to do," she said.

Chapter 11

Cavigal

THE FLYER I HAD SEEN FOR Cavigal Football featured a girl kicking a ball, her pony tail flung to one side. Tryouts were the first Wednesday after the start of school. Bring cleats and shin guards. On their website I had noticed that they still needed coaches. Experience and diploma required. I emailed them anyway. They also had boys' teams starting at age five.

We got to tryouts early. A fence of metal spikes surrounded the club. Inside, more fences and gates: one around the full-size soccer pitch, another for the locker rooms. Chain link covered a smaller training pitch like a giant cage. Zari and Dio stuck close to me as we navigated through the throngs of parents and children decked out in soccer kits of their favorite teams: Barcelona, OGC Nice, Man City—but not a single kit from Monaco, Nice's biggest rivals. Trainers in matching Cavigal jerseys walked through the gates and closed them behind them.

A man with close-cropped hair wearing a red-and-black Adidas track suit opened the gate. Any child born in 2009, he said, over here. 2008, over here. Anyone for the girl's team, over here. A flurry of activity as people pressed forward. Each child separated from his or her parent and squeezed through a space wide enough for one child at a time. Dio clung to me but I reassured him, everything would be fine. The head coach announced: "You cannot come into the facility but must stay out here till the training is complete. Please do not interrupt or talk to your child during practice but instead allow our trainers to do their jobs."

My children walked out onto the pitch. Dio shuffled to a line of other terrified five-year-olds. He had never been on a soccer pitch before. A man wearing a white cap yelled in his face and pointed to where he should be standing. Zari was thrown in with a group of girls several years older than her and the speed and complexity of the game was beyond her ability. Soon they put her in goal. When the ball came toward her, she covered her face with her hands.

Maybe I had made a mistake.

During the tryout, I approached a gray-haired man with a pleasant face and an air of responsibility who was making his rounds among the trainers. We shook hands. I had emailed about helping with coaching. "I wondered who that was—who was this Canadian guy emailing me?" But he was sorry, the girl's team was already staffed. However, they still needed someone for the under-6 boys' teams. "Do you know soccer?" I played in college, I told him, and I had coached my daughter's team for two years now. Did I have a diploma? No, well that might be a problem. It's a big time commitment. What did I do for a living? "I'm a writer," I said. My time was flexible. "I can't promise anything," he said.

The guy was brushing me off. And my kids were getting trounced. I wondered what would happen if my kids didn't play soccer. It was unlikely that they would improve. Would they feel confident enough to play in pick-up games at the park? Zari would lose a pivotal year in her development. But the level was so advanced and the style of training so different from back home, that I worried that they'd never catch up. My children liked to succeed. How would they cope with being average? Or even terrible?

One of the key differences we had noticed with systems in France was how little they tried to inoculate children against failure. In the US, our children constantly received recognition for their exceptionalism, like just about every other child in their orbits. They got prizes for participating in class, prizes for doing their homework. At Zari's school, home to the Nicholson Knights, students would have an elaborate knighting ceremony for a variety of reasons: being a good citizen, not talking in the hallway, or reading their first book. In sports, the threshold for rewards seemed similarly low. Everyone was a winner! In France, the opposite often proved true. If your kid wasn't good enough now, what made you think that they'd improve? If they failed, no amount of telling them that they could do it would help. The motivation had to come from within, not from some gold star. Failure built character.

I was also wary of the evident machismo in the sport. As a child growing up in rural southern Alberta, I turned to soccer as an alternative sport to the small-town staples of hockey, basketball, and football. Soccer was fun because it didn't carry with it the same male politics of submission and domination that I saw in other sports. But here? Every time the trainer yelled, pointing at where Dio should be—ho! pay attention! get your head out of the clouds!—I recognized the same masculine tendencies to belittle, to beat down, to motivate through fear. The children would internalize these behaviors. As much as I loved the sport back home, I didn't know if I could handle my children navigating such a gendered space. Why, for example, were there no girls' teams till age eight? Why were they even separate at that age to begin with?

At the end of the practice, I waited with the scrum of parents for the club to release our children one by one through the gates. This wasn't the place for us. We could find something else to do on Wednesday afternoons. Dio came through first and hugged me. "I scored two goals!" Zari was next. How was it? She was thrilled by the speed of the game, how fast the girls played. My children's hair was wet with perspiration, their hale young bodies thrumming with energy. "The coaches said to come again next week." OK, I thought. If they really wanted to. But only one more time.

Chapter 12

Life without a Car

BEFORE THEY CAME TO VISIT, my parents asked what they should bring. I said snorkel gear and they were surprised. They thought they'd swim, but snorkeling? It wouldn't compare to the tropics, I told them, but it would still be worth it. Plus I had decided that I would try spearfishing. I had spent too much time watching videos and practicing my breathing not to. It was a wise investment, one that would pay off as I caught kilos of fish that my children were hungry to eat. All I needed now was someone to come with me to make sure that I didn't hurt myself.

I had researched the different brands of spearguns: Beuchat, Imersion, Mares, Cressi, Omer. I found another dive shop—a big one on the Port with a wall of arbalètes—and the owner told me that they were all accurate, that they would all catch fish, that the most important thing was my technique and how I handled the thing. I still wasn't ready to buy—just looking for now—but I had started to accumulate enough knowledge that I was close. Longer spears were more versatile and could be used more effectively in deeper water. Smaller spears were best for chasse au trou. I had looked on websites and finally settled on an entry-level speargun about a meter long with a 130-cm spear. Nootica.com had by far the best prices, so I filled up my virtual basket and was ready to buy when I noticed that the store was in St. Laurent du Var, just outside of Nice. The website allowed for direct pickup from the warehouse, no shipping and handling fee. I thought, time for a little trip.

Our decision not to get a car when we came to France was deliberate. As Midwesterners living in a small town, we felt trapped by our car. Even though we lived in the city center within walking distance from most amenities and my job, we still had to regularly use the car if we ever needed to go to the grocery store or to Indianapolis or to any outdoor activities. Public transportation didn't exist. So when the opportunity came to live in a city with an extensive network of trams and public and regional buses, we took it. It would, after all, be a more décroissant way of living. No car.

But as I charted a route to Nootica, I wondered if our no-car idealism was misguided. Some places in France are designed especially for the automobile. They're often the most forgettable places: the big department stores or bland suburbs or industrial parks filled with warehouses and parking lots and not much else. Still, even though Nootica was nestled among similar boxes of aluminum and concrete, three bus routes passed by either side of it. There were the 706 and the 707, two St. Laurent buses that stopped right next to Nootica, and the 52 which looped around after which you could catch the 51, not too far away. Bingo. I grabbed my bag. Did anyone want to come? Dio piped up. It was early afternoon, just after school, and I hoped to be back for supper around six.

We walked hand-in-hand to the bus stop near the Lycée Masséna. The 52 was frequent and it passed along the Promenade so it was fairly direct. Dio was chatty. We settled in two back seats. What had he liked so far in school? The ancient Greek-themed class was going well and right now they were learning about plants that they would grow. Later they were going to cultivate a garden. What kinds of plants? "Tulips," he told me in a French accent. He switched into French and I tried to keep the conversation going to hide my excitement. His French was very light and unaffected. It came out naturally in even cadences without the usual American diphthongs of a second language speaker. Soon we entered the maze of Nice Cap 3000, a huge shopping complex reminiscent of American malls. We stayed on the bus till it turned up north and we got off where we could supposedly catch the 706/707.

That's when things started to go wrong.

I didn't look up the hours for the 706/707 before we left, assuming that a local St. Laurent du Var bus would have similar hours to a city bus in Nice. But now I found that they came only every hour and we had missed the most recent one. If we wanted to get to Nootica before it closed, we'd have to go on foot.

Dio still bounded next to me, eager as a puppy. He was out on an excursion with his Papa and didn't seem to care that Papa had no idea where he was going. We were on the route of three buses and would take one if it happened to come along. We jogged on the sidewalk alongside cars zipping toward their destinations. We passed an Intermarche grocery store and then turned right to meet up with the Boulevard Georges Pompidou. Now sidewalks disappeared. We crossed lanes of traffic at a huge roundabout and cut into a parking lot. A girl in cleats walked with her mother toward a soccer stadium. We were near a junior high and cars pulled out taking children home. We passed the Hotel de Ville and a theatre and a municipal swimming pool. After walking or jogging a kilometer or more, Dio started to complain. He didn't want to run anymore. We found a bus stop and within five minutes a 42 came by. I asked the bus driver—what was the closest stop to the industrial park? Next one, he said. He drove us up a couple blocks and we got off. From there, he said, just continue up to the left and take the 51. If we were lucky we'd still get to Nootica in time.

We walked up to where the bus driver indicated. Luckily, a 51 came by and we waited for the stop that would bring us closest to Chemin de la Digue. It was 6 p.m. now, closing time for Nootica. But we were so close we decided to keep going instead of turning around. We passed a Tae-Kwon-Do club and fields of orange groves and homes in the country. Soon, the flat-roofed buildings of the industrial zone started to crowd the landscape. We were there. I pressed the plastic button on the metal bar and we slowed to a stop.

I recognized the area now from Google maps. We just had to go around the corner and find the road that led into the complex. Cars and scooters whizzed by us after finishing work. They weren't used to seeing pedestrians and drove faster than in town. We hugged the shoulders and checked the corners before proceeding around them. Soon a metal gate opened to an expanse of asphalt and warehouses for every imaginable industry. Next to Garage Abrigo we saw a red-and-black sign. Nootica. A concrete ramp descended to the store.

Both Dio and I still wore our summer clothes: board shorts, t-shirts, and sandals. Dio is almost white-blond and he wore a handmade tie-dye shirt. We looked distinctly un-French and out of place, especially in this boxy industrial park that was wrapping up for the day. A woman in leopard tights, her hand looped through the open visor of a motorcycle helmet passed us, jangling keys. It was past closing but two men smoked outside the entrance. Were they open? What was it for? I was looking to buy a spe-argun. Yes, yes, they said and led us through the glass doors. The guy was friendly, a twenty-something youth with a round face and black curly hair. I was interested in the Beuchat Arker and the Imersion Pro Challenger, I said. I was a beginner but I wanted something that would still be relevant after I improved my technique.

Go with the Challenger Pro, he told me. You can't get a better arbalète for the price. I took him at his word and purchased it with my credit card. We opened the plastic sleeve and he showed me how to arm it by pull-ing the elastic down and notching it into the spear. It was stiff and almost impossible to get the elastic to budge. Not here—only in the water, he said, and he gave me a card. Any questions I might have, even about good fishing spots, they were here to help.

And then the thing was done.

We walked out into the waning sun with my speargun in its plastic sleeve. Dio wanted to carry it. It was taller than I thought it would be, stretching up to my chest. For Dio it was like a black-and-white walking stick with a pointy tip. He wrapped his arms around it like he was cuddling a teddy bear and the handle kept knocking against his knees. The whole industrial park was closing down. I was tempted to ask someone if we could hitch a ride back to Nice. But the speargun made me extra self-conscious; shouldn't we be the kind of people who already had a car? We wouldn't be walking so awkwardly if we had miles ahead of us, especially not dressed the way we were.

I'm hungry, Dio said.

It was already seven. It had taken us almost three hours to get here and I knew Dio couldn't hold out too much longer. We still hadn't quite adjusted to the French custom of eating around eight. Our kids were usu-ally in bed by then. We passed an empty snack place and I asked if they were open. "Sorry, only at lunch," a comment that worried me all the more. We walked back to the bus stop and I read through the schedule. The last bus for the day had already come and gone. We were going to have to walk the kilometer or so back to where the 52 looped around—the stop we should've gotten off at to begin with.

I had a thought—a fleeting thought that I pushed to the back of my mind: what if the 52 was similarly done for the day? The buses here seemed to cater most to the people who needed it: workers who finished at the industrial park by seven. There would be no reason for the buses to be running any longer. If that was the case, we were stranded. No food, no transportation, no shelter. When it was dark it would get colder and then what? A taxi would negate the money we'd saved. Alone, I could jog back to St. Laurent, push my hunger down into my gut. But not with my five-year-old son.

I took the speargun now and held Dio's hand since there was no shoulder and we were vulnerable to passing traffic. It was getting dark. We needed food. We were out in the country and I couldn't remember seeing any place to eat on our way in. I felt incredibly stupid. My kids might not have much experience with failure but now they were going to get it through me. My dumb phone could run out of batteries and then where would we be? We could starve, be hit by a car, freeze to death, any number of calamities. I could trip and impale myself on the speargun. I'd plug the gushing blood from the deep wound and give instructions to my son so he could find his way back home. "Tell your mother I love her," I'd say, my hand holding the dead phone.

My failure also felt emblematic of all that was not going well so far during our year-long sojourn. We were burning through money faster than we realized and now I'd purchased a potentially unnecessary item for the promise of saving money on food later, putting us further in the hole. Other failures abounded: my young adult novel wasn't developing the way I'd hoped. I found myself trapped in a confluence of bad plot choices that were leading to a gratuitous disaster. Our calculated plan was causing our children to suffer. Zari was struggling to fit in at school. Dio and Zari would get crushed in soccer. Guidebooks warned over and over again about French schools, the conformity, the ways that outsiders get branded as different and become targets of ridicule. Now the speargun was a symbol of my lack of ability to provide even the most basic necessity of food.

But then, like I had planned it, a gravel drive opened on our right to a parking lot and there was a Multari bakery, open for business. It was like a mirage, an oasis in the desert. No, it was real—bricks and mortar, a chain bakery with sandwiches and meals-to-go. "Do you want some pizza?" I asked Dio. We ordered and got two slices, a Tropezienne patisserie and a can of Orangina. Not the healthiest dinner but he was thrilled, especially about the cream-filled Tropezienne. We sat on the terrace with my spe-argun leaning against our square café table. Dio ate the Tropezienne and licked the thick cream off his fingers. Powdered sugar dusted his lips. "This is really good. Thank you Papa." We hadn't eaten any street food since our first night here when we had to grab some socca, both times from a feeling of necessity. But we had to get back on the road. It was almost eight and the sun was low on the horizon. We only had about another hour of light at most. We bagged the rest of the pizza and walked back out to the road.

Orchards and vineyards appeared. A bus stop fronted a stone fence. Overhanging grape vines bore globes of ripe muscat. I picked one and tried it: very sweet with tiny seeds hard as stones. The flavor was com-plex and dark. We filled our bag with the fruit and continued down the road single file.

"Mama's going to be so happy we found grapes," Dio said. He ate one after the other and spit the seeds on the ground. I thought, yes she will be. Grapes were in season now and this haul would more than compensate for our two bus tickets. We kept walking. I used the speargun like a hiking stick. At the end of the stock was a flat foot that helped me gain purchase on the gravelly shoulder. Up ahead the Tae-Kwon-do building appeared and I knew that we were there. The posted schedule said that the 52 came every fifteen minutes till ten p.m.

When we got on the bus it was already dark. Dio and I munched away on our grapes and we laid the speargun at our feet. During the trip, Dio fell asleep on my lap. I scratched his back till he was happily snoring. The bus filled and emptied. Near the end of the line, we emerged from the bus to the Lycée Masséna lit up like a medieval fortress. We walked home holding hands. He burst through our apartment door and told Rixa what a trip we had.

Chapter 13

Making It Pay

I GREW UP IN A FAMILY with a very socialist view of money. As a child, I had a paper route while my father was in graduate school on a grant from the Canadian government. We were a family of eight. All the money from my paper route went to pay for family expenses: school clothes for my sisters, a new (used) washing machine when ours broke down. Sometimes I would be on the receiving end: money for violin lessons, or for going to a movie with my friends. In high school we treated money like it was in a big tip jar that we'd sometimes take from and sometimes replenish. We had occasional squabbles or negotiations, but far less than you'd see in most governmental meetings about dispensing public funds.

A friend of mine had a similar upbringing but with very different results. As a teenager he supported a single mother and two siblings. But his constant support, unequal contribution from other family members, and a parent who had substance abuse dependency issues forced him to make desperate choices early on. By high school, he was the gatekeeper, hiding income from his mother in order to keep the rest of his family afloat. The experience made him aware of the power of capital. Preserving it could ensure your well-being. Squandering it could leave you destitute.

Over-extending ourselves had made us more aware of our expenses than ever. Till now, we'd always been able to balance our expenditures with our income, like our own version of a tip jar that we could use when we needed to, always confident that money would return. But now expenditures were adding up, depleting our savings. Another transfer to our French bank account drove home that our current spending was not sustainable. Our addiction to France was costing us our livelihood.

"We have to stop hemorrhaging money," Rixa said. The Euro was falling against the dollar and yet we were still struggling. My half salary for sabbatical compounded our problems. Now everything in our lives had monetary connotations. The 50-euro speargun was an investment on the kilos of fish it could presumably help me catch. The bags of grapes Dio and I had picked on the side of the road helped justify our impromptu take-out meal. Now our kids wanted to do soccer, a year-long commitment that would cost 135 euros per kid—an amazing deal by US standards, but more than we could currently afford. We had spent money on furniture, on snorkel equipment, on school supplies, and on groceries. We couldn't justify leisure activities if it meant that they were going to put us further in the hole.

"I thought you wanted to go skiing," Rixa said.

"The fee includes their uniforms and all the games on the weekends."

"I don't see how we can do both."

"Tryouts are still free."

Fine. We could make the decision if they were able to get in.

The next Wednesday, the kids dutifully suited up and followed me to the tram. On the way, Zari complained about how she was fed up with French school. Her experience hadn't improved. "We don't have any playground equipment," she said. "And we don't have enough activities. All we do is work and my teacher is mean." In the tram, we held to a pole and jostled among other passengers. Cavigal was about a fifteen-minute ride, past Vauban and the St. Roch market.

"I love school," Dio said.

"You're just saying that to make me mad," Zari said.

"Les enfants. . ." I said.

A pattern had been developing. Zari, who had always thrived in school, now complained that if it wasn't in French it would be "easy-peasy." Her teacher shouted too much and spoke incomprehensible English. Dio's Greek-themed class was fun and engaging. He'd made friends. Later on in the year they would be putting on a play. Before school started, we had been more worried about Dio since he had never gone to preschool. His French skills were weaker. But now he was enjoying himself and this seemed to exasperate Zari all the more. "It's not fair!" she said.

At soccer, I worried the negativity would carry over into the tryout. I braced for another letdown, determined that this would be the last week. But when I got to the closed gates and anxious parents, one of the trainers motioned for me to come in.

Dio and Zari split off into their respective groups. I recognized the trainer with the clipboard from last week, the expeditious organizer who had divvied everyone up like a Hogwarts sorting hat. He was Jeremy, the head trainer. "I hear you're willing to help us out with the under-six boys?"

"If you need me," I said, using the formal register "vous." The president of the club must have been more impressed with me during our short meeting than he had let on.

"We should tu-toi each other," he said. "It would simplify things."

"Okay."

"We have an informational meeting today for new parents, but after it's over I can introduce you to the rest of the coaching staff." He shook my hand. I was in.

Jeremy led the informational session in the top room of the clubhouse. He stood next to a stand with a computer projecting onto the wall. This would be my last experience as a Cavigal parent as I transitioned to becoming a soccer coach in what I would soon find out was one of the most competitive clubs in southern France.

He started his lecture explaining how kids at this stage needed support and to have fun, not feel like their parents were pressuring them to become the next Zinadine Zidane. "Cet esprit ludique," he said, "est très important."

Then he showed a PowerPoint.

The first slide outlined a "philosophy of life" containing "keys for success" that the club would teach to the twenty-four chosen five-year-olds lucky enough to make the cut. The next slides covered the club's history, and showed its variety of teams and activities throughout the year. It lauded its trainers, its facilities, its engagement, its organization. Cavigal would cultivate respect and perseverance. Kids would learn rules of life through trial and error. They would experience defeat but also victory.

But remember, one slide said. Soccer is just a game.

I looked around the room to gauge people's reactions. Even with the background music, Queen blasting "We Are the Champions," nobody seemed to think what we were seeing was in any way over-the-top or unusual. They had obviously known about Cavigal's reputation before they came here and tried out with the other hundred kids hoping to make it. Just a game, yes, but more than that at this club. The last few slides reinforced this attitude. One showed the transitional period from "Football School" to "Pre-Formation." From U6 to U9, the three eight-sided teams were in the recruitment phase. After that, they would receive a diploma that detailed their weak points and noted opportunities for improvement. Players were judged according to four criteria: comportment, technical skill, speed, and play. In U10 and U11, the teams went through a period of "brassage," literally meaning "brewing" but more akin to a slimming down or galvaniz-ing the core team as they went from three teams of eight to two teams of ten. After that, recruitment again for U12 and U13 as they went back up to two teams of twelve. Then at U14, another recruitment to two teams of fourteen, then a big "brassage" down to one team of eighteen for U15. Every year after that, recruitment and brassage, with one team ending at U19, with most or all of the players now integrated into professional teams. Some other milestones along the way contributed to their development: the first, regional tournaments and classification at the U10 level, then na-tional tournaments and classification starting at U13. At U16, partnership with OGC Nice. This is when kids would also begin signing with agents and have their first loans out to professional clubs.

Just a game.

Parents had plenty of questions. If their six-year-old eventually en-tertained offers from professional teams, when should they move? Would their kid need to enroll in one of the sports-only boarding schools? Jeremy responded as best he could. "Family support is essential. Of the research we have, children are best off if their families follow them. Sending a child off without family support puts their chances of development at risk." For proof, he clicked back a few slides and pointed to the "Family" bubble that was tied to both the educational "Football School" time period and the "Pre-Formation" period. In order to effectively make the transition, Jeremy said, kids needed their family nearby. For example, Messi. He moved from Argentina with his family and didn't even live with the other students at boarding school. Though he was a product of Barcelona's program, it was unlikely he would have had the same success without the extensive family support. So many other kids had moved for the promise of a future with a club and their success rate was abysmal, the kids like playing cards were lost in a shuffle.

A woman raised her hand. If Cavigal wanted her son, when should she expect a *devis*?

I was unclear exactly what the woman was asking—a devis was an estimate, but an estimate for what? Jeremy's response made it clear: if we want to sponsor your child, when the time comes, we will approach you and not the other way around. Now I got it. Her six-year-old was a soccer star and she wanted to get paid.

I wandered out of the informational meeting in a daze. Before this day I had never even considered that my child would be or even should be a soccer star. I wanted my kids to be kids, to have fun, to play. Although Jeremy's PowerPoint emphasized the importance of developing a "ludic spirit," pressure from the other parents made clear that this wasn't their motivation for bringing them here. With all the money in international soccer now, a child who showed early promise could be a meal ticket later on. Just that year, Italy's professional team Roma had signed nine-year-old wunderkind Pietro Tomaselli. And if a professional club felt that they were able to identify true talent at nine years old, why wouldn't they at six? Now I was a part of this club, something that made me feel both simultaneously proud and worried that I'd be unmasked as a fraud, a guy who was literally way out of his league.

After the meeting, Jeremy walked me out onto the pitch. Two trainers wrangled kids out of different-colored pinnies. Practice was over. One trainer was tall and graying with a red-and-white Cavigal shirt tucked into a pair of Adidas track pants. "Alain," he said, shaking my hand. I recognized him as the trainer who yelled at Dio over and over again last week when he wouldn't move from one spot to another. "I didn't realize Dio was a second-language speaker," he said. "Practice went much better today." The other trainer was a bald and portly man with a beard, an ex-pro player who now worked as a mortgage broker. "Jean-Yves," he said. "You and I will be taking the second and third teams."

Most of the kids had removed their pinnies now and were sitting dutifully in a square designated by four cones. This would be our "maison," the home base where kids would sit in between exercises and scrimmages, where they would have to refrain from touching the nearby bags full of size-three soccer balls. Alain shepherded the kids with military precision. And like a drill sergeant, he'd yell if they got out of line. Both Alain and Jean-Yves tutoyed me right away; we were on the same level now, the same team. The formal register "vous" would be something reserved for parents, for discussions about their child's progress, or to console them when it wasn't working out and their child needed to find another club.

We lined up the kids now, each with their arms on the shoulders of the one in front of them in a human train, and walked them to the gate. We called parents and then handed kids through one by one. Next week I'd have to be there early to help set up the cones and get the goals in place. I'd need to get my official trainer "license" which included a doctor's visit for a bill of health. The kids would similarly have to get one now that they were officially Cavigal players, my position as trainer securing them spots on their respective teams. We were about to be welcomed in to a different kind of French experience now, an exclusive club of athletic elites. And like many clubs with a certain threshold of belonging, the rules applied differently for those fortunate enough to make it. For unlike the children of stressed parents who had been grooming their six-year-old for football stardom since before they were born, my kids wouldn't have to pay.

Chapter 14

A Son in Nice

OUR BEDROOM NOW LOOKED like the inside of an abandoned public bathroom with the urinals torn off the walls. The floor was a composite marble but it was stained and dingy. Naked plumbing crooked out from the wall at odd angles. An old sock plugged the shower drain. Our only furniture was the double bed that sat about a foot off the floor. The high ceilings made the bed seem like an army cot in some bombed-out building, a temporary arrangement till we could find something less exposed.

My parents were coming to visit next week. And yet, we weren't embarrassed but excited for them to see this place. Sometimes I felt like Nikolai in Chekhov's "Gooseberries," chomping away on the sour and unripe berries as though they were the tastiest things in the world. We had spent our livelihood on this place and perhaps we merely wanted people to see why we would risk our financial wellbeing for such a dive. But our apartment embodied a philosophy about space and scale that went contrary to the tide of popular opinion back home. We didn't need four bedrooms and a two-car garage and bathrooms on every level. We were les décroissants. So our family of six lived in 700-square-foot apartment. That didn't mean that we couldn't also accommodate guests.

Living in a small apartment made us question some of the core assumptions we have about living, a vision of middle-class bliss that is dominated by the single-family home. Go to other countries outside North America, and people don't use the term "single-family home." A single family could live in an apartment, for example, or a row house. And what exactly is a single family? Does that mean a single generation? Or does a live-in grandmother count? Real estate listings are especially interesting for the kinds of values inherent in their descriptions. In the UK, listings describe the type of building rather than make assumptions about family makeup. In France, listings are even more complex, choosing instead to mention the number of rooms, whether or not the kitchen is "equipped" or separate from the rest of the apartment or house. Details like the square meters over the "loi carré" and the amount of balcony or storage space can drastically change the perceived value of a property and its appropriateness for a couple or a multi-generational family. Their system is more bureaucratized and impersonal but less judgmental. A single family home. Only in North America would we have such a widely-used designation that so directly normalizes middle-class expectations.

So when we bought an apartment in the south of France, one of our prime considerations was how to accommodate people. Even in our tiny apartment, we could give visitors privacy and still have room for our own four children. Why not? With the bedroom/half-bath in the front and the bedroom/bathroom in the back, our apartment naturally divided into two distinct areas. The narrow hallway reduced noise and gave each area a feeling of separation. The attic bedroom where I wrote with its nooks and storage space was even more private, the perfect place to put a bunch of kids.

But I was nervous about my parents' visit. As their oldest son, I had been coming to France for almost twenty years and each trip spawned stories of its grandiosity. I worried that I had created unrealistic expectations. And now they'd be in a tiny apartment, sleeping in our front bedroom with its exposed plumbing and stark furnishings. But the evening that my mother walked into our apartment, she said, "Wow!" in a voice melodious and sing-songy. She looked closely at the details, the oiled wood antiques and the mahogany bookcase filled with Bernard's leather books. Our children were asleep in the back rooms and so our conversation was more muted than usual even though I could tell that the place had already begun to bring about my parents' transformation. My mother grew up on a farm in southern Alberta. My dad was the son of a vacuum cleaner salesman. All their married lives and during my childhood, they had struggled with money. Now they were in the south of France, a place unlike anywhere they had ever been. They opened the windows and looked up and down the street. They were shocked to see others across from us, close enough that we could toss a rope and tight-walk the expanse. They should've been tired, it was the early morning back in Canada, but still they wanted to explore. They only had seven days to experience it all.

Did they want to see the Mediterranean?

As recent retirees, my parents took every opportunity to go anywhere with a beach. After a recent trip to Florida, my mother said, "I love the waves coming in, the energy—it is just soothing to me—there is something about the sun shining on the water." My parents associate the sea with re- laxation, leisure, and peace. So that first night at our apartment, we went to the Promenade des Anglais and sat on the rocks. Nearby, teenagers teased out a few songs on a guitar and a family with two kids built stone cairns parallel to the shoreline. The waves were small, slowly tumbling pebbles back and forth. It was like the shores of the Great Lakes on a calm day. "To have this all right here!" my mother said.

Over the next few days, my parents hiked, went to museums, visited perched villages and swam and snorkeled. In the afternoon, when the kids were out of school, we took a trip to Eze and Monaco. As grandparents, they seemed to take most pleasure in those activities that included their grandchildren. They walked our kids to school, watched their soccer prac- tices while I coached, and offered to babysit one evening so we could go to a movie. When we were not with them, my parents seemed more adrift, more like virginal French tourists. For years, they had heard me idealize French culture. Now that they were finally here, it was impossible for them to cram all those years of learning the language and altering my life to ac- commodate a new world view and ideology. France had affected my palate, my habits, my attitude around strangers, my leisure activities, my sense of self. For them it was merely where their son lived. Every time they came back from a walk I pounced on them, asking: did they enjoy the open air market? Had they tried socca yet? How about the belle-époque-era opera building? Did they know that Auer was one of the oldest candy makers in the world? It was Queen Victoria's favorite! They always answered posi- tively, telling me how great it all was. "What a neat place!" my dad said, over and over. "You know, you really should write about it."

Still, I couldn't help feel that their visit was primarily for me. For the past ten years or more, I had invited my parents to come, to see France, and always there was some competing event—a family reunion, another vacation, an ailing relative. Each invitation strengthened their resolve till finally, after we bought the apartment and my brother found them plane tickets too cheap to ignore, they made the trip. So now they were here. How could they hope to receive the approbation of their eldest son? Again the sea would provide the best opportunity.

Chapter 15

First Catch

JUST ACROSS THE STREET FROM our apartment, *en face* as the French would say, is a small grocery that's open late. Next door to us is a halal butcher run by a man named Mourad. Around these core businesses are two art galleries, and "Media Cité," a community organization that offers free French classes for second-language speakers and helps immigrants adjust to life in France.

Mourad is the most ubiquitous of our neighbors. His shop is always open at 7 a.m. and he closes only on Tuesdays because the Palais Lascaris is also closed, greatly reducing foot traffic. Every day he smiles, greets us in his white smock, pacing in front of his rotisserie machine where you can buy a roast chicken for five euros.

The butcher stopped me the day I convinced my parents to visit the calanques on the other side of the Port. I carried my new speargun without a bag so it was hard not to notice. "Oh, un harpon!" he said when he saw me.

"Arbalète."

"Bien sûr! Une arbalète! Oh elle est belle."

We started talking. Mourad was an avid angler who fished every Tuesday with his friend Laurent on the west side of Monaco. They caught Liche and Tassergal, the kind of fish people mounted on their walls. He was familiar with the arbalète I had purchased and he said that it was a speargun for going deep. Could I go that deep? I hope to, I said. Did I know where to go? The best place was the point past Coco Beach. "I always see spearfishers there," he said. "Dorades as long as my arm."

My parents nodded and smiled, the cordial Canadians, and we said goodbye and walked to the Port.

I had scouted out a few places to start fishing near La Réserve restaurant. The beaches here were tiny coves nestled among white and tan rocks. Stone stairs led down from several points along the boardwalk. Beach towels and sunbathers filled every moderately flat space. I wanted to get to a pristine pebble beach that was only accessible by water. From there I could swim in the bay or over to the point that the butcher mentioned. We took the stairs down, navigated through the rocks and then sloshed through the water holding our bags and my speargun above our heads like Marines.

We laid out our beach mats and snorkel equipment. I hoped my short wetsuit would keep me warm. It was late September and the water had been getting cooler.

"This is gorgeous," my mom said.

For a moment, we sat and soaked in the sun, drying our legs that were wet to the thighs. The cove secluded us from the crowds that were so visible from the boardwalk. Now looking at the sea we had the impression that we were all alone: just the rocks, the sun, and the water lapping the shore.

"I'm going out," I said.

I zipped myself up, spit in my goggles, put on my travel fins. My parents would follow behind me to give me space. I pushed off and a little water entered my suit from the back. Already the marine life and clarity was impressive. Off to the left, a small sea cave and a gigantic rock encrusted with coral and sea urchins, promised fertile fishing. But first I had to arm my spear.

At Nootica, I had stretched the elastic but I didn't attach it. The guy just showed me where the clasp hooked into the teeth at the spear's base. Now, in the water, I pulled the elastic with the speargun handle pressing into my thigh for support. I could only stretch it about half way before the speargun slipped off my leg. I tried again and this time wound up submerging my head so my snorkel filled with water. Ugh. How was I going to go spearfishing if I couldn't even arm the thing?

My parents treaded water behind me, watching the show.

I needed more leverage. This time I put the handle on my abdomen. I clenched my abs and pulled the elastic down, down. I was almost to the first rung, suddenly aware of the amount of tension I was about to release. If I didn't get it to catch, the metal clasp in the middle of the elastic could slice off my bare fingers. Another inch and it clicked into place.

73

Done. I pointed the speargun away from me. It was like a ticking time bomb. I was careful not to bump anything, to destabilize it and send the spear rocketing out. I gave my parents a thumbs up.

My acrobatics in arming my spear had scared all the fish away. Now all I saw were rocks. Maybe the fish were hiding? Up near the submerged rock the size of a house, I took a deep breath and dove. I descended ten, fifteen, now twenty feet. I pinched my nose and pushed the air out to equalize my ears. A couple labres flitted around the base of the rock. They were striped and colorful with purple, gold and green hues. They glided away from me like little submarines. Any effort to get closer sent them darting away, like I had just zapped them with electricity. Soon I was out of breath. I kicked up to the surface.

This was going to be much harder than I thought. At the dive shop, the owner had said that fish were *mefiant,* and I remembered thinking, really? I seemed to be able to get close enough to them when I was snorkeling. He emphasized the importance of having a black mask, a camouflaged wetsuit, gloves and neoprene socks covering every possible inch of exposed flesh. At the time I thought he was merely trying to make a sale but now I saw how he may have been right. The fish seemed to intuit that I was a threat.

I tried anyway. Chasse au trou. The online videos made it look so simple: just watch where the fish goes and then find the hole, shoot your spear into it and voila! Fish on a spear. Maybe it was the location I had chosen but here the rocks were piled on each other, leaving holes within holes, little crevices that led to others, making it almost impossible to find a fish once it had gone for shelter. I dove down, looking for the fish, only to realize that it was probably on the other side of the bay by now, having navigated an escape route through the rocks that was invisible to me.

Chasse à l'indienne. This proved more promising. I hovered above schools of fish and then dove, hoping to reach them before they were entirely aware of my presence. But I didn't yet have the breath to sustain much of a chase. When I snorkeled, this was how I often got closest to the fish but now that I had a shiny spear pointed in front of me, the fishes' blind spots didn't seem to be as large. Too often, they saw me coming.

Chasse à l'agachon. I tried this once and lay on the sea floor for a pathetically short period of time. My suit buoyed me up so it was hard to stay in one position. Instead, I had to keep kicking, skimming the sea floor like a shark till I found a rock I could hold onto. After one dive, all the fish were miles away.

I considered randomly discharging my spear into a school of saupe. There were about thirty or so, nipping at some vegetation. Anecdotes existed about saupe as hallucinogenic; markets sometimes refused to sell them for fear they'd send their customers on acid trips. During the Roman Empire, socialites would serve them for their orgies. But every angler I knew would take them. They had a strong flavor and a firm white flesh, perfect for a bouillabaisse or en papillote with olive oil and herbs. I fired. My spear few into the rock and the fish scattered. Nothing. I pulled the spear up by the string and inspected the dented tip.

Fish: 1. Me: 0. I poked my head out of the water. My parents were already back at our secluded beach, lying out in the sun. Despite my failure, or maybe because of it, I wanted to try again. I kicked hard back to shore and beached myself at my parents' feet.

"How'd it go?" my mother asked.

"I think I need to go out farther."

"Take your time. We could sit out here all day."

Whatever ethical quandaries I had been having, my actions had led me to do this thing: to catch a fish that we would take home to eat. In several ways, I was still unprepared. I had the basics—a spring suit, a mask and snorkel, a speargun—but I lacked gloves to protect my hands and a weight belt to compensate for my wetsuit-assisted buoyancy. I was an amateur who was hoping to luck out, to find a fish willing to give itself for our sustenance.

I decided to swim out further, to the point that the butcher had mentioned. The sea floor receded till I could barely make out the beds of sea grass. Out in the open like this I felt small, a little like prey.

It gave me vertigo. The Bay of Angels where I usually snorkeled didn't have such clarity and depth. Now white calanques appeared before me, plunging fifteen, fifty, a hundred feet or more to the sea floor. I was at the point. Small fish nipped at coral or seaweed coating the rocks. Further down I could see a school of mulet and another of saupe. I wondered if this is where I would find those monstrous dorades that the butcher hinted at, fish that could strip all the flesh off my wiry frame in a couple minutes if they had a mind to.

I practiced my breathing, filled up my lungs, and dove.

Nothing. My snorkel gurgled as the air siphoned through. I had armed my spear but the high visibility meant that the fish saw me, my shiny spear like a flood light. I was going to need patience and stealth in more quantities than I possessed. I tried hiding as the rocks turned corners. But if I didn't keep moving, kicking my flippers to send me lower, my air-filled lungs and wetsuit pulled me prematurely back to the surface. Fish flitted away, out of reach with every kick, every move, every glint of light.

I'd been out now for almost two hours. My thighs were starting to cramp. I was unable to stay submerged more than a few seconds. The whorls of my fingers had puckered like raisins.

One last dive. I aimed for a small shelf. I could wedge myself under it and get a fish coming around the corner. I bent at the waist and plunged headfirst. I kicked down and positioned my shoulder against the rock, using my buoyancy to keep me stable.

Then I waited. A few seconds, maybe ten. A roucaou finned its way toward me. I had read about the roucaou, *poissons de roche*, the anglers called them: rock fish. They were plentiful and largely undesirable for anything but soup. It was still out of range but it didn't seem to see me as a threat. It came closer. Three feet, two. My lungs were on fire. Then it turned so it was transversal, almost like it wanted to give its body up to me.

I fired. The spear drove through the back of the dorsal fin. I pushed off from the rock and shot to the surface.

I pulled the string attached to my spear. The fish was still alive and smaller than I thought. The depth and distance had distorted the size. Its stripes were green with flecks of purple and blue. The colorful ones are males, the peacock of the labre family, and its beauty filled me with regret. I could eat this fish no bigger than my hand but I knew it would be bony, not large enough to develop the thick filets I craved. Plus I had barely nicked its dorsal fin. I completely missed the head. If I let it go, it would heal.

The roucaou still wriggled on my spear, trying to swim away. I wondered if I really had the temperament to do this thing. The complicity of buying fish at the market was so much easier. Spearing fish felt like losing my life force, like I'd somehow killed a part of myself. I maneuvered the fish, the spines of its fins pricking my fingers. A couple strategic pushes and it slid off the spear, swimming vigorously back into the depths of the sea.

Chapter 16

Nice Life on a Budget

MY PARENTS WERE GONE. We moved back into the bombed-out front bedroom.

"It'd be nice to have just a little more space," Rixa said.

We were thinking ahead to renovations we wanted to complete. It was October now and all we had done since our arrival was demolish a shower.

"Maybe we could add a mezzanine?"

One of our favorite features of the apartment was the high ceilings in the front rooms. You opened the door and boom: fourteen feet of open space with ten-foot-long windows looking out over the street. But the high ceilings also meant that there was room to build. Apartments in France would often feature either built-in mezzanines or furniture that found innovative ways to use the space: an elevated bed with a line of drawers and a ladder, or a bunkbed with a hide-a-bed or a couch on the bottom. While we admired the practical ingenuity of this kind of furniture, we generally disliked the aesthetics, the mass-produced, disposable quality of these products. The ubiquity of this furniture on Leboncoin solidified our resolve: we would only choose this route as a last resort. Till then, we should think about adding a mezzanine.

We differed on the particulars. I was thinking a mezzanine in the bedroom, something tall enough to accommodate an armoire and maybe a writing desk underneath. Rixa was surprised. "I thought you enjoyed writing in the attic?" Her idea was more ambitious: take the existing attic space and extend it to our front room. It could create a larger play area that would look out to the front. She didn't want to put a mezzanine in the bedroom. "If we're just going to have a mezzanine for a bed it makes more sense just to buy the furniture." But didn't we also want to put in a shower/sink in the bedroom like we had before?

"It would be too dark," Rixa said. One of the more interesting details of our apartment was how it capitalized off natural light. About eight feet off the floor, three windows opened up to the kitchen, brightening the room. Putting a mezzanine underneath the window would cut out most of this light, making the room feel *sombre*, the French call it—dark with a more depressing connotation.

"What about a mezzanine after the entryway?" Rixa said.

"Then where would we put the staircase? Only the kids would use it and they already have the attic."

"I just don't like the idea of losing our only natural light."

"We still have the back window."

We were at a stalemate. In the past, deadlines had always driven our renovations. But we didn't want to start something that would take too much time and money to finish. Finances were tight. And although we'd done this kind of work before, we hadn't ever dug holes in rock walls that were hundreds of years old. We would likely need to hire someone which put the project out of our budget.

Meanwhile, a peer group seemed to be forming around children from Inga's class and their parents. Every day after school now, we went to the coulée verte instead of the beach. The closest playground equipment was the great wooden pirate ship and the treehouse with the ropes course, both installations designated for children over twelve that our collective three-to-seven-year-olds blissfully ignored.

"How come Vincent never comes to the park?" I asked Samira. It had begun to occur to me that I was often the only man around. All Inga's friends came with their mothers: Sandra, a taller version of Audrey Tatou who always wore enormous round sunglasses, Sabine, a young single mother who was chronically late, and the Muslim woman Kahina, whose youngest was also in Inga's class. Two Anglophones also came regularly: the musician Allie with blue hair smoking her e-cigarettes, and Themla, an Irish woman with two daughters.

"All the screaming drives him crazy."

Today the city had a series of ateliers for children set up around the coulée verte. In between games of freeze tag—called "trap-trap" in French—our children got their faces painted, made candles, and then learned to identify species of fish by their fins. Before dinner, they watched a Guignols performance in a temporary theatre—a traditional puppet show like the one in Truffaut's famous film *Les 400 Coups*. Like many of the activities in Nice, we stumbled on them by accident. What was the occasion? An inauguration? Neighborhood party? Maybe a maritime festival since so much of it revolved around the sea. There *was* a lot of screaming— always seemed to be with children involved—but it was worth it for how much they benefitted from the experience.

"You going to the *spectacle* this evening?" Sam asked when we started to leave for dinner. "Maybe we'll see you there."

Rixa and I talked about it when we got home. Ivy was still not sleeping through the night, waking up four or five times to nurse, leaving Rixa feeling depleted and exhausted. I was able to compensate by taking the children out and giving her time to relax but today we'd been at the park all afternoon and a late night meant cranky children the next day.

"It's Friday, though—no school tomorrow."

"You're not the one who has to get up in the middle of the night."

"It starts at seven. Maybe if we just go for an hour?" We wrangled the kids into their shoes and jackets, a process that always felt a little like Whack-a-Mole as one new concern popped up just as another was resolved. My sandals are rubbing—I want to wear my shoes. I forgot to go to the bathroom! But soon we were out along the Promenade du Paillon, walking past the playground equipment and the statue of André Masséna, the Napoleonic military commander from whom the Place Masséna derives its name. Crowds started near the miroir d'eau. The spectacle was advertised as an "aerial fantasy" but until we arrived, we had little idea what that meant. Two large translucent helium balloons were tethered to the ground. Nearby, women in metal corsets stretched ahead of their performance. A little jostling near the end of the promenade and soon the spectacle began.

The French are often known for their "son et lumière." Music will accompany a light show in front of a cathedral, a chateau, or some other historic site. Versailles sets its famous fountains to music for scheduled periods of time, requiring tickets weeks in advance. The chateaux of the Loire valley often have son et lumière set to baroque music with people marching around in medieval robes. We had expected something similar—the fountains going during a light show with some musical accompaniment. But as the dancers attached themselves to balloons and floated into the air, I knew we were in for something different.

When does kitsch become art? All up and down our street in Old Nice, artists plied their wares in galleries or studios: stencils of famous figures in Yves Klein blue or watercolor paintings of Niçois streets. Every day we opened our door to tourists snapping photos on their phones of the Palais Lascaris or the Place Rosetti. In 1885, the renowned photographer Jean Gilletta took the first photograph of our street, the floor-level of the homes around the Palais Lascaris crowded with businesses. Our own front door was the entrance to a mattress maker. Were any of the tourist photographs of our street through the years really all that different? Here was a place in time, represented to jog the memory, to remind the viewer of a fleeting impression at a particular moment. Art only used repetition to poke fun at it, the novelty of combining mass production with expectations for "high" art. Otherwise, meh. Kitsch. Seen it before.

My parents had suggested writing about Nice. I resisted the suggestion at first—there were no shortage of memoirs or guidebooks about the famed Côte d'Azur. Repetition wears out its subjects. Behind their suggestion was also the sting of disapproval for the more difficult literary collections that I had already written. A book about Nice—why not? Try writing something that people would actually read.

Plus my approach could be new, like this Cirque-de-Soleil-like performance set against the backdrop of fountains where our children sometimes splashed around in their underwear. It transformed a place we already knew well into an entirely different environment. The dancers were attached to circular harnesses that allowed them complete liberty to twist and flip acrobatically in mid-air. Men in bowler hats and vests and slacks maneuvered the giant helium balloons that held the dancers aloft. Suspended above the fountains, the dancers twirled in and out of the light, sometimes slicing through jets of water spurting fifty feet into the air. Our children were transfixed. Ivy sat on my shoulders, her eighteen-month-old hands yanking at fistfuls of my thinning hair each time a dancer swooped above our heads.

It was a moment for me, dear reader, where my fears of repetition died away. Nice may be a subject that has been repeated so long, subjected to hundreds of years of representations by artists recording their moments spent here. But pastiche, collage, context. Even with Nice as my backdrop, I knew I could write something new. For what was the story of my family, my hours spent under the sea, the pressure of money and time but a petri dish of ingredients for a book, the algal bloom of a family memoir in a location where it just wasn't supposed to happen.

Chapter 17

Working Out

A FEW WEEKS AFTER COACHING at Cavigal, I posted a photo of my kids and me before practice on Facebook. We had just received our official uniforms: my kids with red Adidas jerseys and shorts and me with my black-and-red trainer's uniform. Almost immediately, a friend of mine posted a photo of Ben Stiller with his tennis-star hopefuls in *The Royal Tenenbaums* in matching Adidas suits. So it was a joke then. Every day I was self-conscious as I donned my trainer's jacket and striped track pants. It was like wearing a costume. Sometimes I'd arrive early to practice and Alain and Jean-Yves would shake my hand and apologize for their civilian clothes before they ran to the changing rooms. I was embarrassed in my newly minted Cavigal skin while they were embarrassed without it.

The transformation also brought with it perks that belie an underlining French generosity that is often lost in most of the guidebooks or memoirs about France. As trainers, we were constantly invited to activities. Parents brought us homemade desserts. The club provided us our sports equipment and our uniforms, as well as free drinks and tickets to professional games. Our weekend tournaments always resulted in trophies or medals for the kids, a French "gouter" or snack, and photos and memorabilia. Becoming part of Cavigal was like becoming part of an extended soccer-crazed family. Before each match, we'd rally our five-year-olds together in a circle, and one child would shout: "Cavi-cavi-cavi!" to which everyone responded: "Cavigal!"

I didn't realize how unusual my experience was till I was talking one day with Vincent and Sam. "French clubs don't just let new people in like that," Vincent said. "You must have done something." I'm still not entirely sure what it was that convinced the president to take me on. But the effect since has been at times amusing. Whenever I wear a Cavigal jacket or warm-up suit, people make remarks. Youths have approached me, reverentially vousvoying me to find out what they needed to do to make it into the club. While I kicked a size-four ball around with my kids at the park, they'd dribble through a score of defenders to try to impress me. Maybe I'd see something that Cavigal needs? A special skill or affinity for the ball to help replace a weak right-winger? Often these kids came from competing clubs like St. Roch or Villefranche that were used to getting trounced in games by Cavigal every weekend. For them, Cavigal represented a potential career. I found myself in the awkward position of a gatekeeper who likely knew less about the whole process than they did. "I work with the six-year-olds," I told them. "I can't promise you anything. But you're welcome to come and try out."

Cavigal also demonstrated for me how an expensive and exclusive city can become affordable the more you give to it. While the wealthy decry France's high taxes, the middle-class benefits such as free healthcare or family allowances are substantial. Many French are surprised when I tell them that it's actually easier in France to move from one socioeconomic class to the other. Access to healthcare and education helps the French cross borders that are near insurmountable for many Americans.

But what about Bill Gates? they ask me. Facebook? I tell them, yes, it's true, but even these anecdotes about bootstrapping success don't tell the whole story. They don't mention the connections or the trust funds or the exclusivity of places like Harvard. People with a dream can succeed in the US but often those people have access to education and money. France is a place for your average person to get an education and a job and usher them into the middle class. It has its own problems with racism, with impenetrable bureaucracy and cripplingly powerful unions, but on the whole it's significantly better at providing for the physical health and fiscal well-being of its citizens. Vive la France moyen.

Now after the first few months of self-imposed austerity, our budget was balancing itself out. We had stopped buying furniture. Cavigal was free. Rixa started making bread to offset the price of daily baguettes. I salvaged anything of value from the garbage depot and sold it on Leboncoin. I had started catching fish with regularity now, getting over the moral quandary of providing the most expensive part of our food budget ourselves. Even though it was painful for me, it was better than the complicity and price of buying fish that had been killed who knows how sustainably by some third party. Most importantly, the dollar had risen in strength against the euro and we hadn't started any renovations. We were getting by. Then in November, I got an email.

> Hi Eric, My name is Jen and I work with the casting team on House Hunters International.
>
> I wanted to check in with you to see if you're still interested in being a part of the show and also to learn how far along you are in the process of moving. At this time we're looking for candidates who are very close to closing on/renting a home or are already living in one.
>
> If you are still interested, and get picked to be on the show, we would need you for 4–5 days straight to film in your new city. The shoot days can include the weekend, but we do ask that you keep your schedule completely flexible during the days that we're filming. This means taking off of work, school or any other obligations that you may have. Additionally, you may be asked to return to the country you were living in previously to film what we call the "backstory"; this would be a 1 day shoot.If you think you might still be interested, please let me know. Thanks so much, Jen

Chapter 18

Maeterlinck

TODAY WAS THE FIRST DAY my children were not coming home for lunch. We had decided to sign our kids up once a week to experience the *cantine*, the French-style cafeteria with its varied meals and restaurant-style dining etiquette. It would provide more full-day immersion so they couldn't slip back into English, that two-hour respite every day becoming more like a crutch. Today for lunch I ate a small *casse-croute* and I had finished writing. After her walk, Rixa said that the sea was smooth as glass and clear. I suited up to go out to Coco Beach, to continue past the point where I released my first fish, to the place where Mourad said you could catch dorades as long as his arm.

I bounded down our stairs with intrepid enthusiasm. I carried my speargun in one hand, a bag with my wetsuit in the other, and my weights, snorkel, and fins in a mesh backpack. I wound through the back streets of Old Nice, up Rue de la Loge and down to Rue Ségurane and through the construction for the new tram down to the Port. I wore a pair of board shorts that I bought for twenty-five cents on clearance at an Old Navy fifteen years ago and a t-shirt that I found on the sea floor. I glued my no-name sandals together with shoe goo that was crusted along the sides. My reusable shopping bag was the same kind that homeless people used to haul around their clothes. I had capped the spear on my naked gun with a cork.

So people gave me looks. I jogged with my speargun held vertically like a baton in a marching band up the Boulevard Carnot and down Boulevard Franck Pilatte to Coco beach. Sunbathers covered the tiny pebbled beaches. The water was calm and silent; not even an ebb of current lapped the shore. I passed the La Reserve restaurant and the tiered ruin that teenagers scaled to dive off. I circumnavigated the bay, past the beach to the *sentier littoral*, the trail that cut through the rocks along the coast, east toward Villefranche.

I had never been here before. Mourad told me that I hadn't gone far enough. He had spent the past couple weeks scrutinizing my catch, the less desirable rock fish, saupe, or mulet that I generally ended up with. My attention had shifted to sar, dorades, and rouget, the tastiest fish in the sea. "Go as far as you can till you can't go any further," he told me. So I did. I climbed down the stairs to the trail, followed it past two men pushing hooks into dough. They were fishing off a cliff for saupe and their bag was already bulging. I walked past them till the trail wound through the rocks. Off to my right, the white calanques met the sea and the rock face was a blue veined slab down to the sea floor. Two more men fished off the point, their lines stretching into the water.

I passed tourists plodding along with hiking poles that clicked against the stone path. Stairs climbed up and down. Above the trail, luxury apartments rose up out of the rock. Gated private entrances occasionally met the rugged natural coastline. I almost stopped when I reached a point. A bay with inlets of sea grass and shoals promised fertile fishing. But three spearfishers were already there, eating a sandwich lunch. Still the path continued. I hiked for another five minutes. Finally the pathway ended. A tiny footbridge crossed an inlet and I could see down a hundred feet. It was like I'd fallen through time and descended upon a secret fishing hole. A wire fence and a sign blocked the way. This had to be the place. Up ahead was a concrete slab like for the foundation of a building. Nude sunbathers spread out on the surface and arcades from a residence far above looked over the private terrace. I clambered down the rocks till I found a flat enough spot to change and enter the sea.

I once dated a woman who insisted we hide our watches whenever we went out. She didn't want anything measuring the time we spent together. Now when I slid on my flippers and attached my mask and pulled on my wetsuit like a second skin and slipped under the water I was as far away from any conventional understanding of time as I had ever been. I had no idea how long it had taken me to walk here. Breaths, a heartbeat, and the angle of the light through the water were all I had to guide me.

I started at the surface and swam away from the nudists to the steep inlet and the dramatic cliffs. Being out in the open clear water sometimes gave me vertigo. It was like being on an urban skywalk looking down beneath my feet. I didn't see any fish to speak of—the occasional small sar or rock fish—but not the cornucopia that Mourad had promised. I dove a couple times and stretched out on the sea floor with my spear in front of me. I was sure any significant fish could see me from a mile around and so the motions were merely practice. But I was deeper than I had ever been before.

I decided to head to the nudists. The sea floor filled with coral-encrusted rocks that rose up to meet the shore. A nudist treaded water in the shallows. Then I saw the fish.

My youngest daughter Ivy learned a few signs from DVDs we got her last year. Say "fish" and she would wiggle her hand forward and try to find my laptop. She loved watching YouTube videos of fish, even the three-hour static mood videos of an aquarium. We had looked at all the Mediterranean fish together as I learned which fish were game fish, which were restricted, and which were more to look at than to catch. All were here now, flitting in between rocks, diving for deeper water as my dark shape hovered above them. I saw several species for the first time: a spotted vieille, a young black-and-yellow Moray eel, and a bright green merle. Other Mediterranean fish were out: beyond the usual saupe, sar, and oblade, there were also schools of tiny blue castagnoles and multicolored girelle paon. Orange starfish and brown sea urchins dotted the rocks. I felt like I was in a giant Mediterranean aquarium. I swam on the surface barely kicking my feet. I had already seen some big sar and I imagined that with all this aquatic diversity, the game fish I was seeking couldn't be far away.

The other side of the concrete slab sloped into deeper water. The visibility was still fantastic: I could see the floor over a hundred feet down without a problem. I took a big breath and dove. My ears equalized without having to pinch my nose. I puffed out some air into my mask to keep it from sucking into my face. On the sea floor, a large brown fish with mottled yellow spots hugged the cliff. It was a mérou—a grouper—a protected fish that had been making its recovery in the south of France for the past several years. It was almost three feet long. It was astonishing to see a fish so large after so many pan-sized game fish. Next to the grouper, a couple swoop-backed corb swam into holes in the rock. But I was already so deep I couldn't seem to find them again. I hovered for a moment and then resurfaced.

That's when I saw the dorades.

The first three led me to a school. I had never seen this many dorades before and never this large. Some were larger than any I had ever seen in the water or the fish market, over two feet long, corpulent, the black spots behind their gills the size of my fist. The horizontal bands of gold between their eyes formed enormous crosses on their sloping foreheads. It was like swimming near a school of oversized piranha.

About fifty dorades combed through the rocks, heading up to shallower water. The dorade was farmed and cultivated as one of the tastiest fish of the Mediterranean. Live-caught dorades are prized as energetic game fish. But they are predators with the muscle and dexterity to keep them well out of range. I dove down to try to hide among the rocks and the school dispersed, fanning out around me. I waited for one to turn back to me out of curiosity. Most of them moved to the shallows I just left. They circled around and headed for deeper water. I swam back up and the fish gathered again beneath me. This time I hovered on the surface for longer till they passed by. If I dove and they behaved as they did last time; most would go to the shallows and then circle back to the safety of deep water. If I waited long enough, I might just get one on its way.

Live-caught dorades this large have disappeared from the daily fish market in the Place St. François. Too precious. Any angler lucky enough to pull one from the sea keeps it as a trophy, mounts it above his mantel. Now a school of them wound its way through the rocks, the yellow bands on their foreheads wiggling like yellow glo-sticks in the light. I hid behind a boulder but they somehow intuited that I was there. Maybe they saw the glint of my spear or the lenses of my mask. They swam up above me and I angled my spear and the elastic sent it whizzing by the closest one. I was too far away. I surfaced and dove again, trying to repeat what I had just done. And then again and again. Each time I lurked behind a boulder they gave me wide berth. Then as soon as the school appeared, they were gone. I dove again, this time circling back to the nudists. Maybe they were tired of being hunted and now combed the shallows for their own food? But even when I searched in holes, I found only labres or sar. Perhaps they had gone deeper? I poked my head above the water to get my bearings.

A diving boat sat in the middle of the bay. It must have drifted in while I was hiding on the sea floor. They were debutants, learning with safety cords attached to more experienced divers. I moved closer. Divers hovered in the water, their bright equipment and bubbles and bulkiness like depth charges announcing their arrival. The dorades probably saw them long before me, took off for safety as soon as the boat turned up.

Weeks later I purchased a used camouflaged wetsuit from a spearfisher I met on Leboncoin. He gave me the name of the beach where I saw the school of dorades: Maeterlinck. It was named after a luxury residence in the area, the home to my nudists, which was named after Maurice Maeterlinck, the Belgian Nobel-prize winning author who lived in Nice for much of his life. It was fantastic, I told him, so much fish! I tried to convey the size of the dorades, the way that they combed through the rocks and avoided me where I hid à l'agachon for them to approach. It was a good spot, he told me, but he found the fish too skittish there, impossible to catch.

"Why's that?" I asked.

"It's overfished."

Part II

UNDER WATER

Nothing can be delicious when you are holding your breath.

—ANNE LAMOTT

Chapter 19

HHI

MONTHS BEFORE WE MOVED to France, my colleague Warren suggested: why didn't we try to get on House Hunters International?

I demurred. I thought of yuppy couples or retirees with engorged bank accounts moving to the Maldives or some isolated Greek island. Why would someone want to see a large middle-class family cram into a tiny apartment?

"We're huge fans of the show, you know," Warren said. "You guys would be great in it."

So that night, I scoured the internet for the odd episode and I watched.

My first impression was this: the contributors looked like props for a narrative that wasn't entirely of their making. The twenty-minute reality TV show relied on artificial tension that built between commercials. The contributors had three properties to choose from—only three—and then they deliberated on screen and eventually settled and made an offer, with the narrative picking up after they had lived for a while in their new home. The show made it seem like the contributors had done about zero research and were just following the realtor's three choices like sheep. No house-hunting for me had ever been so simple, so neatly contained within such tight parameters.

Well, surprise, it turns out it wasn't.

A little bit of web research also revealed that each show was carefully constructed, with the contributors often having already purchased one of the three properties. Threads of comments afterwards discussed the merits of a show about house hunting that reconstructed the narrative of a search after the fact. Was it ethical? Were the participants just actors? If they had already bought a house, what about the show was actually real?

Only after reading through the comments did I search out the production company and click on the link to provide our information. To be on a show that followed our move to Old Nice had some appeal, but to be on a show that *recreated* our story, playing to the expectations of a viewing public bent on consuming a false and sanitized version of what really happened had even more. What kind of story would HHI's audience want to see? And what version of our life in France would the show project? Who would be our TV selves?

France is replete with idealistic representations. All during our house-hunting process, we were confronted with images of rural village life, with stone Provençal farm houses and vineyards and fields of lavender. My mother-in-law couldn't understand why we wanted to buy a home in a city; why not go to the southwest where we could get a house in the country for half the price of a tiny apartment in Nice? We'd have all that space and the inspirational solitude to go with it.

When we worked for a study abroad program, we saw firsthand the effect of Peter Mayle's bestselling *A Year in Provence*. Our program was in Oppède, a tiny village a couple kilometers from Mayle's old home. Every stone *mas* or farmhouse with pastel-colored shutters and cedars reaching for the sky seemed to be trying to recreate Mayle's vivid descriptions of the area. The narrative of southern solitude and quirky village life now bore the weight of hundreds of Anglophone expatriates from the UK to Australia trying to replicate these same images by buying summer homes or moving to southern France. This was the stereotype of a place for an artist in the south as much as a tiny garret under the roofs of Montmartre was for Paris.

The city of Nice has a kind of romance, from the stories of jazz-era revelry and luxury yachts and casinos to the light and color championed by artists such as Renoir, Matisse, and Chagall. But the romance of the area doesn't often correspond to most Americans' image of a place to raise a family. A stone farm house in the country, maybe. The palm trees and restaurants and urban nightlife isn't exactly the backdrop that most people would expect for a family of six.

This juxtaposition would become central to our narrative of French expatriation. After House Hunters emailed me back, after we had already bought our apartment and moved to France, they asked us to put together a casting video that would then be pitched to the show's producers. Our production editor emphasized the importance of being upbeat and excited and showing how we had integrated into French society since our move. The first couple scenes of the five-minute video show the brick single family home we left in the states. It has everything a middle-class family of four could hope for in America: a large kitchen, plenty of space, a yard and a garage and an attic playroom. Then the video cuts to promotional stills of Nice: the Promenade des Anglais, the Place Masséna, the terra-cotta rooftops of the Old Town. Over an image of our daughter holding a floor-plan of our tiny apartment, Rixa says, "700 square feet, four kids, and we love it."

While this juxtaposition inspired some, it provoked ire in others. For every retiree chucking our kids under the chin, others behind them shook their heads disapprovingly, moving to get out of the way as our children careened past on their scooters. Four kids didn't belong in the same space as Michelin-starred restaurants or fashionable clothing boutiques. Once, a retired woman berated our children for throwing rocks into the sea. She handed us an article from the *Nice Matin* newspaper about the tons of rocks hauled onto the beach every year and how local taxpayers were footing the bill. For these people, our children were like a virus or Cocteau's *Enfants Terribles*, children who left unchecked in a civilized space could destroy it with their games. Others cautioned us on our decision, seeing the Old Town as a site of danger. Like our taxi driver, shopkeepers, parents of my kids' soccer teammates, and people I'd meet from Leboncoin would tell me: Old Nice is no place to raise a family. You couldn't pay me enough to live there. I'd rather live in the projects than in Old Nice.

The people who seemed most pleased with our move were other foreigners, fellow expatriates, or vacationers who couldn't see past the pastel colors and trompe l'oeil facades. For them, we were part of a postcard-worthy tableau of crooked pedestrian streets and medieval churches. Who could live in a fairytale place like this? Here we were, the proof, our Nordic-looking family linked in a chain of hands, blocking a delivery bike with a basket of baguettes on the back.

Then there were the other locals, the bohemian French artists and musicians with families. Some of my children's teachers had lived here their whole lives, raising their own children, feeding them midday meals for two hours on school days, watching them grow up and then move away.

Talking with these people, I got more practical reasons for living in Old Nice: they could walk everywhere; it was close to shopping, the beach, the market; they didn't need a car; the schools were good. And beyond that, there were the less tangible reasons: the aesthetic beauty of the place, the light, the proximity to others who braved the late-night partying, the drug trafficking, and the limited parking in favor of charm and character, a unique place to call home.

The complexities of this narrative are lost in our casting video. Instead, we show idyllic family living, scenes of our children climbing the wooden playground on the coulée verte. Besides our nod to the challenge of living in a tiny apartment, we focus exclusively on the benefits of living here. We cram into our attic to read books together. At the playground, I toss my children into the air. The last shot is a still from the monastery gardens in Cimiez with our Sunday-best-dressed family in front of a stone portico bathed in afternoon light. If we're critical of the romantic stereotypes, we try not to show it. We've swallowed the Francophile pill and we're living the dream whole hog.

We finished the casting video and sent it off to House Hunters International along with our responses to a detailed questionnaire. We would hear back in January, and then if they liked us, we'd film in March or April. At this point, we were guardedly optimistic. We had scoured the internet for other casting videos that past participants had uploaded to YouTube. Several were simply one long self-taped interview of a couple talking about their move while sitting in a park. We edited our video to show a variety of locales narrated with a snappy voice-over as our children romped in the coulée verte.

It was a fun video for us to watch but it was hard to know how a casting producer would respond. They had already filmed Nice in previous seasons, making it a difficult sell for a TV show trying to highlight a diversity of experiences. Part of me was worried that we would seem too cavalier as I tossed my children into the air or let them dangle their feet out the attic window. Were we concerned parents? Or maybe one of those free-range families who let their kids wander the streets by themselves? We couldn't change the familiarity of the place, but we were hoping that our narrative would be interesting to House Hunters' viewing demographic. Because already through the casting process we had learned that our experience differed from what House Hunters expected.

For example, budget and renovation.

At first, House Hunters wanted to consider us for two shows: their well-known House Hunters International and a new off-shoot show called House Hunters International: Renovation. The second show combined the interests of moving abroad with home renovation, both narratives that wove through our own experiences. The show was longer: forty-five minutes compared with HHI's twenty-two. The compensation was also larger, as was the amount of time the show would spend filming our apartment. In opening negotiations, HHIR was excited about our story. A family of six renovating a tiny apartment in Nice while they're living in it? Sign me up!

But soon after, the narrative started to break down. When we gave the figures for how much we were planning to spend on renovation, the show balked. What could we hope to accomplish with such a small budget? We countered that we were doing the lion's share of the work ourselves. Another problem, they said. They recognized that we had experience with DIY renovating in the past, but they were more inclined to work with contractors who were legally bound to get the job finished within the show's timeframe. Unless we were willing to spend multiple times our budget and hire professionals, it's unlikely that we would get the green light.

So we threw our lot in with the more competitive show, HHI, even though we knew our chances would be slim. This decision carried with it the seeds of a very different narrative: a story of access and privilege more in line with mainstream expectations. It wasn't our story, but the story of a family and their sudden move, a family uprooted from America's heartland and thrust into a gilded storybook life amid the gardens and beauty of southern France.

Chapter 20

Jad

AFTER HOUSE HUNTERS SELECTED US, we knew that we needed help. Outside our local hardware store, Rixa saw an advertisement for a handyman who promised unbeatable prices. We phoned him up and he came the next day for an estimate. Jad was a little over six feet tall, large and thick with a neatly trimmed goatee and a more than passing resemblance to Peter Sellers. We liked him immediately.

We still hadn't settled on a plan for the mezzanine but Jad let us know his preference: just the bedroom, please. Opening up the wall to create a larger mezzanine connecting the attic was too ambitious. "You never know what you're going to find when you open a wall." Plus Rixa was warming to the idea of having a shower *underneath* the mezzanine, giving us more space for maybe some built-in cupboards or an armoire. And if we calculated it right, we should also have room for a writing desk.

So, how much for a mezzanine and installing a shower? It would be a large undertaking by small apartment standards, requiring holes in six-hundred-year-old stone walls and a staircase. We would need new electrical, plumbing, and a mezzanine that was sturdy and level. In the back bedroom, we had some other work as well.

Jad stretched out his measuring tape, made a few calculations. Were we going to supply the material or would he need to pick it up? A few minutes of scribbling in a notebook and he gave us an estimate well below our expectations. I can come tomorrow, he said.

Thus began our relationship with Jad. Jad the sledgehammer. Jad the family man. Jad the dreamer. Jad had come to France only recently after living for ten years in Italy, lured by the more robust social net and the promise of a construction job in Monaco. Both the job and the social net panned out but after two years of what he called abusive conditions he decided to light out on his own. He was keenly interested in our project of buying a dilapidated property and renovating it. Were we planning on renting it out? He'd heard too many horror stories of French squatters to want to rent out a property to anyone for more than a couple months at a time. But vacation rentals, if you were in the right area, could bring in even more than a standard rental contract. He'd been looking at properties in St. Sebastien where he lived, a quarter of Nice that climbed up into the foothills. This would be his first time working in Old Nice, a much stronger market for what he wanted to do.

The first day, he took out a painted wooden range hood in the back bedroom. Our apartment used to be two, separated by a narrow hallway that was divided into closets. The bedroom used to be a kitchen. The last vestige of its previous life was a wooden range hood that jutted out over the bed like a miniature renaissance canopy. We would have left it had we been able to find some aesthetic or practical use that made it look less like a range hood and more like an integral part of the room. But it always stood out. As the room's focal point, it blocked us from putting anything else there, from adding bunk beds or rearranging the furniture. In a couple hours, he effectively demolished it, patched the spot with plaster, and re-attached the fiberglass wallpaper to match the existing wall.

"Ready for the big stuff?" he asked.

Yes, please.

He started with the mezzanine and shower. Most days, he kept to himself, hammering and cutting and re-plumbing. When he worked construction, he was mostly a plasterer, one of those professionals who could take a twelve-inch blade, slap on a couple glops of mud and feather out an edge so it barely needed any sanding. But his inexperience with the other work was starting to show. For part of the re-plumbing, he had to add a drain that exited the apartment, hugged the wall of the stairwell, and entered a wrought iron drainage stack. We wondered how he was going to do it—cutting into wrought iron was beyond what we had for tools—but we didn't have to wonder long. Before we knew it he had banged into the thing with a chisel and then mortared it so it was flush with the original stack. It looked good—clean and sealed, and with a lot less debris and trouble than we were anticipating.

"He just mortared that up with cement," Rixa said.

"Maybe that's what you do in France?"

We let it go. The shower also went fairly quickly. He installed it and chiseled off the plaster for electrical lines. For the vanity lights, he couldn't get the two-centimeter-diameter channels into the wall so instead he embedded the wires directly. Again, done so fast that we couldn't object. About four months later, after House Hunters had come and gone, after we'd renovated most of the apartment, the electricity to the shower and vanity would suddenly stop working. Jad's connections, which he had secured with tiny "dominoes"—the French name for electric connectors—would come loose. An electrician would have to rewire the whole thing. But initially we saw Jad's work as efficient and clean, enabling us to meet our deadlines for the upcoming shoot date.

Soon Jad started on the mezzanine. Here, he literally hit a wall. "These are solid rock," he told us. He wasn't anticipating that. Armed with only a hammer and chisel, Jad lunged and whacked and beat at our unforgivably solid rock walls. He didn't have a rock saw, didn't think he'd need one. We'd leave, get groceries, pick the kids up from school and he'd still be there, whacking away at a watermelon-sized boulder to try to open up enough space for one of the four transversal supporting beams. The minutes turned into hours which turned into days. Our neighbors complained about the incessant hammering. At the rate Jad was going, he was way over his time estimates. We expected him to get surly, to swear or want to renegotiate his contract, but he kept on hammering, chipping away, all part of the job.

But when it came time for him to put together the staircase and landing, we realized that he didn't exactly know what to do. "Could you help me out with this one?" he asked me. He wanted me to hold a board parallel while he sent a screw shooting into one of the plywood stairs. "I don't think that's going to hold," I said. "I got the longer screws," he said. He held his fingers open to show how long and then held it up to the stair tread. It would go in about three inches every side. He'd marked where each tread needed to go. But I knew that the plywood would splinter over time. Didn't we need some supports under each tread? Like the ones going up to our attic? "It should hold," he said.

Rixa had something sturdier in mind for the stairs. We were behind schedule now and we needed to get started on the back bathroom, a demolition job that required wall building—more his expertise. We could finish the stairs ourselves. Would he be interested?

Jad hitched up his pants. He'd see. Couldn't promise anything though. Wasn't that wall load-bearing? He had already seen the Jacuzzi that crowded the corner of the back bedroom. We had bought it on Leboncoin brand new but it was bigger than we thought and wouldn't fit through the doorway. Now we wanted to open the wall. Right now the back bathroom was like a cave with very little room to move around. Ventilation was terrible. Opening the wall would make the space more livable, like a small master suite opening directly to the bathroom. It was impossible to tell how thick the wall was but it looked to be thinner than the solid rock of our bedroom. And even if it was load-bearing, we could put in a header and it should hold up just fine.

"I don't like opening up walls but I will do this for you," he said.

We were going to need more help.

A few weeks prior, I visited Franklin University in Switzerland for a reading and workshop with students. On the way, I picked up a hitchhiker in my rental car, an American who had been traveling around Europe for months. To minimize his expenses, he set up work stays through HelpX.net, a website designed to connect people wanting to travel with homeowners in need of specific skills. The majority of these opportunities were farming or rural renovation projects but some were as varied as music tutoring for children or leading tour groups at a private chateau. HelpXers agreed to work a certain number of hours per day, usually 2–5, in exchange for food and housing.

It was the kind of thing I would've loved to do before I was married with children. It sounded fantastic: a month in a vineyard in the Vaucluse, meals with local ingredients and a chance to see a more authentic version of France in exchange for a couple hours of work per day. Most appealing about the service was the self-regulated interface. A neglectful host or a disrespectful HelpXer would get bad feedback that would limit their ability to continue with the program. But who would want to come to our tiny apartment with four kids? We already had plenty of experience sharing tight spaces with guests but that didn't mean that everyone would enjoy it.

"You'd be surprised," the hitchhiker said. "If you live in Nice, you'd have no problem getting helpers."

Turns out he was right.

The first time we advertised with HelpX, we put all the projects we wanted to complete: two bathroom renovations (tiling, plumbing, painting), some electrical work, scraping and painting the attic, and installing flooring. We were up front about our living situation. We could give HelpXers their own bedroom with their own shower and sink. But the apartment was small and we had four young children. If you were allergic to toddler tears, you need not apply.

The first two weeks, we received on average a HelpX request per day. We were the only opportunity available in Nice. Most HelpX hosts lived in remote locations, with barns to erect or grapes to pick. Ours was one of the only urban opportunities and one of the few where HelpXers would be living in close quarters with their hosts.

The conditions didn't seem to bother people. We were most drawn to a newly-retired couple, northerners with family in Antibes who wanted to escape the dreary winter. Their profiles were amazing: Adilah was an accomplished cook and seamstress and Jean was a French handyman who had done everything from fine carpentry to kitchen installations. The quality of his workmanship was high and hosts raved about his efficiency. A blank patch of land became an A-frame garage in two weeks. He liked to get up early and work through lunch, sometimes putting in five hours a day without complaint. Previous projects showed him mixing mortar in a bucket shirtless. Leveling beams with precision. Sheetrocking a new wall. Raising a glass with contented hosts in the summer gloaming.

A few clicks and some emails back and forth and now they were coming to help us renovate the back bathroom. Before then we'd need to finish the front mezzanine/bathroom and at least get the back tub hooked up so we'd have a place to shower ourselves. Now we only had a week before Jean and Adilah were scheduled to arrive. Rixa would work on the mezzanine staircase. Jad and I would do the demolition.

We started by tearing out the old cast-iron tub and hauling it down the stairs and through the pedestrian streets to the garbage depot. Then we chipped off the tile with hammers and chisels. Jad bashed a sledgehammer into the wall, trying to open it up, sending gravel and debris into the room.

The only other sound was the tick tick of my hammer and chisel and the breaking ceramic tiles.

I probably haven't conveyed effectively the size of our work area. An average US bathroom in new construction is now a whopping 200-square feet, a third the size of our whole apartment. This bathroom was just a little larger than the Jacuzzi we were about to install, with a narrow hallway and room enough for a tiny vanity and sink. In centimeters it sounded much larger: 160 cms by 210 cms. But in feet, not so much. A meter is about three feet so the space was about 5 x 6 feet, smaller than the standard US bathroom size in the 1950s. Each swing of a hammer or pressure exerted on a wall had to be calculated and negotiated not to knock the other person over. Jad himself seemed to take up all the space with his linebacker's girth and sledgehammer. When the wall started tumbling down, I backed out of the room and watched the destruction unfold.

Each chunk of the wall now was more substantial, cinder-block-sized with plumes of dust that would spray from the growing hole. Unlike walls back home that were hollow, these walls were filled with earth and gravel, making any disruption messy and tedious to clean up. I ran into the kitchen to get some heavy-duty reusable grocery bags and I filled them by hand in the swirling dust. I opened the bedroom windows and turned on fans but still we coughed and felt the dust in our clothes and mouths. Jad was undeterred. He attached a bandana to his face and whaled on the wall till I was worried he'd cave in the ceiling of our attic floor.

But soon he was done. I scrambled to pick up more debris. Bags of gravel lined the hall outside our apartment. I think that does it, Jad said.

After that first day, the settled dust left a film over everything. While I swept and continued chipping away at the cemented-in tile, Jad ran conduit for the electrical. On the ground, I found a curved triangular chunk that looked like the rim of a stone pot. I handed the chunk to Jad and he examined it.

"How old are these walls?" Jad asked.

I estimated mid-1500s, a period of building and renovation in our neighborhood. But the Rue Droite was one of the oldest streets in Nice, appearing on maps as early as 1344. Who knew how old the wall could be?

"Keep your eyes open. You never know what you're going to find."

Jad then told me a story about a job he'd done not too long ago. It was in a villa up on the *corniche fleuri*, an old provençal mas that had been around since the mid-1800s. He demolished a wall like ours, full of dirt, and found a brass tube with a lid, a foot long, about the width of a baseball bat. He had to pinch the metal to get the lid off and inside were several official-looking documents in a language that he couldn't read. Instead of turning the contents over to the owner who was, in Jad's words, a real *connard* or asshole, he kept the sheaves hidden in his toolbox and took them home.

So what were they? I tried to keep out any judgement—if Jad felt comfortable telling me that a previous employer was a connard I assumed that he didn't feel the same way about me. Still, Jad swiped the curious papers that had been hidden possibly for centuries, mortared into a wall, and kept them for himself. Buried treasure. He took them to an antique dealer and the guy gave him a couple hundred euros.

He felt kind of stupid now. Why would someone cement in a tube of documents like that if they weren't valuable? Jad must've felt the pressure to unload his find, no telling what trouble he could get into. But he couldn't help think that their value was much more than what he received. One of his friends told him that he should've talked to an expert who could read the language. Maybe they were deeds to a property or stock in some long-lost company. Who knows? For the antique dealer to lay out 200 euros like that for a few pieces of paper, they must have been worth more. Jad could have been rich.

The only tiles left now were coming off with a layer of mortar behind them almost an inch thick. I'd need more bags. What I had hoped would be a quick job was becoming longer and longer the more I hammered away. I didn't know how we'd get the work done before Jean and Adilah's arrival in less than a week.

"No, no," Jad said. "Like this."

Jad picked up his sledgehammer. I had been chipping away, trying to work off the individual tiles like a jewel-cutter getting every facet perfect. Jad swung at the wall and the mortar underneath the tiles cracked, forcing large chunks to give way. Each swing split the air like a rifle report. In a few minutes, he'd cleared half the wall. I took back the hammer with a new reverence, like it had suddenly acquired magical powers. I swung hard as I could and while I wasn't able to reproduce the spectacular force with which

Jad demolished the wall, I was at least able to keep the pieces coming off in sizeable chunks.

The rest of the week, we worked in tandem till the space started to take shape. Jad framed the wall using flat boards and forms attached on either side of the irregular wall with bent pieces of re-bar that acted like clamps. He dumped concrete into the forms then finished off the edges with plaster. I cleaned up the debris from the tile and made multiple trips to our local plumbing supply store Ets Simon. Its convenient location right behind the Mediterranean-palace-like Lycée Masséna meant that I could go there repeatedly if I ever forgot something or a seal broke loose. The store was filled with tiny wood cubbies like the inside of an old apothecary and the two guys who ran it were both master plumbers with a story to tell. When I showed up with a brass fitting with a hairline crack, they whistled and examined it.

"You cranked it too hard. Busted it wide open."

"It was leaking."

"It leaked because you didn't put the Teflon on the right direction. Has to go with the threads or else it bunches up. I'll get you another."

When it came time to re-plumbing the room entirely—something I was hoping to avoid—they provided me with all the material and an electric crimping tool commonly used by professional plumbers. Even though the job was small, they lent it to me, free of cost.

When Jad saw the crimping machine, he was impressed. "Those things cost a thousand euros," he said. "You sure they just lent it to you?"

"They said I have to have it back by Friday."

"That'll make the job go faster."

And it did. Originally I had wanted to do brass soldering, a process that would have taken much longer and cost far more. Now we had these custom fittings. All we had to do was crimp them to the PVC pipe—pipe that we could cut in a few seconds with a hack saw. I calculated and measured where we needed to mount the tub faucet and then the bathroom sink and cut and crimped, finishing the plumbing the first day.

Jad started on the sheetrock mud. He feathered out the edges and sanded so it was a smooth rectangle, the corners sharp and clean. Between the moist plop of mud and the scrape of his blade along the surface, Jad told me how he first came to Europe in the hold of the cargo ship. His family hadn't wanted him to go, especially his uncle who owned the family estate.

Till his departure, Jad had been a good worker, someone who kept things running smoothly, who took care of the livestock and performed repairs on the outbuildings. But even after getting an education, Jad wasn't given any further responsibilities. He couldn't invest or make any decisions. Under his uncle, he'd be an underling stuck doing the same job for the same boss the rest of his life. So he left.

His uncle tried to talk him out of it.

If Jad held out, he could come into a fortune. According to his uncle, the estate hid millions in gold. When his great-grandfather first purchased the land, he buried his wealth in secret locations all around the estate. After he died prematurely, the secret died with him. The sons fought among themselves to try to divvy up the property while each of them conducted their own covert mining operations. The gold had to be somewhere. But after years of digging and finding nothing, the brothers gave up.

Then an archeologist came along. The archeologist asked permission to do research in the area; he'd studied Jad's great-great-grandfather's exploits in the Middle East and he wanted to recover some rare artifacts. But this guy was intelligent, knew that the brothers would never trust each other or allow him to conduct his research unsupervised. So he formed alliances and pitted the brothers against each other. By the time they figured out how they'd all been played, the archeologist had left, taking with him a sizable part of the grandfather's fortune. He'd use the money to fund a whole wing of a university and never had to work another day of his life.

"My uncle thinks there's still treasure somewhere on the property."

"What do you think?"

Jad let go of the conduit he'd been bending around the corner and rocked back on his knees. "There might be gold. But I'm not going to search for it. If I'd stayed I'd still be looking."

It wasn't the last time that Jad would tell me an outlandish story. We still had a few days of work before we'd get the bathtub installed, before he'd have everything hooked up and the wall milky smooth. We'd reach our goal of having the bathroom ready before Jean and Adilah came, the first in a long line of visitors who would use the front shower while we sat inside our Jacuzzi tub and alternately washed and then rinsed our bodies waving a hand-held showerhead.

In all the stories, Jad appeared the unlucky recipient of his mediocrity. Everywhere else people rose to fame, succeeded, bought yachts, and hired servants and lived the high life. Always he doled out critique, showed how his path was the nobler one: *I could've been a millionaire if only I'd agreed to work for a crook who turned out to be a mafia boss!*

Some of the stories sounded like something out of horror or sci-fi, like the well on his grandfather's property that accounted for the deaths of several villagers. When open, it lured people into its depths like the loudspeaker for a siren song. I also learned something about myself. With every upstanding choice, every outlandish connection, every hard-luck story Jad recounted to me, the closer I felt to him. I nodded, exclaimed in amazement, and laughed along with him. The more bizarre the story, the more I felt Jad trusted me. Each passing day built a house of cards that could topple if I expressed my disbelief. It was a touchstone of my character, a willingness to believe people when they needed me to. And now my gullibility was invested in a project that I hoped wouldn't get the better of me.

Chapter 21

Western Art

IN THE WINTER, NICE UNDERGOES a transformation. At the turn of the century, winter was when Nice geared up for high season, readying its boardwalks and parks for the influx of English aristocracy. The hot and dry summers would see multiple businesses shutter and hotels lay off their seasonal staff. After the 20s and the Jazz Age and writers and socialites like the Murphys and Fitzgeralds made summer swimming and sunbathing fashionable, the industry shifted to accommodate them.

As travel became more widespread, Nice expanded its clientele to include the middle class, becoming a destination for mass tourism throughout most of the twentieth century. By the 60s, the summer was overcrowded, the pebbled beach a patchwork of towels and sisal mats, while in the winter, Nice emptied and went back to les Niçois. In the 70s and 80s it became a haven for the newly retired, filling up assisted-living facilities and Cimiez villas till the city reached its peak of about 350 thousand people, a number that's stayed more or less stable since then. But even with this influx of people, winter in Nice still felt empty.

When I first visited in the early 90s, the city was in dire financial straits. Its famously racist mayor, Jacques Médecin, escaped to Uruguay under suspicion of corruption and had just been extradited to France and convicted on charges of fraud. Although Médecin had built museums and tried to make Nice a cultural destination, it didn't succeed until very recently. Now Nice is growing again, resulting in a dense urban stretch from

Cannes to Monaco, home to more than a million people. The winters are still calm, but they're not as calm as they once were.

Our neighborhood in Nice has perhaps experienced the greatest shift in demographics, becoming more pronounced as the city gradually empties of tourists. Long a center for drug trafficking and prostitution, Old Nice is now increasingly popular with families. In 2014, the current mayor, Christian Estrosi, finished a spate of renovations designed to turn the center of Nice back to the "Nice of his childhood." The Nice he is referring to is the Nice pre-1970s renovation that saw the destruction of the Ritz-Carlton-style hotel "Le Meridien," the Casino Municipal, and the building of a bus station and above-ground parking garages that would block the Old Town from the New for more than 40 years.

The Nice of Estrosi's childhood was a Nice with an open skyline, a Nice with both sides of the city connected by the covered Paillon River. This was a more unified Nice, a Nice where people came together, using the center of town for markets, gatherings, concerts, and festivals. Most importantly to us, it was a place to play, where children could kick a ball around or let loose.

The aptly-named "Promenade du Paillon" represents more than three years of continual renovation over thirty acres in the middle of Nice, a project that included dismantling the bus station, parking garages, and existing fountains and parks. The resulting Promenade winds its way from the grey marble national theatre of Nice through the Place Masséna to the sea. Along the way, the city of Nice constructed the "mirior d'eau" that my brother and his children had so enjoyed, a hectare-large rectangle of fountains that shoots jets of water from an obsidian surface, modeled off the award-winning 2006 Jean-Max Llorca model in Bordeaux. When the fountains aren't running, water pools in a millimeters-thin glassy mirror that reflects the buildings lining either side of the park. The fountains cycle through various choreographed combinations, spraying water into the air while children gambol and splash about. Other sections of the park are open grass or artificial turf where families and circles of friends gather for picnics or to play music.

Further along in front of the Lycée Masséna are a series of wooden sculptures, playground equipment with signs designating the age for which they are suited, signs that everyone disregards. Each sculpture is a hand-crafted work of art from the atelier of David Steinfelt and Natalie Massot in a maritime theme. There's a wooden pirate ship, a wooden whale, wooden octopuses, wooden sea turtles, wooden dolphins. Each incorporates some familiar playground element: slides, swings, a jungle gym. A tire swing gyrates between the tentacles of a giant octopus; children crawl through the corded belly of a whale.

Nothing exists in all the south of France to match both the aesthetic beauty as well as the sheer size and number of playground installations open to the public. Its current iteration represents something even better than the Nice of Estrosi's childhood: it represents all the vision and imagination of what it could have been. Whereas the previous parks and structures segmented the various quarters of Nice, the new park invites them into one open common space. It's like the Dude's rug in *The Big Lebowski*, a kilometer-and-a-half-long green carpet that really ties it all together.

The park has had a tangible impact on Nice. Nice is a dense urban city, with over 95 percent of its residents living in apartment buildings. The surrounding hillsides and the proximity of the French Alps make building away from the city center expensive, with most development following the Paillon or Var rivers that empty into the Baie des Anges. The improvement of public transportation, with a first tram uniting the northern and southern quarters of the city and a second one recently uniting the east and west, has made it easy for people to come into the center of town. During the day, the parks are generally limited to tourists, but the end of school brings a flood of children, from kindergarten up through high school. On the weekends or school holidays, the numbers triple.

The Promenade du Paillon's influence is most pronounced on the areas immediately adjacent to it such as Old Nice. The buildings fronting the once-traffic-congested Juan Jaures with its unseemly bus station and tiered concrete parking garages, now advertise the view and the calm and serenity. We ourselves were partly drawn to the area because of these amenities. And we're not alone. The streets of Old Nice are now filled with the laughter and screams of children. The École du Château, long a school accommodating overflow from more populous neighborhoods, is bursting in local enrollment. Among school-aged children and their families, various sections of the Promenade du Paillon, or "coulée verte" (green strip), have come to have their own topographical designations. A playdate could be at "la baleine" or "le bateau." If you're meeting at "la fontaine," you know to come in swim clothes. Always bring a soccer ball "en mousse" since regular soccer balls can cause injury to bystanders, as one of the Segway-riding park police will tell you.

Every day, children in Old Nice have the choice of several outdoor activities: the coulée verte, the splash pad (miroir d'eau), the chateau, or the beach. If it's one of the few days a year that it's raining, there are also indoor spaces like the huge municipal library or the Piscine St. François, all within about a two-minute walk from each other. Sometimes we'll switch to one of these locations during good weather just to change it up a little.

These amenities have reinforced Nice's reputation as a year-round vacation destination. The city of Nice has also tried to diversify its offerings through festivals and events. During the winter months, the town builds a temporary Swiss village in the Place Masséna, complete with a Ferris wheel, outdoor skating rink, and carnival rides or ropes courses. Russian tourists and locals break out their designer poofy parkas and Hermès scarves even though it's still a balmy 60 degrees. Probably the most pronounced changes come along the sea front, on the Promenade des Anglais. The seemingly natural stone beach succumbs to winter storms, dragging many of the gray pebbles into the sea. Outdoor restaurants and bars are dismantled, leaving bare concrete slabs. Detritus from previous years of beachgoers are suddenly visible, uncovered after the summer layer of rocks is gone. Boulders on Castel beach, once hidden, are now bare. Anglers replace bathers.

Winter feels like a reclamation. The Niçois often leave during the summer, renting out their apartments or leaving them vacant till the rentrée scolaire. Nice in the winter is busy as ever but it's the people who live, learn, and work there who dominate the parks and the sea. These are places of outdoor socialization and recreation, where residents are back in majority numbers. It's where we form peer groups, solidify friendships, and invite each other over to each other's homes.

Navigating friendships as expatriates poses certain challenges for us. Enclaves of Anglophones permeate Nice and often we felt like satellites being drawn into their orbit. Enrolling our children in public schools helped to stem this attraction but still we felt it. It's an odd kind of person, my brother Kent said, who preferred being with people different from themselves. Most of the time, we felt like we were these people—wasn't that why we were drawn to Old Nice to begin with? The demographic of Old Nice and the families who sent their children to the École du Château represented a racial, ethnic, religious, and socioeconomic potpourri from several different nationalities. But we weren't immune to the homophily that Kent decried. Other expats chose Old Nice for those same reasons, making them ironically just like us.

Our closest expat friends were Johnny and Natalie Gent. Natalie taught at the International School in Monaco and Johnny was a visual artist. His last show in Dubai drew on previous experiences in the south of France and he wanted to have a go at it again. And now they had kids: Otego, a son Dio's age, who was in the same kindergarten class; and Alba, a high-energy girl the same age as Inga.

Johnny made an impression.

He wore his blonde hair in a topknot and sported white cotton button ups and orange pants. When it was cooler, he wore an artist's trench coat. Probably his most arresting feature was his face that bore a striking resemblance to Jodie Foster: intense, round eyes, angular nose and mouth. It was enough of a resemblance that he'd joke about it in interviews as the camera panned over, getting his "good side—his Jodie Foster side."

We first met outside the elementary school. He was worried about his son feeling like an outsider. "Otego's teacher—did you see what she did?" He felt like Otego wasn't welcome. Discovering that Otego barely spoke French, the teacher had thrown up her hands in frustration. Not another one! He was coming in late September, three weeks after school had started. He had missed the detailed orientation, the explanation of how their Greek-mythology-themed school year would go. I told Johnny more about her: she had received a grant from the state to do hands-on instruction where children would garden and learn Greek myths alongside other aspects of ancient Greek culture. Her pedagogy was innovative and engaging. And didn't the French often wear their emotions on their sleeves? Give her a chance, I assured him. She's great. Dio comes home every day thrilled with what he learned.

OK, he said. I guess if Dio can help him out.

Still I could tell that leaving Otego in the school made Johnny uncomfortable. Otego was their oldest child and had it not been for another family, a family somewhat like his own, he probably wouldn't have stayed. Schools can be as much a tool of social networking for the parents as they are educational experiences for children. Wouldn't Otego be better off in a bilingual international school like where Natalie taught? But if they did that, it was unlikely that he would really learn French. Plus Natalie didn't want him picking up the entitled behaviors of her students. They liked the bohemian diversity of the École du Château. Our family and children became anchors for their experience: look, here was someone else doing what they were trying to do. It was reassuring. And that reassurance formed the seeds of a strong bond.

The first time Johnny invited me up to their apartment was after a playdate. Otego came to our place once and now it was Dio's turn to go there. I buzzed the interphone and Johnny's top-knot appeared out of a top-floor window. "Why don't you come on up?"

"That's OK."

"Just for a minute. The kids are still playing."

"All right."

Seeing the apartment was the first, most direct encounter with privilege we'd had in our neighborhood. While Old Nice is known for its expatriates, for moneyed foreigners like Russian oil magnates or retired bankers, we had managed to integrate ourselves mostly with the shop owners, restaurateurs, boat mechanics, waiters, and teachers who worked there. Our children spoke French and went to public school. But although Johnny and his family weren't immediate inheritors of wealth, they had spent enough time on its periphery to feel like they should be. When they visited Nice in the off-season, they stayed in the Negresco, automatic upgrade to the penthouse when they found a hotel error in their reservation. They drove an Audi and filled their cave with expensive wine, their pantry with sea salt from the Camargue and delicacies like foie gras and truffles. They made decisions on a whim and once they did, they were all in with a fierce intensity.

Their apartment itself was, for them, good *enough*, but not what they had hoped for. Their first choice was the villa of an investment banker—one of Johnny's clients—on Cap Ferrat. They'd been to visit it at a party: huge veranda, verdant gardens, an on-site caretaker, a pool, and private access to the sea. Most of the year it was empty and his friend had said that they were welcome to it. But then a Saudi prince, a business connection, needed it for a few months. He thought maybe they could share it—it was big enough for thirty people—but his friend said, no—he throws parties all the time. Would be awkward with a family there. And so they ended up in this pied-a-terre apartment of another friend of a friend with too much money who didn't mind if they stayed a while.

Compared to our own standards, the apartment was luxurious: three full-sized bedrooms, a great room that opened to the kitchen with vaulted ceilings and exposed beams, a Viking stove, and an open marble bathroom as big as our living room with a claw-foot tub in the center. But for them, it felt cramped. Johnny needed more room to work. It wasn't the Cap Ferrat villa they were hoping for, but it would do. He paid for their rent with a painting. Stay as long as you like.

In Johnny's apartment, Dio and Otego were both dressed in full-body superhero costumes: Dio as Spiderman and Otego as the Hulk. Their green and red padded muscled bodies wrestled and kicked in the air. Johnny and I sat at the table in the great room while the kids continued their rough-housing. A couple paintings leaned against the wall. One in particular stood out: a painting in a gilded gold frame of ships at sea. It was a print that Johnny had painted over, adding flags from various Anglophone countries: the UK, Scotland, the US. "Boys on Tour" was written in thick yellow gouache in the middle with his name writ large in the corner. The sea was a blood-red swirl. I didn't know it yet, but the painting would one day end up in our apartment.

"So you're a writer. That's great. What sorts of things do you write?"

"Short stories. Essays. Literary stuff that nobody reads."

Talking about my work could feel like dangerous territory. Sometimes I would avoid the conversation entirely, preferring instead to say that I was an English professor on sabbatical. But here was a painter—a bona fide visual artist—and if there was anyone who would understand what I did every day, it was him.

"I wish I could be a writer," he said. "I just read this fantastic book. Everybody's reading it—*Stoner* by John Williams. He was an English professor in the 60s and now it's this international phenomenon."

"I haven't heard of it," I said, embarrassed.

"It's about academia. An English professor."

We talked some more about books; I'd just come off reading Donna Tartt's *The Goldfinch*, a book about beauty and the value of art, centered around a lost painting. The irony wasn't lost on us: I had just read a book about his métier while he was fascinated by one about mine. When Dio finally peeled off his Spiderman costume and put down the light sabre he'd been brandishing, we shook hands knowing that we'd see each other again.

And so began a period of intense collaboration and cross-pollination, a friendship that thrived on sharing and conversation. Could I have developed a similar relationship with a francophone Nice-based artist? A contemporary Matisse or Chagall? Maybe. But part of the reason we were drawn to each other was because we were both expats with young families in the thrall of similar artistic concerns. Nice and its surrounding communities were hotbeds of material; our art navigated the clash of socioeconomic groups, the high rises and empty villas, the racial tension. We walked the Promenade when a Muslim woman immersed herself fully clothed in the sea, her thick clothes clinging like shrink wrap to her form while teenagers in thongs pressed their cleavage together for bikini selfies. I gave Johnny a copy of *Hemingway on a Bike* and he shared with me his work, pre-showing, in private vernissages. A series of paintings using Japanese ink produced black-and-white tableaux of Monaco that differed from the pastel watercolors and Provençal kitsch in the markets or boutique galleries. Dark smudges of a woman masturbating in a hotel room. A drunk in a suit half-asleep on a bench. Spires of Monaco's Grand Casino as foreboding as a gothic cathedral. Dogs humping next to a fountain. The paintings were loosely representational—I could discern the figures and locations if I looked hard enough—but the paintings were mostly mood, beyond impressionistic. The ink felt accidental, like tea stains or pens washed in the laundry, and each one negated the glamor one often associated with Monaco. These were sordid pieces. Beautiful, and honest.

My own work addressed the ironies and the injustices of our environment more obliquely. My memoir had started to take shape, addressing not only our social and cultural integration as we renovated our tiny apartment, but the way that this place exemplified a new way of living in the world. Over and over I'd been confronted with subtle forms of racism, the silent complicity that occurs as people schedule play dates and get jobs and try to carve out an existence. I was more conscious now than ever of our reasons for moving here and for our growing cadre of expatriate friends. We were beneficiaries of a legacy of social and racial privilege. Our benign and welcoming conversation with the immigration officer for our visas was a stark contrast to the shouting matches and aggression that we heard in adjacent rooms. "I've always wanted to visit Canada," the immigration officer told us as she happily stamped our passports and fawned over our golden-haired child. We were welcomed to the country because we fit a profile, welcome to partake of the stereotypes of French food and culture and beauty and communicate them back to the privileged masses back home eager to consume them.

Although we came to Old Nice partly because of the diversity, it was still difficult to avoid being drawn into circles of people more like ourselves. Johnny's family and ours became friends. Yet it was still a challenge to persuade him to give the public schools a try. Most expats tended to keep their kids in the École du Château only for the three years of *maternelle*, then put them in private schools where they were more likely to find students of the same socioeconomic class. Bohemian parents with Mohawks and tattoos flocked together, as did the women in headscarves with multiple children. It was hard to break these habits. The other day, a Muslim woman approached Rixa with some trepidation, wondering if she'd be interested in meeting on occasion for an English conversation group. "I thought of asking some of the other English-speaking women but you seemed more approachable." We knew the parents she was referring to: the lead of an Irish punk band who wore combat boots and a nose ring and her other expat groupies. The buffer of our several children made us more like the Muslim woman. Approachable. None of us are immune to the pull of people like ourselves.

But I wanted our story to be for others. My short story collection was finally coming together. I chose a title: *Invisible Men.* I hesitated choosing it, the deliberate nod to Ralph Ellison's classic, but I wanted a title that memorialized the narratives of the marginal and dispossessed in its pages. And now my memoir was starting to become equally conscious of the plight of the underdog and the social systems that kept us apart. A man like Jad could become my friend as we labored together in our dusty bathroom but he was still a paid worker, the terms of our arrangement temporary. Economic and social machinery could create resentment and animosity. Indeed, much of the rise of extremism against the West comes from governments offering repeated blank checks that are never filled. Benefits from social systems are often just ways of keeping the masses at bay, saying, aren't health care, family allowances, and unemployment benefits enough? Positions of power in industry, education, and government in France are still vastly controlled by white men who went to one of the elite grandes écoles. And that gendered and racial consolidation of power corresponds with a global sense of French pride and cultural superiority. France's glass ceiling is made of Lalique crystal.

For now Johnny and I absorbed these ironies and injustices and expressed them in art. Images channeled our discontent in ways that arguments could not: a painted toenail beneath the folds of a formless dress, French youth doing wheelies in front of a Mercedes, our Tunisian butcher Mourad cleaving thick slices of overpriced Halal meat. These were our ways of accounting for the tensions that we saw, of saying: this is how democracy works. We enrolled our kids in public school, invited Muslim families over for English conversation, tried our best to integrate, to become productive members of our society, to share in this space we call our community.

But soon, the first of several experiences showed us that even our most well-meaning intentions could be a kind of imposition on others. Some people saw the same ironies of exclusion and privilege but instead reacted out of hate, maybe even saw us a symbol of everything that was wrong with the world. For that January, after Johnny and I turned racial tension and ironies into art, after play dates and birthday parties and trips to concerts, after Johnny's family followed the long tradition of seasonal nomads in Nice and moved away, two brothers, Muslim extremists, forced their way into the offices of Charlie Hebdo in Paris and killed eleven editors, writers, and cartoonists—people like us—shooting them execution-style in the head.

Chapter 22

Jean and Adilah

THE DAY BEFORE OUR FIRST HelpXers arrived, Jad temporarily installed the tub in the back bathroom. It was the last of a spate of renovations
we'd been staying up late to complete: constructing the mezzanine staircase, installing the shower in the front bedroom, and prepping the back
bathroom for tiling. All the kids surrounded the tub when we tested it. Jad
turned on the water and we watched it fill and immediately kids were pressing buttons and removing their clothes. Downstairs I paid Jad in cash about
20 percent more than he'd asked for. The job had taken longer than both
of us had expected and we'd become friends. We shook hands and he left
down the Rue Droite, stopping to talk to Mourad. It had been a grueling
few weeks but now everything was functional. We were ready.

Theoretically, we loved the idea of HelpX. Human exchange. A demo-
cratic space with no regulation except for our own online reviews and story
of working together. We had a family but that didn't need to be a liability.
It was a new experience and we were willing to welcome others into our
home if they were willing to come.

But our first HelpX experience almost proved to be our last.

Jean and Adilah would be with us for two weeks to help with our
bathroom renovation. Our correspondence before then had been ami-
cal and positive, albeit somewhat overly detailed. When we asked about
any dietary concerns, Jean gave us a long list, including what kind of table
wine he preferred and when he liked to eat (late). We said that we would

accommodate his requests as best we could. But our children went to bed early and so our dinners would have to follow suit. Not a problem, he said.

It's hard to know exactly what turned this experience so sour but by the end of the two weeks, I think both parties hoped we never saw each other again. Jean was as competent as his profile indicated but he was also used to working alone and not having to deal with budgetary constraints. All of his projects to date were in the pastoral French countryside and not in an urban environment. Now he was in a tiny bathroom, a box of crumbling grey concrete without any windows and poor ventilation. But worst of all, he was having to share the space with me.

The first couple days passed in strained cooperation, everybody putting on their best show. The living arrangements weren't what they expected. Adilah had never slept in a mezzanine before. Why hadn't we mentioned it in the advert? (We had.) She was worried about having to get up in the middle of the night to go to the bathroom. So we pulled the mattress down and laid it on the floor. But it was fine, no problem. Jean liked to be working by 7:00 a.m. and didn't realize that the kids wouldn't be up yet. They would need the back bathroom and access to their clothes to get ready for school by 8:30 which meant he couldn't realistically start tiling till then. No matter. He would take a late breakfast and wait till they were gone.

The first day Jean and Adilah showed up, we were excited, a little anxious. The kids had decorated a sign saying "Bienvenue Jean et Adilah!" in multi-colored crayons. In their minds, our guests were like Grandma and Grandpa Freeze or Spencer, people whom they adored. When Jean and Adilah crossed the threshold our kids threw their arms around them like they were long-lost relatives. "Such beautiful children," Adilah said. "I have two grandkids myself."

Therein lay the heart of our problem, a factor that I don't think either party had entirely considered. Both of us assumed that the interactions would be similar to our own experiences. Rixa and I came from large families with grandparents who were used to double-digit numbers of grandkids and who had a built-in tolerance from years of exposure. Jean and Adilah had a couple grandkids each from previous marriages, children who they saw over holidays with a high adult-to-child ratio. Near the end of the two weeks, Jean said, "When you first sent us your schedule, I thought, now here is a family that is put together and organized," the implication being that the opposite proved to be true. "We're just not used to all this."

While Adilah still interacted with our family the best she could, Jean took more and more to staying in his room, watching episodes of French comedy shows on Netflix rather than endure the noise and activity of our kids. His solutions about how to live with us often relied on the exclusion of our children. And like nagging grandparents, they injected our family with an overdose of French criticism.

Here were some of their complaints:

Your oldest daughter is vain. She doesn't care about anyone but herself. I can't believe you let her treat Ivy like that.

Inga never eats her supper. She's never going to eat on time unless you force her.

Your kids come and go from the table like they're at a playground.

Tensions reached a head during a game of hide and go seek. Since I was working with Jean most of the time, slathering walls with mortar and cutting tile in the hallway, I couldn't be with the children the way I used to. And Rixa was busy sewing cushion covers and throw pillows. Hide and go seek seemed like a good diversion, a way that our children could amuse themselves without having to rely on one of the parents to keep things going. But halfway through the game, we heard a scream. "Get out!"

"Your daughter is *mal élévée*," Adilah yelled. "Badly raised." Zari ran into the room and buried her head in my side, sobbing and shaking. We had never yelled at Zari so forcefully. "She can't just go walking in on people like that. I was *à poil*. Naked. She didn't knock, didn't even act like she'd done anything wrong."

"Oh, Zari," I said. "Is this true? You know that's not our room anymore. It's Jean and Adilah's."

"I was looking for Dio."

"Your girl needs discipline."

Initially we reinforced Adilah's response. Zari had no right to go into their room and we needed to ensure that our guests had at least a modicum of privacy. Recounting this experience even now, I feel a mix of sympathy and shame. But then we began to see how Adilah's reaction to Zari was more complex and nuanced than we had originally thought. Adilah came from a family of three girls. Her older sister was the most beautiful and she was self-centered and emotionally abusive to the younger two. Adilah brought these experiences up repeatedly in a way that meant they mattered to our own household of three girls and one boy. Zari was the oldest in our family and attractive, with thick blonde hair and a lithe figure, a beautiful smile, straight teeth. I couldn't help feeling that Adilah attributed her sister's negative traits to Zari, along with her residual disdain and jealousy. Here was another girl just like her sister, tormenting her younger siblings. Adilah tried somewhat to make amends for the screaming reprimand that had by now so obviously traumatized Zari but each compliment rang hollow. Such beautiful hair, Adilah would say, but what we heard was: yeah, she's pretty but your child is rotten to the core.

By the end of their stay, we had adjusted our behavior to fit theirs and not the other way around. We made dinner early for the children and then later for Jean and Adilah. We bought them whatever they wanted to drink or eat. When we worked, I would try to leave Jean alone and find another project I could work on simultaneously. At every turn, for every decision, we felt their disapproval. Jean complained about the quality of our tools, for not having a strong enough drill or an accurate enough level. "I should've given you a list," he told us near the end of the project. "If you didn't have everything on the list, I wouldn't come." For him, attitudes that we had absorbed from the south of France were largely to blame. He'd lived in the south before and observed how sloppily things were done here. His frustration was compounded by our own; for unlike his other projects where he muscled a garage or barn to completion in record time, now he was falling behind, taking twice as long to finish projects that we would've completed more quickly ourselves. When we started tiling the bathroom, he insisted that the tiles needed to be back-buttered with mortar to help them adhere to the wall. Placing each tile became a huge production with minute adjustments to the spacing made ever more difficult by the overabundance of mortar causing the tiles to slip around. We slowed to placing just a few tiles per day. Whenever I suggested a cleaner or more efficient route to finishing, Jean would snap. "If you only knew the amount of tile I've laid," he said.

One afternoon I decided to finish the tiling myself. I had also laid tile, redoing bathrooms, entryways, and kitchens in six different homes in the last ten years. I had worked with granite, marble, and ceramic. I knew how to set mosaic and cut horseshoes freehand with a wet saw so that they fit around baseboards or pipes. So that afternoon when Jean and Adilah changed and left for one of their daily walks, I stopped the painting project I'd been working on and took over. I laid the rest of the tiles in a couple

121

hours, double the work we'd been doing in about half the time. But when Jean came back and saw what I'd done, he was convinced that he'd have to rip it out and start over. "It's your apartment," he said. If the tiles magically fell off the wall, I'd have to live with it. No way was he coming back.

The last couple days we looked at what we had left to do before HHI. What we realistically could complete kept diminishing. We needed to glue up the fiberglass "papier peint": literally "painted paper" or wallpaper. Most of the apartment was already covered in the inoffensive cross-hatching-patterned stuff, but installation also meant painting it. And if we were going to paint the new wallpaper, didn't it make sense to paint the rest of the apartment too? In some ways now we wondered if the HelpX experience had really helped all that much after all. The tiling took longer than we thought and we still felt like we were entertaining guests, making meals a more time-intensive, sometimes laborious affair that would trail on into the night, hours that we could have spent working.

The day before they left, we took Jean and Adilah out to Le Bistrot Gourmand, a Michelin-starred restaurant on the other end of the Old Town with a reasonable lunch-time menu. They dressed up like for one of their walks: leather jackets, polished shoes, scarves, designer sunglasses. Hipster grandparents. For a moment we could all forget that we lived like rodents in the same sixty-five-square-meter space with four kids and sheet-rock dust and tools all over the place. Earlier that day, Jean had burned out the motor of our electric drill while churning plaster in a bucket, calling the thing a piece of *merde*. I mixed it by hand with a trowel, hoping that it would satisfy his desired consistency. But no matter: this was the end. I wondered if they would give us a bad review, if they would ever come back to the south of France.

"You'll have to send us pictures when you're all done," Jean said. "And let us know when House Hunters airs."

I imagined the final pictures up on Jean's HelpX profile, along with our smiling portraits in the back bathroom, troweling gobs of mud onto the walls. We would be another success story, another family helped out by his impressive slate of skills. He had a project coming up in a couple months, a vineyard in the Languedoc that needed a barn razed, a chicken coop built. "We'll probably stay a month," he said.

As soon as they were gone, we had more work to do: wallpapering and repainting the apartment, tiling the backsplash in the front bedroom, tiling the toilet room, installing two sinks, building a casing for the plumbing, putting up trim, and cleaning, cleaning, endless cleaning. Because in less than two weeks, a film crew would be there to witness the final product.

Chapter 23

Jean de Florette

THE NIGHT BEFORE THE FILM SHOOT with House Hunters International, I decided to cut the legs on the stand for the back bathroom sink. I was trying to think through the lens of a camera, to find what in our apartment would look finished and what needed work. The height of the stand was less of an issue than the bare wood at the bottom of each leg. Why paint what you're going to cut off anyway? But now I imagined how it would look on TV and so I got out the handsaw and set it up in the bedroom. Although the mitre box and clamp ensured a straight line with minimal waste, I was still cursing our frugality and wishing for an electric compound mitre saw. Each snag sent my already sore shoulder and triceps into paroxysms. I cut the back legs a few millimeters shorter to accommodate the gentle slope of the bathroom floor and propped it up against the wall. The stand's once milk-smooth surface was now marred with holes and scratches where the pre-painted mahogany wood showed through. I sunk my fingernail into the paint and it wrinkled up, un-adhered. "I'm going to have to strip and re-paint it," Rixa said. "I don't know why the primer didn't work."

But there was no time. We started filming tomorrow. I grabbed the cellophane-covered brush from the paint cupboard and applied the first of the three coats to the holes. Hopefully the camera wouldn't pick up the brush strokes or the pockmark scars. I unwrapped the sink—a heavy piece of solid grey stone like a giant split geode—and placed it atop the stand. There. The faucet hadn't yet arrived but we figured we could prop up the one from the other bathroom when we filmed to make it look like it was done. It was midnight now and we could hear our children's muffled breaths from the attic. Thankfully they wouldn't be filming our apartment till Friday because we were nowhere close to being finished.

I tried to think where we went wrong. The work with Jad? Jean and Adilah? But those were the experiences making progress on the apartment, renovating it, getting it ready. In January, our producer Melissa interviewed us via Skype. They had loved our casting video. Her advice not to mention the sabbatical and instead say that we were moving to France permanently seemed to have worked. It was a compelling narrative: two academics giving up their secure university jobs take their family of six to live in a tiny apartment in the south of France so that I could write full time. HHI also had some questions or comments about the video. Could they film in the attic space? They loved the idea of getting some footage of our family crammed under the low ceilings. We mentioned that we were in the middle of renovations. Had we finished with them? Not quite, we assured them, but we'd definitely have them done within a month.

Now, standing in front of the botched sink with its unattached plumbing and missing calk and trim, I wondered: were we in some kind of breach of contract? They'd invested too much in us for them not to go through with the shoot. Whatever final product they got would have to be magically pieced together in the editing room.

No, it was the other activities that had sent our project off the rails. Our children had school and soccer matches. We wanted to go skiing. I spearfished with a friend and was still going into the water even as the cold caused my legs to cramp. I had finished my terrible young adult novel and was now submitting my short story manuscript, *Invisible Men*. Our lives were so much more than HHI and that's why we weren't finished. Now those same activities felt frivolous and unnecessary. We should've spent every waking moment getting our apartment ready and not enjoying this place where we lived.

"It'll be OK," Rixa said. "We can just move the faucet from one bathroom to the other. Nobody will ever know it's not hooked up."

"I haven't even attached the tub skirt yet."

"Maybe we can just push it into place?"

"It needs the hardware to pull it tight."

For weeks the tub skirt had been lying on the floor next to the bed. The bathroom area was hundreds of years old and nothing was square. We had leveled the tile and now we were having difficulty getting the tub to line up. Every adjustment to the metal feet pushed it off kilter somehow. None of that would show up on a TV show. But the bare wires and plumbing, the motor and fiberglass would. The tub was a display model without the hardware to attach the skirt and now it was late at night and we had to make do with whatever we could find in the house. No 24-hour stores in the south of France. I looked at the vanity legs I'd just cut off and had an idea.

Several points of the tub had wooden supports, mostly underneath the lip where the skirt was supposed to attach. What if I screwed the bits of wood left over from the vanity into these supports? I could leave a tiny gap in between them and then wedge the skirt in. If I did it in three or four spots, it should be enough to hold it, at least temporarily.

One film that haunts me, that I think about from time to time while I'm in France, is Claude Berri's adaptation of Marcel Pagnol's *Jean de Florette*. In the film, Gerard Depardieu plays the sanguine Jean de Florette, a recent inheritor of a French estate in the south of France. He is the quintessential outsider: a moneyed northerner with a different accent, effete social manners, a can-do work ethic, and a city slicker naiveté. He tries to make a go of it as a farmer, suffering through one of the worst droughts in recent memory, unaware that his property conceals an underground spring that could irrigate his farm. Everyone in town knows about the spring but they keep it from him out of mistrust, jealousy, and greed. He is an outsider after all, and although he displays all the characteristics of success, all the affability and goodwill of a French everyman, it's not enough to invite him into their inner circle. The work and the conditions eventually kill him, crushing his dreams and the hopes of his family.

Many French stereotypes reflect this isolationist attitude. Open almost any guidebook on France or exposé on French culture, from *Bringing up Bébé* to *More More France, Please* and the French are distant, believe intrinsically in their cultural superiority and way of life. There are important reasons for this; besides being the most frequented tourist destination in the world, France also has a long history of cultural commodification, of visitors coming and staying and then exporting the best of what the culture has to offer without giving much back. If anything, the cultural distance to outsiders comes from a general fatigue of having accommodated so many cultures for so long. Contemporary groups such as the far right Front National express this fatigue by trying to draw arbitrary lines in immigration history, with the "true" French on the one side and immigrants on the other.

Some guidebooks are more positive narratives about how friendly and inviting the French can be. "Learn French and your experience will be different," these guides tell us. We often find ourselves in the latter camp, contradicting the negative stereotypes over and over, falling instead into the equally damning trap of over-idealization or romanticization of French culture. "Everyone here has been so accommodating," we say. "Not closed-minded at all." But if I examine the terms of our acceptance, a more disturbing picture emerges, one that pollutes and distorts even my most well-meaning intentions.

The story we were creating with HHI was starting to bother me. First, our narrative bespoke a level of privilege that the show intentionally exaggerated. A couple weeks before the shoot, Bart told HHI that he couldn't find comparable properties at our price point because they didn't exist. And now that we had done renovations, the value would be even higher. The properties that they wanted us to consider in the show were more than we could afford and we would have to price our apartment accordingly. Our already privileged narrative was now even more unattainable, ironically pricing us out of our own apartment.

The show also latched on to my artistic pursuits in a way that corresponded with other idealized narratives of expatriation to France. It was *my* dream, *my* romantic longing, *my* muse-contemplating solitude that accounted for the move. Melissa wanted to know: what drew me to the south of France? Was it the wine, the food, the culture? The picturesque Old Town? The nightlife? From where did I draw my inspiration? I wasn't a starving artist but a moneyed foreigner who had already made it, a writer who could afford to sit by his window all day sipping coffee, waiting for the words to come. To say that the move was primarily for my kids, for the bilingual education I felt compelled to provide felt disingenuous, or even outright false. And now my own blunders that had led us to this point, our dwindling savings and our obsession with trying to save money, made me wonder: was this really for them after all? Really?

So far, the demise of Jean de Florette didn't seem to be happening. At least not to the parents. I have read many examples of families who have tried to integrate into the French system and found it overwhelming. The level of conformity is great and there often isn't room for American exceptionalism. Our second youngest started the maternelle at the age of three. Every time she got on her coat, she flung it on the ground like she was laying a bedspread. Her class taught her that she needed to then bend down and put her arms in the holes and flip it over her head so it slid on her back with ease. Go to any maternelle in France and you'll see this same trick repeated over and over. Voila! Coats on backs. Other aspects of the children's lives were equally regimented: this is how you sit, this is the kind of crayon you must use, this is how you walk in a line, etc. At the school cafeteria, children eat one dish and then it's whisked away and replaced with another. Children eat everything or they don't eat at all. The expectations become even more conforming once the child starts reading and writing. Zari was shocked to be learning cursive already and struggled to get the loops and serifs exactly right so that it met with her teacher's satisfaction. Any French child's writing after the second grade is astonishingly homogenous, the size and shape of the words so similar it's like they've been Xeroxed.

So far our children had been faring well enough but some struggles continued. Zari was still not enamored with school and her complaints continued into the winter. And while our other children had play dates and plenty of friends, Zari seemed to be having more difficulty socially.

I started to watch how she behaved around her peers. Once I was paying the cafeteria bill and a balcony looked out over the elementary school cours. To the left, the dramatic blue crescent of the Baie des Anges cut along the Promenade des Anglais. The terra-cotta rooflines and winding streets of the Old Town completed the picture. But what the school had in its million-dollar view, it lacked in kid-friendly amenities. The cours was a cement holding pen with walls and metal barriers and no playground equipment. It was break now and I looked for my daughter's tell-tale blonde braid. There she was, standing still as a crane, looking at something at her feet. Clusters of girls passed around cell phones with attached earbuds. Boys kicked a foam soccer ball. Zari navigated this already gendered space alone. She didn't talk to anyone. She walked to a tree near the center of the cours and jumped to try to grasp one of its low-hanging branches and then climbed her way up.

A couple weeks later, Zari came home upset.

"Someone cut my shoelaces."

She took off the offending shoes. We had picked them out together from a second-hand store: a pair of barely-worn DC skate shoes with black-and-white skulls on the laces. The shoes were Goth-skater in good condition and she especially liked the skulls. They were also very much unlike the pink-studded shoes the other girls her age wore. And now someone had taken it upon themselves to cut the laces through the loops, rendering them useless.

It was the first time I had ever talked to a teacher about negative behavior at school. When I explained what had happened, he seemed shocked. "She is always so attentive," he said. He had a class of almost thirty students. I wondered if the attention was reciprocal.

The challenges continued as the school year morphed into winter. For her birthday, we dutifully made invitations and she gave them to everyone in her class. But only two kids came to her party: an awkward Russian girl from her class and Otego, along with the rest of Johnny's family. Now I wondered if my children would become casualties of our forced integration. I might succeed where Jean de Florette could not, but what about my kids? And if that was the case, I couldn't imagine a worse failure, worse than all the botched filming caused by our half-renovated apartment.

Now I screwed in the wood blocks with coarse sheetrock screws, leaving a gap the width of a quarter. I wedged one end in while Rixa supported the other end of the skirt. I pushed in the middle, then the other end. Neither popped out.

I stood back. The skirt hovered about an inch off the ground—the tub still wasn't quite level—but all along the lip the skirt sucked in just right to cover all the mess underneath. It looked good, professional, even though I knew if you punched it in the right place it would probably pop out. But like our idealistic image of our family in France, I hoped it would hold.

Chapter 24

Petit Papa Noël

WINTER IN FRANCE ALSO BROUGHT changes to the sea. By the end of October, the kids no longer ventured into the water for more than a few minutes. When the sun was out and the wind was low, we'd still suit up and trek to Castel but the kids spent most of the time combing through the rocks for junk that winter storms would push up onto the beach. The exception was Ivy, our youngest, who would strap on the arm floats and diving mask and jump in till her body started to shake. I still had my spring suit and could tolerate a good hour or more if I was kicking around to keep warm. By November, I was the only one getting in the water. Soon we rarely went to the beach except to observe storm swells or skip rocks. By December, my spearfishing was starting to suffer.

Still, Johnny had heard about my spearfishing and wanted to try.

"I'm a beginner," I told him. "But you're welcome to come along."

He was ecstatic. For him, there was something heroic and Hemingway-esque about spearfishing. I imagined our exploits being memorialized in one of his paintings. Tubes of gouache squeezed out to resemble a fish, a spear, the glinting corner of a diving mask from behind a coral-encrusted rock. I still felt shame every time I caught a fish that gave itself for our sustenance.

We waited for the right conditions. Even in winter we could occasionally catch a 65-degree day in the early afternoon when the sun was out in full force. Beach-goers were minimal now except for the leather-skinned retirees who would lie where the rocks met the stone wall of the Promenade, the angle magnifying the light and heat. After lunch, I would drop the kids off at school, then walk out to the Promenade and look for the clarity which made for the best spearfishing. Any crescents of milky-white blue meant that the undercurrent was strong, kicking up fine particulates that gave the Baie des Anges that striking, almost fluorescent blue color. On a day when the sea barely lapped the shore and I could see submerged rocks from the Promenade, I called Johnny up and met him at his apartment.

Did he need anything special? Johnny wore a pair of Bermuda trunks and a white linen shirt open at the collar and rolled up at the sleeves. A pair of sunglasses acted as a kind of barrette for keeping his long hair out of his face. He wore a pair of Lacoste sneakers without socks and slung a blue-and-white-striped towel over his shoulder. He looked more like an actor getting a few minutes of sun in between screenings at Cannes than a guy ready to dive into the frigid depths of the Mediterranean.

"Maybe a plastic bag. In case we catch anything."

I took Johnny over to my favorite spot off Rauba Capeu. Till now I'd mostly hugged the coast, searching for big sar in holes or spearing saupe as they clustered around vegetation. But the winter had sent the fish deeper into the water and I was finding it more difficult to get as close as I once did. It wouldn't be till the late spring when I would really realize the potential of the point and learn to venture further from shore. For now, I dove down my ten or twenty feet, poked around and searched in holes till I ran out of breath. If I happened to nab an octopus or a cuttlefish, anything that swam in the sea, the outing was a success. But recently, I'd started to come back empty-handed.

We took the stairs down and navigated out to the flat rock where I'd stash my clothes in a hole. On the way, two tiny caves were littered with bottles and refuse, evidence of a homeless squatter. A tiny inlet led into the rocks. When the waves were more substantial, the inlet became like a giant toilet bowl that would suck you out and scrape you against the submerged rocks if you weren't careful. But today the water was flat and calm.

"You going out very far? I'm not a strong swimmer."

"You'll be fine."

We stripped down and I put on my spring suit. I hoped it would be enough to keep me from freezing. Lately I would start to get cramps, making my ascents to the surface agonizingly long and painful. Sometimes it was a calf or a quadriceps. Sometimes a cramped hamstring would leave me doubled over, kicking one leg and trying not to scream.

We left our clothes in a pile where we could see them, on a flat rock a couple feet off the shore. On one side of the inlet, rocks formed a vertical wall that largely held against any swells. Out about thirty feet, a submerged rock the size of a truck almost broke the surface. When the water was calm, you could stand on the wall and dive into a deep natural bowl between these two structures. The bowl was also fertile fishing. If I was quiet and careful I could usually catch a fish as I came around the corner of the inlet. I slithered out into the sea, thinking Johnny would follow me, but instead I heard a splash. Johnny had cannonballed into the bowl.

I pulled my snorkel out of my mouth. "You just scared all the fish away."

"Oh it's cold. Damn cold." Johnny treaded water in the bowl and adjusted the mask that had slipped off his head. "What do I do now?"

"Wait."

My legs from the knee down were gradually going numb so I kicked hard for a while to warm up, then I armed my spear. Johnny was behind me reluctant to follow. I took a few deep breaths and pushed air out through my snorkel, purging my lungs of CO_2. I gulped and packed down fresh oxygen, then dove.

Nothing. Or at least nothing of size. I'd become bewildered by the relative lack of fish as the winter wound on. Did they all go into hiding? Like some weird fish hibernation? I had looked up winter spearfishing in the Mediterranean on the internet but they told me almost the opposite of what I seemed to be seeing: the fish were in shallower water. The water was less crowded. Perfect season for bigger game fish like the loup.

But for whatever reason, the rocks and crannies where I usually found my sar or mulet were empty. I saw tiny rockfish and labre, schools of small saupe but nothing that would amount to more than a couple mouthfuls of fish, nothing I'd be willing to spear.

And then I started to cramp.

With another swimmer nearby I was more willing to push my body to see what I could handle. By myself, I was always conscious that if anything happened, if I got stuck on a rock or trapped by old fishing line or remnants of a fisherman's net, nobody would be there to rescue me or even witness my demise. Johnny stayed in the bowl, sometimes locked on to the peak of the rock like an overgrown barnacle, but always within sight. When my calves started to ball up, I worked out the knots, no big deal. All fall, I'd been regaling Johnny with stories of underwater adventures, like the time when I saw a school of a thousand barracuda that surrounded me like they were going to have me for lunch. I stayed completely still then thrust out my arms so the barracuda scattered, and the sound was like an underwater train. Another time I saw a fish as tall as me skirting the rocks, a powerful tuna-like fish that I later found out was called a liche. I dove, then dove again, ignoring the pain.

Then my hamstring cramped.

I was on the sea floor, about twenty feet down, crawling around a rock and hoping to surprise something—anything—on the other side. My legs were partially flexed, ready to kick down, when the long tendon along the back of my leg tightened and wouldn't relax. I grabbed the leg with my free hand and tried to knead the muscle as best I could. I was running out of breath.

I kicked to the surface, one arm clutching my leg. Johnny was already on shore, shivering in his striped towel. I stretched along the surface but couldn't get the knot worked out without feeling the twinge again. I was done.

I slipped back into the inlet and pulled myself up onto a rock. Bending my leg seemed to aggravate the hamstring, so I asked Johnny if he could help me with my fins.

"I just realized I never let you have the speargun."

"That's all right. Got cold pretty fast."

"See much of anything?"

"What are those striped fish called. I saw one, torpedo-shaped. Huge."

"Probably a sar."

"I just hung out on that rock most of the time. I could have got him, you know. He came right up to me."

"Next time you take the speargun and I'll watch."

"I think I'll get my own. I'm hooked."

I unzipped my spring suit and pulled it off like a rubbery second skin. My body shook like I'd just plugged myself into a car battery. I had been in the water for less than an hour.

At home, I started to look for full-body wetsuits. I needed something to keep me warmer if I didn't want to end up painfully cramped from now on. The cold was just too much. I was a father with four children and I didn't need to be taking those kinds of risks. I had caught enough fish to pay for my speargun several times over but a wetsuit was an even bigger investment. The very cheapest I could find on Nootica were still almost 200 euros for a 5mm suit, the bare minimum that people recommended for winter fishing. And now that we were in the middle of renovations we were feeling the financial pinch more than ever.

"You getting me anything for Christmas?" I asked Rixa one evening. We were thick in our preparations for HHI, all the materials and expense of having Jad do the mezzanine cutting into what we'd set aside for the holidays. We still wanted to get some presents for the kids, but I knew that neither Rixa nor I were counting on anything.

"How about an apartment in the south of France?"

"I'm worried I'm going to kill myself if I don't have something to keep me warm."

"I don't see how we can afford it."

I let it drop. Other concerns: celebrating our first Christmas with just our family, the prospect of skiing, and the renovations leading up to House Hunters took over. Johnny was serious about getting started spearfishing until he was not. Natalie's job at the International School of Monaco wasn't going as well as she had hoped. Their son Otego still wasn't learning French. And now the XVA Gallery in Dubai was calling, asking if Johnny would like a position there? They could give him a studio and access to clients he was having a hard time attracting in Nice. The week before Christmas they decided to finalize the move.

"You want to help us get rid of some of our stuff?"

Like Johnny, we had a similar anti-consumerism attitude toward stuff. Back home when it was time to downsize or move, we gave everything away to friends or put articles on Freecycle, a website where you could get rid of anything from toilet seats to carpet remnants. It was liberating. As the only grandchildren from both Johnny's and Natalie's families, their kids had, in Johnny's words, "way too many toys." They wouldn't have room in their luggage for the boxes of Legos and books, the puzzles and light sabers that they had accumulated. With Christmas coming up, they'd have everything they could ever hope for in Dubai. Really, we'd be doing him a favor. And could we also store some things for them for when they came back in February?

Well, OK, we said.

Their generosity provided a respite amidst the chaos and disappointments of the winter. We dutifully wrapped Otego's old toys: a bin of Legos, a pirate puzzle, a Star Wars Angry Bird game with conically-shaped Angry Birds dressed in Jedi robes. We felt an undeserved abundance that holiday season. We brought some of the toys to a second-hand store, hoping that other families would also benefit from Johnny's departure. But their leaving also left a hole in our lives. I would lose an artistic collaborator and a friend. Although we'd make efforts to work together or visit throughout the years, we'd never be able to walk the block or two to each other's apartments.

On Christmas morning, our children unwrapped the presents, decimating the paper and cardboard and Scotch tape. Each plush toy or puzzle was met with the same wonder regardless of its provenance. Who cared if it was second hand? It was a great Christmas, the best, made even better by the lack of anything to compare it to. Other years, surrounded by cousins and aunts and uncles with differing levels of consumer tolerance or budget or affluence, our kids became conscious of what they didn't have, of trends and toys that possessed no more intrinsic value than these second-hand gifts except for what consumer culture said was important at that particular moment in time. On our own, we were surrounded by a bounty. Forget the unfinished bathroom, the crumbling plaster, the half-laid floor or botched plumbing or all the underwater marvels to ponder on my solitary dives. We were a family. Just us. Now, in this place.

That evening, we walked the Promenade du Paillon past the wooden dolphins and turtles, past the stature of General Leclerc and the splash pad to the winter village. All during the winter, we had ignored our children's demands about the prominent Ferris wheel in the middle of the Place Masséna. The town of Nice had put up a temporary skating rink complete with rental skates and booths selling hot chocolate. The Ferris wheel sat above it, on a platform, and at night it lit up the square as it rotated round and round, a great eye through which you could see the Mediterranean on one side and the town of Nice on the other. Tonight, we said, the whole family was going up, a gift from their Grandma Spencer. Merry Christmas.

We stepped up the wooden stairs, paid the attendant and squeezed into a pod with two facing benches. The motor whirred to life and the spokes of the great wheel started to move, taking us up and up till we were high above the skyline, looking down on the whole *place* and its winter lights. The kids sang "Petit Papa Noël," a song that had been playing in all our heads ad nauseum for the past month: Quand tu descendras du ciel avec tes jouets par milliers, n'oublie pas mon petit soulier. When you come down from the sky/ With toys by the thousands/ Don't forget my little shoe.

After another rotation, the wheel stopped, keeping us perched above downtown Nice. Zari stepped out to the middle of the pod, arms out like she was balancing, surfing a wave. We could see everything! Where was our apartment? We were on top of the world. But after a few moments teetering in our cocoon, the wheel started its descent.

Chapter 25

House Hunters

THE HOUSE HUNTERS CREW had arrived. I met the fixer first. I was waiting in the lobby of the 4-star Hotel Masséna when he pulled up in the minivan rental half-filled with production equipment. I bolted out the door and got in the front seat and we shook hands across the stick shift. "Laurent," he said, and right away in French I asked if we could tu-toi each other. "Good idea," he said and soon we were chatting about the shooting location. "The sound guy thought the Promenade was too noisy," he said. "So I suggested Coco Beach." It was the same beach where I spent the first days learning to spear-fish with my parents diving in and out of rocky coves. It'd provide a more scenic backdrop than the Promenade and it was quiet and calm in the winter.

"So what exactly does a fixer do?" I asked, not realizing that he had more or less already told me.

"I'm the liaison between HHI and the local community. I make sure that everything goes smoothly."

Over the next few days, Laurent would bound down the narrow streets of Old Nice to see if a restaurant was open. He would bring around the car just when we needed it or negotiate with police who were curious about our filming, showing them all the necessary permits. He went for coffee, introduced us to sheep farmers at the Cours Saleya market, invited us to his brother-in-law's ski resort. Laurent was taller than I was, broad shouldered, with a trimmed mustache and goatee, and I imagined "the fixer" as also having a larger role as the muscle, a man not to be trifled with. I'm from

Canada originally, I told him. I'm an academic and a writer. I was interested in HHI because of how it intersected with my writing projects, particularly a memoir about home renovation in France. But it was more than that. I was also interested in expatriation and identity, about historic preservation and the aesthetics of beauty and the romanticized stereotypes that drew people to France and finding a more décroissant way to live in this world.

He had also traveled and was fascinated by the US. He lived for years in San Francisco, following a partner there. We talked about how living in another culture changed you, how it could distort your perception of where you came from. The difference could cause rifts in relationships. I told him a story about friends of ours, an American who married a French man and then moved from Miami to France. "She couldn't get over not having a two-car garage and a pool," I said. "In the end, divorce." I waited for him to respond and then I realized that I didn't yet know his history. In the ensuing silence, I imagined his own spurned partner left in San Francisco, a tenuous alliance that lasted till the exotic appeal of dating a Frenchman had worn off.

We were finally at Coco Beach. The director Kris, a square-jawed German in khaki shorts and an orange jacket, and a skinny Israeli with a tripod greeted me. "Yahel, enchanté," he said. "That's about the only French I know." But his accent was spot on, good enough to convince me that he knew much more. Last was the sound guy, Thomas, a bald and buff Englishman with a pair of headphones looped around his neck. Laurent hopped back in the car to pick Rixa up. Kris wanted to start with me first and get my version of our backstory before the sun washed out the sea. He had a series of questions. And advice: act natural. Don't look at the camera. Try to speak in complete sentences. We quickly fell into a routine. The sound check. Keeping the light consistent during the take. The three filmmakers had never worked together and came from all over the world: Israel, the UK, Germany. They flew in last night with their own equipment in hard plastic cases. Twelve hours later and here we were on Coco beach, filming my backstory, everyone already comfortable in their roles. Action.

A day or two into the shoot, Kris indirectly told me how happy he had been with the results. "House Hunters does a much better job vetting the participants. Sometimes on 'Under the Sun' we get these people who are so shy they can barely talk." He was very interested in how we came to be on the show and why we wanted to do it in the first place. For me, it was a cultural experience that spoke to my memoir about bringing a large family to France and renovating a small apartment here. What better environment to examine our reasons than a reality TV show? We were more like collaborators rather than subjects or actors. We shared experiences with home renovation: the dust and hassle of refinishing wood floors, the challenges of stripping lead paint, the joy of seeing natural stone laid down. Kris loved filming these shows but admitted he'd rather have our authentic experience than HHI's reconstructed one. Who cared which property you bought or how much you paid for it? His own style was to be more in the background, to follow and observe, to find the narrative worth telling.

But now, filming me, what we got was tension.

"Did you and your wife disagree about any of your criteria?"

"What were some deal breakers?"

"How did you overcome challenges to your move?"

The English professor in me wanted to point out the underlying assumptions behind each question. Did we have disagreements? Certainly, but they were years ago before the conditions were right for us to make a purchase. Our actual home-buying process was infused with consensus. We trolled the local market in Old Nice for years till we found an apartment within our price range. But House Hunters didn't want the narrative of a middle-class couple miraculously purchasing an apartment in a market normally closed to anyone but the wealthy. They didn't want a story of bilingual education, or financial instability, of living with less and the inequalities in immigration. Instead, they want dithering, plot twists, arguments about whether or not the dishwasher matched the fridge, questions about bursting our pre-determined budget, something that would fit nicely into a twenty-minute TV show.

Kris was done with me now. The sun had come up a little and they wanted to get Rixa before the light was too intense. She and Ivy were with the fixer in the tinted-window rental car waiting for their cue.

The crew fussed over Ivy in her hand-me-down brown velour jacket and gingham dress. All but Yahel had young children and she had a face that opened to strangers if they smiled and gave her attention. "You'll have to take her away," Kris said, "for the sound." I took Ivy by the hand and we followed a stone path that became stairs till we were just above the rocks near the shore. Occasional wildflowers sprouted from crevices and Ivy amused herself by picking the colors: jaune, violet, blanc. She held each stem to me till I acknowledged them and repeated the colors back to her. The sea drowned out the sound from Rixa's interview. I wondered: was she being fed the same questions? Would her story corroborate mine? Contradict it? This seemed suddenly important, and I wondered if all the late-night painting and renovations were the wrong kind of preparation. Like defendants in a court case, we should've been getting our facts straight, making sure we agreed on the narrative we wanted to tell.

I was starting to see how these shows blew up.

Before being on House Hunters, we'd only watched one or two episodes and we were surprised by how many seemed to pit the couple against each other. Buying a home abroad was maybe one partner's dream and not the other's. Sometimes petty arguments erupted: You can do without your man cave for once! The more pressure the show was able to expose, the more satisfying the resolution became. Challenges of budget, aesthetics, layout, location, and size were tantamount. Would Kris uncover some hidden bias that Rixa had been suppressing? I knew that he would likely find whatever caused the most conflict, editing the clips to make it seem like we were a couple on the brink of disaster.

Kris waved to me, a sheaf of papers in his hand.

Laurent was already loading up equipment into the van and Yahel and Tom coiled cords and removed microphones. We'd be filming the realty agency next: Bart first, alone, then our surreptitious arrival and greeting. We piled in the car and Laurent the fixer whisked us off back downtown.

So far the narrative seemed to be coming together. We were filming in loosely chronological order. This was supposed to be the moment when we arrived in France to first look for an apartment. It was only the two of us, our children magically absent. Maybe we came over for a house hunting trip and didn't bring the kids along? No, in the afternoon we were supposed to pick them up and act like we'd just arrived, like we were staying in a hotel till the deal went through. But how would we have arranged it so that the move went so quickly? These were questions that the show didn't have time to answer. It was chrono-logical, not logical-logical. No need to worry about cause-and-effect. The viewing audience would align these events subconsciously and make inferences without our help. Don't disrupt the movie magic.

When we filmed at Bart's office, "L'Agence," a place that had become a common stop on my walks, Rixa and I acted like we'd never been there before. Yahel shot us through the window, looking at the listings while Rixa and I mumbled like we were deep in discussion. In truth, we were reading the bad English translations, randomly inserting words like watermelon or heteronormative to make ourselves crack up. We needed to look happy! We were going to buy an apartment in France! When we came in and shook Bart's hand, I said, "It's nice to finally meet you!"

In the aired version of HHI, I was pleased that they captured this first awkward greeting. It's infused with a forced energy. It *is* nice to finally meet you! I am loud with an abnormally large smile. I'm wearing a denim shirt with a skull-and-crossbones pattern and I'm tanned from over six months of living in the sunny south of France. I look like some French hipster and not a gullible North American fresh off the boat. The greeting also belied a familiarity that indicated that we were acting. Finally! It was ironic since we had known each other for almost a year and our communication had always been in French. Hearing Bart's nasal-inflected English, his "i"s like "ee"s and "d"s for "th"s sounded so stereotypical, exactly the kind of thing a viewer would hope to hear from a realtor in Nice.

We went over our "wish list": a fantasy list of things we would've loved to have in an apartment but realistically could never afford. This was where our hopes were so dashed that the viewer couldn't help but feel our disappointment. No ocean views for that price? Oh, drat. Maybe we had made a mistake.

One point of tension became increasingly clear.

We had four kids.

Four?

"It is difficult in the Old Town. That will be our challenge." Every one of Bart's "i"s came out like "ee."

We left the agency pretending to be resigned. None of the things we wanted: a balcony, sea views, lots of light, three bedrooms, location in Old Nice, were likely to exist in our already over-inflated price range. Our one overriding criteria became space. We had four kids and we would need somewhere to put them. We'd be lucky if we could find even a shell at our price in the Old Town, when in truth our budget had been much less. "We will see what we can find," Bart said.

It was already past one and the crew was starting to get hungry. Each scene required multiple takes and then checks for the sound and light. Sometimes a scooter would go by and botch the scene completely. We got used to saying the same things over and over again: "It's nice to finally meet you!" *Less enthusiasm this time!* They were amazed at our resilience. We didn't seem tired. We weren't cranky. What they didn't realize was that for us this was so much easier than patching a wall or repainting the living room, activities that we were doing up till last night. Plus our kids were at the cantine today! What could be easier? Laurent found a reputable restaurant in the Place Rosetti, and we took a late lunch.

It was our turn to ask some questions. I wanted to know about past HHI episodes Kris had done. Who usually tried to get on one of these shows?

"Most of the time, it's vanity," Kris said. "We don't pay them much so they can't be doing it for the money. They want to show their rich friends back home. Kind of like some hat trick or anecdote they can share at a dinner party."

I was becoming increasingly self-conscious about the narrative we were trying to tell. Kris's response implied that we were not among the uber-wealthy he described. Still, I started to question our motivations. Were we any different? Our story was like an elaborate Facebook post, a hyped-up version of our home-buying process. The show would instill envy rather than inspire others to live with less.

The afternoon extended our idealized vision of France. We picked up our kids from school then went home to wrangle them into their soccer uniforms. We would be shooting this next part out of sequence. The weather wasn't supposed to be great the next couple days and HHI wanted some footage of us playing at the park while we still had some sun. After that, we would change again, into a new outfit for our supposed first arrival in Nice. We'd familiarize our family with their new city and speculate about where we wanted to live.

Would our children believe us when we stood on a balcony and pointed to the Old Town like we were seeing it for the first time? When we went to the beach and I held a flat pebble in my hand that'd been smoothed by years of tumbling in the waves and showed them once again how to skip a rock, would they finally learn? The cameras would be on them then. We had signed the release forms and said: yes, it's OK for the world to see our children. Look at the nuclear family tossing pebbles on the beach. Look at the father playing soccer at the park. Look at the mother eager to teach her children about a new culture. Look at the children's braided flaxen

142

hair, their matching soccer uniforms, their unrestrained smiles. Look how happy they all are.

Chapter 26

Life in the Port

THE SECOND DAY OF HHI, we saw our first apartment. It was in the Port neighborhood on the busy Boulevard Riquier, just down the street from the mega-yachts that winter in Nice. Bart showed us some of the pictures: a new kitchen with built-in appliances, two large bedrooms, and lots of neutral taupe. It would come partially furnished with the possibility of a parking spot. It had a small balcony and large windows with plenty of natural light.

We had looked at the Port area during our apartment hunting. The antique quarter and the roads behind the Notre Dame du Port cathedral and the pedestrian road from the Place du Pin up to the newly-renovated Place Garibaldi were always teeming with life: good restaurants, an independent cinema, and plenty of grocery stores. But cars ruled the Port neighborhood. Large intersections crowded the roads heading up to the Basse Corniche and the Moyenne Corniche. Cars nosed through the one-way streets looking for spots amid even more cars, double-parked, their hazard-lights blinking in tandem. It was here that twenty years ago, I witnessed a fatal accident. An octogenarian woman caned her way across the street when a white Mercedes with its top down ran a red light. The crash flipped her over the hood and she lay on the ground with her ivory teeth opened for a scream that never came. I held her hand as her jaw twitched and then stilled. The apartment that Bart was about to show us was just a couple blocks away.

"I would never have shown you this place," Bart said. "It's not at all what you're looking for. But the producer wanted some variety and this is the kind of property that most people want."

We filmed the walkup seven times because of traffic noise. I anticipated when to tilt my head up, taking in the skyline, or when to ask questions about size or amenities.

"There's an Intermarche nearby," I said. "I like the nice clean lines."

The building was one of those concrete boxes so popular during the 60s and 70s. The balconies were small, cramped with AC equipment, and they all looked out onto a busy street.

We opened the door to the building. A tiny elevator at the end of the entryway dinged and a gray-haired man in a flannel shirt and jeans came out. He raised his hand in front of his face like he'd been blinded by a floodlight. "Shit, you fuckers, get that thing out of my face!"

"We're not rolling," Bart said.

"Son of a whore!" The man shielded his face and lunged out the entryway and down the sidewalk.

"All right," Kris said. "Let's do the take again. And remember to be upbeat—we want to keep the audience guessing and it will look bad if you dismiss a property right away."

Luckily the apartment itself gave us more to be excited about. Coming off of a month of continuous renovations, we appreciated a finished space. The counters were smooth, professionally installed, the appliances hidden behind matching veneers. The Kohler sink and grey laminate floors and freshly painted walls seemed like little miracles of uniformity and cleanliness after our dusty old apartment. The bathroom was large with a lacquered vanity and a stainless steel towel rack and light marble tile. Kris filmed us in each of the rooms. We ran our hands along the slick counters, opened and closed cupboard doors. But it wasn't long before one of us delivered the sound bite, the damning verdict that would likely convince most of the viewing public that we weren't interested: I feel like I'm in a hotel.

In our extended conversations about the place, we latched on to this description more than any other. A hotel room communicated a homogeneity, a sameness that we found difficult to associate with being in France. These three rooms, as spacious and clean as they were, could really be anywhere. With the square furniture and modern finishes, we felt like we were in an IKEA showroom. The irony for Bart (and for us) was that this was the kind of home most people were comfortable buying. "It'll be on the market a week or two, tops," Bart said. When we pressed him about it, he gave his reasons: nobody wants to buy a property abroad and then be saddled with a spate of renovations, especially an apartment in a city center. They wanted a place that they could buy and then not have to think about, not have to worry whether or not the stove would break down or the walls would crack. These concerns often resulted in homogenous renovations, in properties that were as forgettable as they were transmutable. This was an apartment that could be anywhere and nowhere, a quality that guaranteed its acceptance to the largest, most multinational demographic possible.

While Yahel finished the b-roll, cataloguing the generic space in magazine-worthy stills and empty shots, we sat on the IKEA Karlstad couches facing the flat-screened TV like a hunk of polished obsidian. Even though Tom wasn't recording sound, we talked in hushed tones as Yahel swept around the apartment with the camera.

"My chair is vibrating." Kris said.

"I hear it too."

What started as a dull hum now reached a tremor-worthy climax. Maybe it was a heavy truck passing? A nearby concrete overpass? We were on the first floor, not a likely place for this kind of continuous noise. But Rixa guessed it immediately: "It's a laundromat."

"I definitely don't think I could ever live here," I said.

As if on cue, the front windows started to shake.

At lunch that day, Kris brought up something that was to dog our plans till the end of the shoot: the weather.

"I just hadn't planned for it to be this cold."

If the météo held true, we were in for the coldest weekend of the winter. Every day it was supposed to rain. Except for this afternoon.

"This may be the only day we can get any good b-roll of the town."

Kris scribbled on his white sheaves of paper, reordering the shoot schedule. If we could keep to our indoor projects for the next few days we could pack the rest of the exterior shots into the afternoon.

"But first we need to get footage of you spearfishing. Melissa was very insistent."

During our early negotiations about the show, our producer Melissa explained how HHI wanted to make each narrative unique. What were some of our hobbies? What in our narrative was different from other expatriates who move to Nice? We wanted to emphasize our family, how people could live in a smaller space than in the states. No plastic houses, three-car garages, and bedrooms for every child. We wanted to show what happened when play space was also public, how apartment living engendered respect for others. We wanted the anti-single-family-home narrative, to show how privacy often led to isolation, whereas being in an apartment forced you to be part of a community. Yes, yes, Melissa said. But what were some things we liked to do? We mentioned hikes and antique shopping and soccer with the kids. Then near the end, I let it slip: I'd been getting into spearfishing.

Melissa was especially drawn to this. Spearfishing in Nice? It didn't correspond with the majority of images she had of the city, the open-air markets, the Place Masséna, the art galleries and Museums and beaches. Seemed more like an activity reserved for someplace far from tourists and pleasure yachts. Would I be comfortable if we filmed some spearfishing during the shoot? No problem, I said. I go all the time.

In reality, I hadn't been spearfishing for weeks. The renovations and the impending deadline of HHI had consumed most of my free time. I hadn't even used the wetsuit I'd picked up from the guy on Leboncoin. And then there was my actual ability as a spearfisher, something I was sure would become painfully evident. I was still a novice. No amount of movie magic was going to hide that. I would be like those films of movie stars fake-playing the violin, the actor magically producing a vibrato without moving his hand.

I left with the crew while Rixa and Bart had the afternoon off. We decided to go back to Coco beach rather than film at Castel. The water was clearer and street noise was significantly less. I toted my gear in its usual Carrefour reusable grocery bag down to a stone staircase carved into the rock. We were on a man-made shelf with a curved stone wall border, like the base of a castle turret. Yahel peered into his eyepiece and panned down to the rocks and then over across the sea. "You're going right over there?" It would be a magnificent shot, he said. The light was a little strong but he would make it work.

I got out a bottle of soapy water. When I first bought the wetsuit, I didn't believe the guy when he said that I couldn't try it on. "You don't have any soap. You're the same size as me so it should fit you." I thought he was joking till he explained. Spearfishing wetsuits were different than diving wetsuits. There was no protective fabric on the inside—just the bare neoprene. If I didn't have some kind of lubricant to help slide the two-part suit on, I'd risk tearing it. Searches on the internet confirmed his advice. The bare neoprene created a better barrier to the water, especially for two-part suits. I watched a few videos to see how it was done and I dutifully did the same. "Hold it," Yahel said. "You mind if I film you?"

I started, self-conscious as a toddler tying his shoes for his parents for the first time. I poured the soap-and-water mixture into the waist and leg holes then I held them shut and sloshed the water around. I did the same with the torso. Then I pulled on the pants, my legs sliding in with a slap. Suds pooled around my ankles. I folded the top of the pants over so a band of bare neoprene covered my stomach. The top was a little harder to get on. I slid my arms in first then shoved my head up and through the hole. I pulled the crotch flap from where it bunched in folds along my back between my legs so it wrapped around and snapped into the other side. I looped my weight belt around my waist and pulled it tight like I'd been doing this for years. I uncorked my speargun and provisionally put my mask on my head.

"We need to get you hooked up first."

Yahel had brought a GoPro with a torso harness and a waterproof case. The way it was set up, I'd be filming straight down, not out in front in my line of sight. A few adjustments and we rigged it to shoot up toward my head. Yahel gave me a brief demo on how to operate it and then sent me down to the sea.

The water was calm and clear. I sat on a rock that tapered down into the water a few feet and then dropped off. A deep sea cave was off to my left and a large submerged rock was just below me, providing plenty of cover for fish. Kris and Tom stood with their elbows up on the stone fence while Yahel squinted into his camera, filming me. I spit in my mask, swirled in some sea water, and put my snorkel in my mouth. I reached down to the GoPro and pressed record.

I skimmed the surface for a while, looking for game fish. A school of saupe nipped vegetation off a rock. Normally when I spearfished, this was where everything changed, where the outside world disappeared and I found myself alone with the creatures of the sea. But this time I couldn't let go. I was on display, a prop for someone else's experience in the south of France. I worried; how would the GoPro footage turn out? Would my head and upper torso appear along the top of the frame because of the wide angle lens? A couple green-and-purple-striped labres skirted the edge of the submerged rock. I slowed my breathing, purged my lungs of CO_2 and dove.

Fine gravel carpeted the sea floor in between rocks covered in coral and vegetation. Goldfish-like apogon hovered under shaded overhangs. The two labres had gone around the tip of the rock so I crept forward, trying to keep as silent as possible. At any moment, they could come flitting into my line of sight. But did I really want to get a labre? I had become picky now, discriminating. Labres took a long time to clean and their flesh was less tasty than sar or dorades. Plus when would I have time to cook it? We still had three days of shooting and our tiny freezer barely fit the ice cream we got last week. But the HHI-watching public would want some confirmation of my south-of-France hobby. They would want to see a fish wriggling on the end of my spear.

Or would they?

I was confronted again with the violence of the thing I was prepared to do. As a child in southern Alberta, I knew one avid hunter who built a small house for his trophies: my scoutmaster. He had bear, moose, elk, and cougar. Even some exotics from Africa and South America. After scouts one day, he paraded us around and we stood under their severed heads while he told us their stories. One was a Jackalope, a common hare that he'd outfitted with antlers from one of his other kills. "Now that there is the rarest of them all," he teased, trying to get us to believe. At the time, I probably laughed and was amazed along with the rest of my troop. But now I wonder—what did it all memorialize? It was the sickest kind of collection, a monument to his ability to overcome the beasts of this world and to put them on display. Was what I was doing now any different?

I thought how the labre would look. It's a striking fish, with a thick comb of a dorsal fin tipped with light blue. The purple-and-green stripes make it look like it belongs in an aquarium of tropical fish. When it swims, it sometimes tucks its fins to its side and glides through the water without flicking its tail, like a miniature submarine. On the sea floor, it picks up gravel in its mouth then spits it out, leaving small clouds of dust that swirl in the water. For every person watching in awe as I stalked and speared this fish, there would be at least one who was horrified. Each time I caught a fish and brought it home, my oldest daughter would stare at its lifeless form in the sink. "It's so pretty," she'd say, and I'd feel her remorse. Did she feel the same passing by the fish market every day? My doing this thing had made her more conscious of where our food came from, showing our role in its consumption.

But these were things I couldn't tell the HHI audience. I couldn't tell them how difficult it was for me emotionally. How each time I fished, I felt the life of the animal as it fought and then died. I couldn't tell them how a part of me was linked to each creature. I didn't spearfish because I wanted to show someone how big a fish I caught and display it on my wall. Instead, I felt a kind of shame, that as a human being, this was something that I felt compelled to do. I ate meat. And ownership of that privilege required that I examine my place in this world, in its maintenance and sustainability. But even though this submarine-like fish that now glided into my field of vision was plentiful, even though it was a male that wasn't carrying the eggs of its next generation, even though it was an adult, large for its species, the perfect candidate for harvest, I couldn't bring myself to pull the trigger. All the audience would see was a vain romantic who had dragged his family to this place, eager to show the world what he could do with his gun.

I fished for about thirty minutes, concentrating instead on the dramatic drop-offs and depth. Sun lit up the orange, pinks, and blues of the girelle paon, the sharp brown-and-white stripes of a serran. The crew was waiting for me. From their perspective, there was probably not that much to see, just the occasional break in the water when I surfaced for air, blowing water out of my snorkel like a whale from his blowhole. Soon I was back at the rock. I pulled off my mask, held up my empty spear. "Didn't catch anything. Good thing I have the rest of my life here."

Kris laughed but Yahel looked up from his eyepiece. "That was great. But could you say it again? A little louder this time."

Chapter 27

Movie Set

ON DAY THREE OF OUR HHI shoot, the movers buzzed in at 7:30 a.m. We'd had a comparatively languid hour already getting showered and dressed and then ushering our bleary-eyed children to the table for breakfast. But as the movers clomped up the stairs to our apartment, the tempo accelerated.

Our apartment was about to become a movie set.

The president of AGS movers knocked on the door. He and the two laborers wore red-and-black coats with the AGS insignia across the back like letterman's jackets. Latex gloves covered their hands. It was our first experience with professional movers, having always relied on ourselves and friends and a moving truck to get the job done. Mr. AGS president re-introduced himself: Laurent. I was more aware of his name now for the potential confusion it might cause with the fixer. We already met him briefly last week when he cased our place for the upcoming move. He brought us AGS boxes, AGS shoe bags, AGS totes, even AGS stationery and coloring books for the kids. Someone at HHI must have neglected to tell him about their no-logo policy. He didn't know that HHI wanted him to be invisible.

"Where do we start?" We told him they would film the front rooms first, so to go ahead and box things up. Everything had to be moved out except our antique mirror that we had painstakingly mounted to the wall. They could move the furniture into the front bedroom. The staircase and back bedrooms were also free game. The movers packed with alarming speed. They covered our dishes in the bubble wrap that would later entertain our children for days. They packed the mugs, the dish rack, our cereal, potatoes, all the contents of our buffet. One mover put both hands on our dining room table. "The top comes off," we said and he smiled, relieved.

The film crew buzzed up. Soon Kris was there, navigating around the furniture piled high in the hallway. Once inside our apartment, he looked forward and then back. We hadn't considered what the entrance would look like. Kris asked us to translate: the hallway had to be empty for the shot of us coming into the apartment. They could use the stairs. Chuck everything into the front bedroom.

The workers complied. They shifted boxes, moved the table so it tilted down the stairs. President Laurent scratched his neck and bobbed his head forward and back. "We have to leave for Monaco by 1 p.m.," he told me. "Ça va pas être evident." It wasn't going to be easy.

No problem, I assured him. We should be done by then.

Rixa left to take the kids up to school. The front rooms were empty now except for our Versailles-sized mirror. The apartment felt like a ballet studio with the open hardwood floors and high ceilings. The minimalist kitchen concealed our food and cookware and spices. In one drawer, our toothbrushes and toothpaste crowded our utensils. The back bathroom sinks still didn't have the plumbing hooked up.

Bart buzzed in and soon we were just waiting for Rixa. The movers excused themselves—when did they need to be back? The first shots wouldn't take more than an hour. Yahel was getting b-roll, squinting through the camera and repeatedly checking the light. We had coordinated our outfits so that they were the same as when we filmed the other apartments. Our whole front room was packed away into the back bedrooms and up and down the stairs. Ready to go.

Except I couldn't find my shoes.

I opened the front cupboard again, just to be sure. Not there. Everyone looked at my bare feet. "I think I put them next to the daybed sofa," I said. Rixa was back now and Yahel had finished with b-roll. In the front bedroom, our sofa and daybed were turned on their sides. Rolled-up oriental rugs leaned against double-stacked kitchen chairs. The armoire, bookcase and trunk shielded a wall of boxes. "You didn't put on your shoes?" Rixa asked. It was a lingering Canadian habit I had: never to wear shoes inside. I only put them on when I was leaving. But now the camera was waiting. "You might not need them," Yahel said. He could movie magic the footage so it never showed my feet. But we were filming the exterior first and it had been drizzling all morning. Did I want to be walking around in my socks in the rain?

I squeezed into the front bedroom and managed to close the door behind me. I was going to have to scale the mountain of boxes. Luckily the movers had put the books on the bottom, making my ascent less precarious. At the top, un-taped boxes yawned open. A vase of pens. A plush monkey. Watercolors in a plastic case. Nothing. For décroissants living in a tiny apartment it suddenly seemed like we had way too much stuff. I started ripping open the taped boxes, hunched like Golem on a pile of bones. Everyone was waiting. Boxes of books. Potted parsley. Library DVDs. I hoped it wasn't somehow underneath it all. I ripped open the last box on the top, by now at the far wall underneath the window. Bingo: my shoes.

Although we were playacting, we tried to look at our apartment objectively, as though we were seeing it for the first time. Bart ran through the particulars: it was a false 3-bedroom with attic storage that wasn't counted in the square feet. It was in the heart of Old Nice but it was over budget, a fabrication that still made us cringe.

About halfway through filming our apartment, Kris told us, "Make sure you balance your impression with some negatives." We had just been through the back bedroom/bathroom suite where only a month ago, the walls were concrete and dirt with chips of old tile still adhered. We didn't have any light and the work lamp we were using gave the impression that we were laboring away in a coal mine. Now a frieze of stone mosaic bisected rectangular tiles placed vertically to give the tiny room a sense of volume. Stainless fixtures with LED lights illuminated the white walls. A Jacuzzi tub dominated the tiny bathroom. A vessel sink carved out of a solid piece of stone rested on a converted antique nightstand. Just before filming, we took the faucet from the front bathroom and propped it between the wall and the vessel sink to give the illusion that it was truly finished. We had agonized over every detail of the renovation. We had bathed our children in the tub and clicked through the Jacuzzi's mood lights in the dark. We loved this room for how it changed the back bedroom from feeling like an old vacation rental to a luxury suite. But Kris was right. We had to pick out more negatives to keep the audience guessing.

"Big tub," I said. "Big rock. Big tub." I repeated the sound bite three or four times for different takes. Bart said, "Unlike some of the apartment where they did the work themselves, they had this room professionally done."

Ha. We hoped that the HD video wouldn't show that the hole for the sink wasn't drilled yet or that a bead of caulk didn't connect the wall and the tub. I thought back to the night before HHI when I rigged the tub skirt with pieces of wood that clipped it into place. I hoped that nobody bumped it in case it fell off. We were still missing a vanity mirror. Negatives. We needed more negatives. Our attention shifted to the gripes we had accumulated after living in the apartment for six months: the geometric way the previous owners had installed the flooring, the sloppy walls and humidity in the bathroom. And there were issues that still concerned us, renovations we hadn't gotten to yet. The steep stairs to the attic, for example.

"I could see Ivy falling down this hole."

"We'd always have to be watching her."

"The mezzanine is another death trap."

"There's moisture here. The kids could be sleeping in mold and mildew."

During the b-roll filming, Yahel hovered for a long time over the moisture damage in the attic. It was the only space that we hadn't altered since we moved in and it was dingy with yellowing shelves and cracked floors. Water had been dripping from the ceiling in places and the space felt cramped and unsanitary. But the attic was what had sold us on the apartment. This would be our kids' room where they could watch movies or play with their toys. Most importantly, it provided the space for three of our children to sleep, opening up the other bedrooms to us, Ivy, and the visitors who were sure to come.

By the end of the filming, the AGS movers were surly and curt. Only Laurent the president was still civil. They hauled our furniture back and forth, piled beds and boxes of books and night tables and armoires only to be told no, not there, more out of the way, try the other room. They were frustrated with the misdirection, the confusion of it all. To empty a room, see it removed of all personality and decoration and then filled again with double the furniture like it had gone from a renovated shell to a packrat's hovel seemed somehow wrong, not in their job description. The usual formalities of boxing and protecting edges gave way to the necessity of moving objects quickly, not to have the camera reveal them like an unforgiving eye. They were hired hands, bodies to sling boxes, part of the invisible machinery behind our show. Now the filming was finished and the film crew wanted to get Bart's impression of the apartment somewhere outside, maybe with a view of the Old Town, and Rixa was off to pick up the children from school.

I was alone with the movers, talking with AGS president Laurent.

"You guys were amazing," I said. "So efficient." All our furniture was back where it was at the start of the shoot, the boxes unpacked, our dishes and glassware in place without a chip or a break.

"*They* were amazing," he said. Laurent had hiked up the sleeves of his AGS jacket and he ran his hands through his graying hair. He had worked in the Philippines for ten years and was still getting used to French formality. I could tell how much he relished the occasional English conversation and being in a multilingual environment. But he was surprised that the crew didn't film any of his work. Didn't they want a few shots of the truck and their men unloading our furniture as though they were moving us in? They had one parked up on Juan Juares—he was game to make a staged show of it, pretending to haul boxes out and down the street. No, Kris said, just get all our stuff out of the way. Now that everyone had left, president Laurent realized that the boxes and shoe bags and coloring books he had given us weren't going to make it on the show. No wide-angle shot paused over the logo of the moving truck. He had no idea how completely absent he would be from our narrative. But he was a meek and understanding man. Before leaving, he said, "If it's not too much to ask, could you have Melissa include an acknowledgment in the credits?" They were off to Monaco to move a sculpture for a gallery, ignoring the usually required two-hour lunch break.

The film crew was back. Rixa and the kids' voices filled the hallway up to the apartment. We needed to go through a time warp. We changed our clothes. Now we'd been living in France for six months, getting used to our new home. Kris started in the living room, plying our kids for conflict; was it strange living in France? What did you miss about being back in the states? We moved up to the attic, the beds and toys now littering the space as though they had always been there. The remaining b-roll went quickly. Everything was back in place now, looking like it should, like we had made this our home. But some of the shots were almost identical to the "before" video of the empty apartment. It hadn't changed enough to warrant another take. "Could we get something to make it seem more lived-in?" Yahel asked. He stood in our back bathroom. There were no toiletries, no decorations. No mirror. We obliged by finding some toiletries but then the space looked cluttered rather than decorated. Rixa grabbed our one nice plant: a white orchid with two open blooms and put it on the flat triangle expanse of the Jacuzzi's corner. The leaves were a deep, waxy green and the orchids were like daubs of milk against the grey tile. It would have to do.

So far during the filming, narrative threads had started to emerge. Rixa fretted about practicalities. I wondered about where I'd write. The last became a bit of a schtick as the days went by. Sometimes Kris would prompt: "And what about your writing space?" I felt pressure to respond like other artists before me. I needed light, a window, preferably with a view, where I could daily contemplate my muse. I speculated about where we'd put a nice antique desk, maybe a traditional secretary that folded up against the wall. "There is so much light here," I said. "I could definitely see myself writing in this space." I stepped away from everyone and held my hands out in front of me like I was measuring, trying to judge the distance between me and the wall, me and the window, me and the book that would surely come.

After we finished filming our apartment, I asked the film crew where they thought I really wrote. "Try to guess," I said. In the living room? The front bedroom? Yahel got it right away: "In the attic," he said. "Away from everyone." I then described my little nook, facing the exposed stone wall. The attic ceiling was low, a child's height. On a plastic chair caked with dried sheetrock mud, I sat with my head almost brushing the rafters. I told them about the old drawer that I'd turned on its side for a desk. It was an almost monastic way to write, the space free of any decoration except the ragged contours of the rock face, the painted rafters. I once visited Balzac's home in Paris, saw the tiny desk where he composed 100 books in sometimes feverish all-night writing binges where the story wouldn't stop. He wrote like an addict, the story the drug. I felt the same way. Pare it down to the bare essentials. All I needed was a tiny corner in my own writer's crack house.

But a writer who could write anywhere didn't create the tension that House Hunters wanted. Where I would write became an overriding question, one of utmost importance, the question that could derail everything and cause the deal to fall through. If we stayed within our budget, I'd have to be creative. In a tiny apartment with four young children clamoring for my attention, a place to write might not exist. What would happen if I couldn't find that one space, that ray of light to illuminate my keyboard, give life to my imaginings? And would I privilege my own desires for creative expression over the needs and wants of my entire family? *I can see myself writing here,* I found myself saying, standing in front of a window overlooking the street of the first apartment. There was traffic noise but a small balcony, light. Our own apartment was dark. Most of the windows opened to the public staircase. Only two opened out to the street and they were marred by views of the opposite building, direct light coming only in the afternoon. Neither space seemed ideal. Didn't Bart have anything else he could show us?

Chapter 28

Soccer Dad

IN BETWEEN HOME RENOVATIONS, preparation for filming HHI, spearfishing, kids' soccer, and writing this memoir, we somehow bought a car.

I had always loved the French family car—their compactness and versatility. Back home we drove the most environmentally-friendly six-seater we could find: a used manual transmission Mazda 5. But unlike the states where the Mazda 5 was the only manual-transmission six-plus-seater on the market, France was saturated with comparable models. Almost all of them had more robust diesel-engines with mpg ratios that made our economical car at home look like a gas-guzzler. French used-car classifieds were filled with cars we loved: station wagons (called breaks) with jump seats in the back, VW mini-mini-vans with fuel economy over 50 mpg, low-slung Peugeots or boxy Fiats or slope-roofed Renaults. I wanted something cheap with low miles that we could maybe buy and then sell when we left, thus minimizing our expenditures. It was the winter when car-selling was at its slowest and I imagined that I could pick up a deal.

The car was a 2004 Opel Zafira Disneyland, a 5-seater with two additional jump seats that folded into the floor. Clean car, one owner. The price was less than half of blue book and it was in our area. I talked to Rixa. It would save us time and money for home renovations and soccer games. We could go hiking and skiing. We could sell it before we left for more than we paid for it. Go into the red for a little while to come out ahead.

"We came to France because we didn't want a car."

Rixa was right. We had come to France in part to escape a society that had embraced the car in a way that no other society had. We didn't want drive-throughs and acres of parking lots and multi-lane highways. Having a car would contrast with how we wanted to interact with our environment. A car was like the transport-version of a single-family home, designed to keep us separate from our community. Often we would joke to our French friends that Americans could do everything from their car. No need to get out and no need to do anything except to feather the accelerator or stamp on the brake. Our daily lives in France didn't necessitate a car except on the weekends or for special occasions, reasons that kept many people—even large families like ours—from ever buying one.

Cars have changed the landscape of Nice. The famed Promenade des Anglais was once used primarily for walking but now was flanked by two to four lanes of traffic stretching ten kilometers from the Port neighborhood all the way to the airport. Most of the changes happened in the 1920s when combustion-engine cars became more the norm. Several Niçois buildings replaced gardens and walkways with parking lots. The covered Paillon River became an open-air market in the morning and a huge *place* for parking in the afternoon and evening. Even the iconic Casino de la Jetée Promenade, a belle-époque-era casino that sat on metal pilings in the sea, enlarged its footbridge to accommodate vehicles.

But the city had recently undergone efforts to reduce cars in town. Back in the 1990s, the center of Nice was dominated by cars. The Avenue Jean Médecin, the artery of the city, was a constant four-lane traffic jam, with buses and cars filling the Place Masséna and roads on either side of the covered Paillon. The center of town became clogged with bus stations and parking garages. In 2007, the new tram system closed the main traffic thoroughfares and turned them into tramways with grass planted between the rails. The Place Masséna once again became a *place*, with grey-and-white geometric paving stones and sculptures from renowned artists. The enlarged pedestrian area on either side of Avenue Jean Médecin and the demolition of parking garages had decreased central Nice's dependency on cars. No longer was a car necessary or even desirable for the majority of its citizens. Buying a car would be like being holders-on to a bygone era.

Then again, maybe not. Like many large European cities, the city of Nice had invested in public bikes and electric vehicles. Electric vehicles got prime treatment: parking spaces in some of the most desirable locations in the city and free charging stations for those who had an annual pass. The municipal Voitures Bleues was Nice's effort to go green. Another service that had helped diminish the number of cars on Niçois roads was a car rental platform called Drivy and a ride-sharing application called Bla-bla car. With services like these, owning a car didn't have to separate us from our community. Besides that, they also offset the cost of owning one.

OK, Rixa said. But only if it saved us money in the long run.

The Drivy website was easy to use. I uploaded photos of our 2004 Opel Zafira Disneyland and listed all its features: cruise control, air conditioning, ABS brakes, and most importantly, 7 seats. For price, I took their suggestion of 32 euros per day. I entered in my contact information and then waited.

The first rental I had was a soccer coach from St. Roch. He was transporting his team to a weekend tournament and needed something cheap with as many seats as possible to take more kids. He came to the Place Centrale where I met him with the Drivy contract and a camera. I got copies of his driver's license and we walked around the car together and signed the paperwork. "I'll have it back to you tomorrow night," he said.

The guy returned the car in exactly the same condition with the gas tank full. Over the next couple months, I'd rent the car for periods anywhere from a few hours to a couple weeks. Part of the car's popularity was its size: for a seven-seater, the car was the same per day as you'd pay for a compact. I picked up families from the airport, met renters at the Place Centrale in Old Nice or nearby at the Place Garibaldi. People took our Opel Zafira to Italy, for day trips up in the mountains. I also met some of my neighbors: people like me with families who didn't want to buy a car but liked having access to one for the occasional trip. One of my most common renters was a group of cops who worked in Nice in the wake of the Charlie Hebdo shooting. France was officially in a state of "vigipirate," the French equivalent of a terror alert. Over the months following the shooting, demonstrators gathered in solidarity with the victims. Machine-gun-toting armed forces walked the streets of Old Nice for the first time in my memory.

And they rented our car.

"There's a reason they're angry," a cop said to me once. The cop was staying at a residence in Ariane and I had agreed to drop him off at the end of his rental. "But no amount of anger justifies what they did."

"How long do you think vigipirate will last?"

"Till terrorists stop killing people."

The real problem, he said, was immigration. Now everyone knew how to game the system. He'd just spent hours interrogating immigrants who claimed not to know where they were from. Selective amnesia, he called it. If they told the officers then they'd have grounds for deporting them home. People coached them now. They could find advice on the internet. Just say you're from nowhere, that you can't remember, that the trauma of displacement has caused you to forget.

I told him, I'm an immigrant.

"Yes, yes," he said. "But you don't really count. These immigrants, they come into the country and try to make it. They can't and so they become radicalized. They forget where they're from till they decide to blow something up."

I pulled up to the residence and let him out.

We mostly used the car for soccer. Till now, we sent Zari to games with parents of her teammates, never being able to return the favor. For Dio's games I carpooled with Jean-Yves, Dio sitting silently in the back while we discussed real estate or OGC Nice's embarrassing 4–0 loss to Marseille. Now we had a chance for reciprocity so that other parents or coaches weren't shouldering the burden of shuttling us around on the weekends.

The first match was for Zari. During the winter, soccer games were "en salle," meaning we'd be indoors even though it was 60 degrees and sunny outside. We took her teammate Sara and her father, a reciprocal arrangement for the last two times they had carted us to games. Sara's father Maurice was a compact smoker with dark hair and a soft voice. He teased me about my "big car" when we drove up to the club house, an investment he knew I was loath to make. Sara hopped in the back. As of yet, Zari had still not made any close friends at either school or soccer. Sara, a girl who was small and fine-boned but tackled girls twice her size, didn't talk much during practice but had opened up to Zari the last time we went with them to a game. I hoped another little road trip would help bring them closer together.

We were headed to Mougins, a privileged hamlet just north of Cannes, about forty-five minutes away. For most of the trip, Maurice mumbled through conversation while the girls chatted in back. He was a painter for the city of Nice. What school did Zari go to? He had just re-painted the gate at l'École du Château a couple weeks ago. How long had Sara been playing soccer? All her life. He still played Monday nights with a senior league. Soccer was something that they could share.

Maurice fit the profile of many of the other fathers I'd seen accompanying their daughters to practices every week. Outside of Cavigal, Nice fielded only two other dedicated girls' teams in Zari's age group—the professional prep team OGC Nice and Carros—whereas over fifteen different clubs offered multiple teams for boys of every age. Girls who played soccer in France played despite pressure to the contrary. They were often called "garçons-manquées" a term for tomboy that literally meant, "failed boy." Fathers of these girls expressed that failure by signing them up for soccer. And like many of the fathers I had met, Maurice was a soccer fanatic with only a daughter, a failed boy, to channel his enthusiasm.

"Will you tell Sara that I play with boys in the states?" Zari asked me in English.

"It's not polite to speak in English," I said.

She asked me again in French.

"Oui, c'est vrai," I said.

Sara pouted. It's not fair, she said. At school I play with the boys but at Cavigal they won't let me.

Both Sara and her father were intrigued by our co-ed system. Compared to France where soccer was the gatekeeper for more traditional gender roles, the US seemed downright progressive. Could this be the reason for their dominance in the women's world cup? This year the tournament would be in my native Canada. Zari and I had already started watching highlight reels of the Canadian national team, past performances of Christine Sinclair, one of my favorite players of all time. Zari had been especially upset by the discrimination leading up to the tournament, the revelation that the matches would be on artificial turf whereas men's games were always on grass. Now both the girls sat in the back of our car, complaining about the injustices, how they were just as good as boys if given the chance.

"Je joue très physique," Sara said.

I know, I told her. I've seen what you can do.

The indoor arena in Mougins was large and new with stadium seating and dedicated indoor soccer courts, a reminder of the hamlet's affluence. Not far away we would meet an American family who had also been on House Hunters International. Like us, they found and purchased their home before responding to a casting call at their local *mairie*. But unlike us, their budget was more in-line with mainstream expectations. Their home was a Provençal mas that they had renovated, a multi-million-dollar property with views of the baie de Cannes and a hundred-year-old olive grove and an infinity pool. Now we were in the city center, at the Mougins gymnasium, a facility likely paid for by their lofty property taxes.

Zari and Sara found their coach and other teammates while I joined the cadre of fathers gearing up to watch their garçons manquées play in their tournament. I recognized all the same teams: the blue-and-yellow-jerseyed Carros, the red-and-white AS Monaco, and the nearby AS Cannes. Mougins itself had a girls' team, an impressive feat considering the size of the suburb and its surrounding communities. If past performance was any indication, our girls would end up somewhere in the middle, not winning against OGC Nice but beating Cannes and Mougins. AS Monaco was always a toss-up, often depending on whether our star player, who was often recruited by Cavigal's Under-12 girls team, showed up.

The tournament started with Zari's team against AS Cannes. The games were short—fifteen minutes—and Zari would start off as a sub. They would play six games this morning and finish around 11. Two other games started simultaneously after a booming announcement over a loudspeaker. Shoes squeaked into action. For the time being, Zari watched the game from the sidelines, supporting her teammates as they tackled and passed and dribbled the ball. Star Player was here and she was already exhibiting her footwork, balancing one foot on the ball before a feint and then a step-over as she rocketed past a defender. Score. Five minutes and we were already up three points. Time for Zari to sub in.

She started out on defense, her least favorite position. In the states she liked playing striker but as coach I put her everywhere. For me, it didn't make sense to specialize in positions so early. Growing up, I had several negative experiences with coaches who didn't give all players equal attention or playing time, often privileging aggressive players who hogged the ball. I wanted everyone to have fun. To play. But here, coaches wanted to win.

Zari wasn't moving in tandem with her teammates. Something about the speed of the passing, maybe, or perhaps a fleeting insult that froze her up? Her first tournament she had been like a firecracker, a perpetual energy machine that would take after the ball regardless of where it was on the field or which side had possession. Now she seemed deflated, even lethargic. She was hanging her head.

In all my years coaching soccer, I'd never seen a player her age act like what I was seeing. The younger players had their own particular set of problems, usually how to avoid clustering like a herd around the ball. A few kids had difficulty focusing, choosing instead to pick dandelions or rip out tufts of turf—grass fight! But this was something different. Zari's action slowed and then stopped. A girl on her team passed her the ball and it bounced off her legs like it had just hit a tree. She wasn't crying, didn't seemed to be distressed, but she would not play. The game swirled around her till Star Player got the ball again and dribbled in for another solo goal. Zari stalked back to her position on defense. Shortly after, the ref called the game.

Zari engaged in some muted celebrations before returning to their bench. I looked for the coach to address Zari's behavior, some huddled aside to find out what went wrong. But there wasn't any time. Their second game was up and Zari started off again as a sub.

"I don't think I've seen anything like that before," Maurice said to me.

"Yeah."

"You sure she wants to play soccer?"

For the first time I wondered the same. Till France, soccer had been an important part of Zari's physical and social development. She looked forward to soccer season and she loved to run, to score goals, to make friends. But maybe the rigidity of the French system, the criticism, and expectation was taking its toll. She wasn't improving as I hoped but instead was now not even playing, just standing around, her golden tresses lying limply down her back. And I couldn't do anything about it. As a parent, I had to wait till she came out of the gymnasium before I could even talk to her. I couldn't shout down or ask what was wrong. It was like I had left her in a cage match and I was only there afterwards to check for fresh wounds. Whatever was bothering her she'd have to overcome on her own.

After the tournament, Zari came over with Sara, happy and flushed after their six games. Only one defeat this time—OGC Nice was still hard to beat—and they were alive with the thrill of their success. We walked back to the car and Zari opened up about her lapse. It had lasted two games and the beginning of the third before she finally broke through and started running after the ball. By that point, I was sure that every parent in the room had wondered about the girl who stood statue-still as the game unfurled around her, the girl likely forced into soccer by an over-zealous father.

"I was feeling sick," she said.

"Sick? Like puking sick?"

"I just didn't feel well."

"Do you feel better now?"

"I think so."

I let it drop. So she was sick. Why didn't she talk to her coach and let him know? Whatever it was, the lapse was over and she seemed to be having fun now, enjoying the conversation with Sara in the back seat. Maurice and I talked about it on our ride back home: the almost casual way that she transitioned from not wanting to play to wanting to, the complete inward focus that for a moment blocked the rest of the world out. It was significant, but my daughter hadn't suddenly become a zombie or completely lost control of her motor skills. Just sick, physically sick, an upset stomach that required her complete attention. It reminded me that sometimes we could be alone and suffering, even when we were surrounded by others. But unlike Zari, most people hid what they were feeling. The pressure to keep up appearances, to run after the ball like nothing was wrong, was too great. We lived in a world where showing pain for everyone to see wasn't normal. Better to hide it, keep the burning down in your gut, and hope that it didn't erupt.

Chapter 29

The Holy Grail

IT WAS DAY FOUR OF OUR shoot and Bart had found an apartment with all the charm and space that we had been looking for. He described it as an artist's loft with three bedrooms, lots of creative touches, south-facing windows, room for outdoor entertaining, and plenty of light.

In the show, the third apartment cost a number far outside of what we could actually afford. But for the sake of the HHI audience, it was the Holy Grail that checked all the boxes. A teaser would set up the showing before a commercial break. Would the Freezes finally find the space and charm to make their French dream come true? Stay tuned to find out!

We filmed the walk up just past the Église de Gésu on our same street. We passed this address almost daily on our way to the boulangerie, the beach, or back from dropping the kids off at school. The Acchiardo restaurant with its vaulted stone ceilings and refined Niçois cuisine was right next to the entrance. The Four à Bois bakery was steps away. With Bart, we turned and pointed to these amenities like we were seeing them for the first time. I loved the little square next to the church, I said. I could see our kids playing here. Just a couple blocks to the beach, Bart said. I think you are going to love it.

You are going to love it. It was a phrase Bart has said several times throughout the shoot, his pronunciation without the diphthongs of an American or British speaker. The "v" in "love" softened to an "f" and his "i"s still sounded like "e"s: "You're going to luff eet!" We quickened our pace.

This could be our new neighborhood, these walls and streets becoming more familiar with each passing day.

We did several takes, trying to get the street as free of passersby as possible. For the time being we concentrated only on the positives. We didn't reveal that the Four à Bois was owned by an English family and had the worst bread in Old Nice. We didn't talk about the three bars at the corner—Paddy's Pub, Au Für et Measure, and the skull-decorated "Rock Eat," known for raucous late-night behavior. Bart talked square footage and aesthetics. The building was in good shape, the staircase wide. An interior courtyard brought in extra light. The trek to the fifth floor was grueling—a downside to be sure—but the advantage was the extra space it would give us and the view it provided. The previous owners used the common areas from the last landing up to the apartment, turning it into an open-air terrace. Garden plants in pots lined the stairs. A bead curtain separated the area from the rest of the staircase, making it feel more private.

"Technically this space belongs to the rest of the building but you'd be the only ones ever using it." We contemplated this like we were actually considering purchasing the apartment. What if a neighbor complained? Our children could be noisy. If we were out on the staircase all the time maybe the residents wouldn't be so thrilled about us using it as a terrace. But already we saw evidence of another family: tiny shoes in rows, multiple hooks hanging coats of all sizes. This put us at ease. We were in familiar territory.

We were closer to reality now than we had been the whole shoot. I had seen this same apartment online about a month ago in a computer-generated alert. It was competitively priced and eclectic, exactly the kind of apartment we would've liked to have seen before purchasing ours. Never mind that it was beyond our budget. If we had a choice and the money, would we have bought it over our own?

The apartment opened to a narrow hallway that led two directions: one to a solitary bedroom where the teenager lived, and the other to the main living area of the apartment. Rafters slanted over the hallway, causing us to duck. Video games and DVDs surrounded a TV with a futon on the floor of original burgundy hexagonal *tomettes*, a desirable historical feature. The apartment felt either claustrophobic or cozy, depending on who took a mind to it, an artist's garret or a kind of squatter's paradise. Off to the left was the main bathroom, a nice corner tub and a stand-up shower under the sloping ceiling. The floor, the housing for the sink, and frame for the shower were all stamped concrete, with occasionally embedded seashells. The concrete was painted pink with turquoise blue accents, giving the feeling of being in an aquarium. Our kids would love this, we said. Our kids, our kids. Indeed, the space felt made for them, their own little hobbit hole with the nooks and play spaces of a treehouse.

Each step of the filming forced us to contemplate every facet of the apartment, to help preserve our surprise for what was to come. Kris wanted authentic reactions: what were we first drawn to? What impression did it make? Copper pipes followed the walls for the water and heat and air conditioning. We noted the fan-shaped wall sconces, the gaudy swatches of paint and rough plaster. Each tiny decoration—a Banania tin, old wine boxes, porcelain knobs and wrought-iron hooks—implied hours of browsing antique markets, looking for the one item that would draw the eye, provide a splash of color. Finally now, we were in the main living room, the winding passageway leading up to the big reveal. Unlike the rest of the apartment, the living room had high ceilings following the pitch of the roof to its peak. South-facing windows dominated one side of the apartment, filling the room with natural light. More windows to the east. I felt a tinge of buyer's remorse.

"I could really see our family living here," I said.

But Rixa wasn't so convinced.

"Where are the kids going to sleep?"

As far as we could see, there wasn't the promised third bedroom. The bedroom on the other side of the apartment was tiny. It had barely enough room for a bed and the sloping roof ruled out the possibility of bunk beds.

"Up here," Bart said.

He climbed a ladder behind the couch. We had been admiring the pebble mosaic in the middle of the room embedded in a clear resin. The floor also had two posts next to the terra-cotta tiles, evidence of a removed wall. The resin mosaic was a way to compensate, to reunite the two sections of floor. We had completely missed the ladder leading up to a sleeping loft.

"The third bedroom," Bart said.

Both of us took turns poking our heads up. The loft was wide enough for a double-bed but not much else. And it was open to the main living room, disqualifying it for a child's sleeping area. Our children still had fixed bedtimes hours before our own, and it would be difficult, near impossible to host people in the evenings without our kids being up at all hours. The other bedroom was on the other side of the wall, also with a door connecting to the main living space.

"There's no place for Ivy," Rixa said. "She needs total silence."

"We could put her with the other kids."

"They won't fit."

"They'll adjust. And in a couple years it won't be an issue."

"It'll be miserable."

The camera rolled. Finally some natural tension! Then Rixa hit me with the killer question: "And where will you write?"

In my excitement, I had neglected my own narrative. This apartment was clearly designed with a family in mind but not for solitude. I loved the open layout, the way that rooms flowed into one another. Several nooks provided space where individual kids could go to read or play. It had two bathrooms. The kitchen was long and new with wood cabinets and stainless-steel pulls. A gas stove. A dishwasher. A family-sized fridge. Built-in seating for a family-sized table. But where *would* I write? At one end of the main living room, a curtain cordoned off a tiny office space. I could write there but I could forget about privacy. The back bedroom barely had room for a bed, let alone a desk. The sleeping loft? I'd have to be lying down. The master bedroom? Again, no room. The living area in the apartment was spacious but so much of the area was public. If we lived in this apartment, I'd have to write at the kitchen table or sitting up in bed or behind a thin curtain.

"Another downside," Rixa said. "The apartment is completely finished. I can't imagine doing anything to it that could increase its value."

It was true. To renovate any part of this apartment would be folly. The previous owners had put so much care into making every space usable. Built-in closets in the bedrooms. Shelves affixed to the walls for books.

"The previous owners received permission to build a balcony," Bart said. He walked us to the south-facing windows. He held up plans for a balcony that would extend from the tiny bathroom off the kitchen around the horse-shoe living space. Having a balcony could be interesting but it would require hiring a contractor for most of the work, an added expense. Plus the common-area terrace made it somewhat redundant.

"I still love the apartment," I said. "It's like we're in an artist's garret."

"It's not practical," Rixa said. "The only place for laundry is off the living room and the washing machine is next to the back bathroom. There's no place for the kids to sleep."

"We'll make it work. It has *tomettes*!"

In filming our separate reactions to the apartment, Kris tried to pick up on earlier narratives, to build to a climax of tension. I had done an about-face in my supposed wish-list. I was advocating an apartment full of old character and charm and without the inspirational sun-drenched corner window writing space that I needed to do my work. I would draw inspiration from the whole apartment, I said. It was designed with a family in mind, with plenty of room for us to grow and develop over the years. It might not be perfect for us now because of our fickle daughter's sleeping preferences, but it had the most to offer our family in the years to come. Rixa had abandoned her hopes for old-world charm and instead focused on the practical. Where would we sleep? Do laundry? She agreed that it had plenty to offer a family but she felt like the low ceilings in the entryway and the sloping roofline would make us feel claustrophobic over time. "It's a great place for hobbits," she said. "But our kids won't be hobbits for long."

Yahel finished the b-roll and we clomped down the stairs from the apartment we would start calling The Artist's Garret. It was an apartment that we would never buy, that we could not afford, and that was, as Rixa continued to remind me, very impractical for our family and difficult to resell if it ever came to it. But it was also the only time in the whole five-day shoot that the camera captured something authentic below our polished responses and rehearsed narratives: a couple at odds about what the future could potentially hold.

Chapter 30

A Story of Privilege

THE MOST STAGED SCENES of House Hunters came when the couple debated the merits of the three properties they had seen and then decided on a winner. They would walk along a beach or through the cobblestone streets of some Italian perched village and discuss. They were obviously being coached and prodded. The location itself was as important as the couple's decision, influencing the overall feel of their choice and reinforcing the narrative threads of the show.

Some finales produced counterpoint: maybe the couple was moving to Bretagne where it was perpetually rainy or overcast and it was hard to find someplace that reflected the euphoria that the couple presumably felt. With an average of more than 300 days of sunshine per year, Nice didn't usually have this problem but for us the filming had been rife with inclement weather. Five days was five days, an investment that HHI had to make pay. Right now our original site was the beach or the Promenade des Anglais, but the recent rains had churned the sea a tannish color and the wind had picked up. A last-ditch effort came to try to get Vincent to let us use Chez Palmyre. The restaurant was indoors with a cozy atmosphere and plenty of traditional décor. He said yes, though reluctantly, since it would require him to open up early, to leave the tables set as though he were ready for service. But he would do it for us.

Yahel walked by the restaurant just to see. "It could work," he said. He rubbed his chin with his hand. "Still I'd rather not be indoors. It's not going to be pretty."

171

"If it's what we have," Kris said. "We can't change the weather."

Like other moments of tension during the filming, the fixer Laurent seemed to intuit the problem almost instantaneously. We had already filmed so much indoors. The forecast said there may be a break in the rain this afternoon, so maybe we should aim for that. Get someplace outdoors that was going to look warm, like we were in a Mediterranean climate and not the Scottish highlands. "Have you thought of the monastery gardens on Cimiez?"

"Where's that?"

Laurent described them. Near the Roman ruins. Next to the Matisse museum. Formal French gardens with flowers and symmetry. Bleached gravel footpaths. Majestic cedars to block the wind.

A Google image search gave Kris some visuals. We showed him our casting video. It ended in a still taken in the Cimiez gardens with our family naturally framed in front of a stone portico. That's it. Kris said. We would do it there.

Laurent scrambled to get the rental car. Tom and Yahel hauled plastic shipping containers filled with audiovisual equipment down our apartment stairs and into the drizzling rain on the pedestrian streets. Laurent would meet us at the Place Centrale and then we'd drive up to Cimiez for the finale.

It was the coldest day of the year. Wind swept across the gardens and down to the Paillon. Both Rixa and I wore our coats and we huddled together on a stone bench while Yahel scouted the area and Thomas miked us up.

"The light is perfect, really makes the roses pop." Yahel was back and Kris laid out where he wanted us to walk. We were supposed to shuffle our legs, like we were walking in place or doing a forward moonwalk. The shot would take us down to a stone bench where we'd sit and then make our grand decision.

"I want you to run through all the positives and negatives for each apartment. Make sure to pick up on the differences to keep the audience guessing."

We did several takes till a cohesive narrative started to emerge. The first apartment was obvious: too sterile. We felt like we were in a hotel, not an apartment in the south of France. But we couldn't agree on the other two. Rixa was drawn to the practicality of the second apartment, our apartment, and the possibilities for doing some renovation. "I don't mind doing a little work," she said, like maybe she could pick up a paint-brush or hammer in a nail for hanging pictures. But I was blown away by the space in the last apartment, the romantic, quirky attributes that made me feel like I was in an artist's garret. Think of our children! They would have so much fun exploring the third apartment and we wouldn't have to worry about them falling down some hole and breaking their necks. Ah yes, Rixa said, but the kid-friendly nooks and sloping roofs might make us feel claustrophobic over time. Even though the square footage on the second apartment was less, the high ceilings made it seem so much bigger. It had more usable space. I started to cave. "I really did like that mirror," I said. "Tell you what—if we can get Bart to throw in the mirror, I'll go for the second apartment."

We filmed the discussion several times and I felt my body drawing blood in from my limbs to warm my core. My lips purpled and my mouth started to shake. Each take we ended with a forced embrace and flopped over onto the grass trying to look spontaneous. "Let's move to the south of France!" Rixa said. It was like it was the first time, a confirmation of so many years of looking forward to this moment. Yes, I said, let's do it.

And cut.

I kept expecting for there to be more, that maybe we would have an-other exit shot or interview but this was it. Job done. Tom and Yahel packed up their equipment. We had already filmed the interior of the apartment with the kids in our supposedly-after-three-months settling-in period. We had already crowded into the attic and pretended to read bedtime stories. We had talked about our adjustment to this new place, how we loved the lifestyle, the proximity of school, shopping, museums, and recreation. Kris had hours of raw footage that he would deliver back to our producer Me-lissa. She would engage the help of editors and production assistants to arrange our narrative for maximum dramatic effect.

Our story of moving to France was now in post-production. What-ever story they constructed would circumscribe our experience and rein-force my romantic idealism and Rixa's pragmatism. It would become the record of our lives at one point in time, a neatly sanitized story about a family who had a dream to move to France, to go from a big single-family home to a tiny apartment and a pint-sized fridge and pedestrian lifestyle. It was a story of privilege, of whiteness, of getting what you wanted through ease and persistence. We augmented the price, wore our most expensive clothes, and dawdled around the morning market as though we shopped there every day instead of at discount grocers. The film crew had asked the scripted questions, followed us around, blocked out where we should stand and sit, advised us on what we should wear, how to talk without looking at the camera. Done. They shook our hands, said if you ever do a project like this again, look us up, and Laurent the fixer drove them back to their hotel before traveling back to Israel, to Germany, to the London suburbs. If this were their story, this is where it would stop: the happy couple, new home-owners in the south of France, waving to the film crew. In some ways, the story would be more complete this way, more whole. We decided to move to France, looked at three apartments, chose one, moved, and settled in. But so much for us was unresolved. Our plumbing still needed fixing, we were mired in debt, and our renovations were only half finished. Tomor-row, another HelpXer would come. We would move our furniture to the sides of the apartment and drape them in sheets, then pound the wall of earth and plaster dividing our front room.

It was once again demolition time.

Part III

SURFACING

We are so afraid of each other, you know? Color, wealth, these things
that don't matter still play too much of a role in how we see one another.
And it's sad, because the thing that least defines us as people is the color
of our skin, the size of our bank account. None of that matters.

—MICHELLE OBAMA

When the seagulls follow the trawler, it's because they think sardines
will be thrown into the sea.

—ERIC CANTONA

Chapter 31

Deep

OVER THE WINTER AND INTO the spring, I never stopped spearfishing even as home renovations occupied more and more of our time. The more interesting game fish were often in deeper water, and gradually, through practice and internet research, I extended my depth to find them. Spots where I wouldn't venture before, down 60, 70, up to 100 feet, now became possible. I packed air into my lungs to the point of bursting and marveled as that air compressed and extended the time I'd be able to hold my breath the deeper I went. My ears adjusted without me even needing to pinch my nose and blow.

My physiology was starting to change.

In his bestselling memoir, *Deep*, James Nestor writes about humanity's connection to the sea. We have mechanisms in our body to help us deal with being under water for prolonged periods of time that make it easier to descend and ascend than scuba diving. Freedivers unlock our innate potential by diving to depths of more than 300 feet without fins or weights. The world record-holders in freediving use sleds to carry them to depths of 800 feet or more. It's a dangerous sport, with accidents and fatalities every year as people test their limits. Like these freedivers, I was becoming more and more drawn to the lure of being in the depths of the sea, occupying the still point you could inhabit on one held breath.

So on Thursdays when the kids ate lunch at the cantine or afternoons mid-week when the sun bore down, I gathered my used 5mm wetsuit and my accroche-poissons and headed out. Free diving and spearfishing had become an obsession. I knew where the fish were, which areas were best.

I made friends with the locals.

A favorite spot was the blocky jetty that led out to the lighthouse guarding the Nice Port. On sunny afternoons in March, I'd often find Jean-Pierre, or JP, a transvestite retiree who chopped his blond hair close to his scalp and curled licks of it to frame his pudgy, made-up face. He always wore a colorful brassiere and a speedo and sandals. When I'd go out, he'd keep an eye on my stuff so I didn't have to stash it in the rocks. When I caught something, he'd admire the fish and talk about his own days fishing. "Have you seen any octopus? A guy last week pulled out a monster." I told him I had, but it had wedged itself under a rock and I couldn't get it to come out. He shook his finger and explained—what I needed to do was get a small fish, then dangle it in front of him. The octopus would relax and gradually pull out. After that, just grab it. It would suck on to my arm. I thanked him for the tip.

One time in early April, I met another spearfisher who was just cleaning his equipment when I walked up. He'd caught a couple dorades but not much else. "Last year, there were hundreds of them," he said. We got to talking. Had I come out here much? What was in the water? I told him about the strings of eggs I'd been seeing, the huge sar that hid in the rocks. I'd found sieche and octopus and lots of mulet, but only a couple dorades and not the schools he was describing. "Well," he said, "good luck."

In the year I'd been here, the only school of dorades I'd seen was out by Maeterlinck. Since then, nothing. I began to wonder: was my spearfishing obsession adversely affecting the fish population?

Fishing has long been a part of Nice. According to legend, the fertile Baie des Anges actually got its name after Adam and Eve searched for a terrestrial home. Two angels bore them to Nice since it was the closest to the lush perfection of the Garden of Eden. Another legend refers to the angel shark which used to be plentiful in the waters off of Nice. The name was for how these angelic bottom feeders glided through the water. Yet another fishing-related legend says that the Baie des Anges was called "la baie des anchois" or the bay of anchovies till it was changed in the 1800s to attract British tourists. To this day, clouds of anchovy flit through the water, sending little slivers of light up to the surface. Anchovies still figure heavily in traditional Nicois cuisine, from the onion-pizza-like *pissiladière* to the *pan bagnat* street sandwich. The prevalence of anchovies off Nice's shores provided the foundation for a thriving fishing industry. Besides netting these tiny salty fish, fishermen caught a number of other fish that preyed on them: sar, dorades, mérou, and loup. And then also on bigger fish that preyed on those, species like pélamides, tassergal, sériole, and liche.

The first time I came to Nice was in 1993. I lived in an apartment in the Port neighborhood and I walked by the Port and up through the Place Garibaldi almost every day. One of the most famous restaurants in the area was the Grand Turin, a fresh seafood-only restaurant that had been run by the same family for generations. In October and November, diners would order plates of *oursins*, purplish-brown sea urchins that they'd pile high on silver plates. But now during urchin season, you never see this spiky cornucopia, even in the still-famed Grand Turin. Occasionally the St. François fish market would have some specimens, but only a handful and at prices that would make you think their innards were spun of gold.

Certain species have also suffered. The French government has put a moratorium on any fishing of mérou and corb. Mérou is the most urgent, since the fish takes so long to mature and reproduce. The mérou are hermaphrodites until about 8 or 9 years old, after which they become male or female. The males tend to grow larger, making them more of a prime target for anglers or spearfishers. Normally, killing larger fish is more responsible since it allows for younger stocks to thrive. But killing large mérou actually led to the species' demise. Without the larger males, the younger female's eggs went unfertilized. The corb's difficulties were more due to their habits, their delicate taste, and their ease of capture, especially for spearfishers. A social and nocturnal fish, the corb emerged from their rocky dens in the early evening. During the day, they could be seen hovering in holes, an easy target. But even in open water, corb were curious and slow. Though not as dire as the mérou, corb fishing has been restricted pending review in five years. If the populations don't spring back, it's unlikely that people will ever be able to fish for them again.

But not all fish populations have declined. Critics of fishing often misunderstand the double-edged sword of human disruption to ecological systems. Introduction of invasive species is as much to blame in the loss of biodiversity as overfishing. Pollution is also a culprit. While pollution can stunt population of some fish, it can prompt others to thrive. Over and over again, anglers cautioned me about catching mulet, the abundant silver-striped fish that could grow to a meter or more. Schools of mulet swam in the Port, living off the detritus brought in every day by boats. Mulet out in the open sea were fine, they'd tell me, but avoid the ones in the Port, especially any mulet of size. These would be bitter, with an almost metallic taste. No good, even for soup. Instead, I should concentrate on the smaller mulet. I could take as many as I wanted. Garbage fish. A similar counsel came regarding saupe, the plentiful yellow-and-green striped vegetarian fish that grew to the size and shape of a rugby ball. Since the seas had been warming, the algae and other marine plants had blossomed, providing more food than the saupe could consume. Saupe were in the middle of a population explosion.

Besides these fish, sar were common and difficult to catch for both anglers and spearfishers, and they competed for the same resources as more desirable fish such as mérou and corb. Catch any of these fish, and I was doing Mediterranean biodiversity a favor.

Then there were invasive species.

It's hard to know how many species in the Mediterranean are invasive since invasion has been going on for so long. The Mediterranean has long borne the stamp of human interference. Shipping and trade brought algae and crustaceans. The opening of the Suez Canal in 1896 brought exotic fish species from the Red Sea. Because of climate change and the gradual warming of the Mediterranean, other fish species have started coming through the straits of Gibraltar making it the most invaded body of water in the world. In Nice, one invasive fish species is the barracuda, an aggressive carnivore that travels in enormous schools to chase after clouds of anchovies or sardines. They're prolific hunters, and prevalent in the waters around Nice. Schools of Barracuda pose the biggest threat to young fish populations. They're also, as I can attest, very difficult to catch.

But everything I read about dorades claimed that the fish populations were stable, even thriving. Farmed dorades had lessened the demand for wild-caught dorades, so competition was limited to other sport fishermen. Nobody was fishing them commercially anymore. My schools of hundreds of dorades should in theory be there.

In the meantime, I continued my dives, practiced hiding behind rocks and going deeper and holding my breath longer. I kicked less, preferring instead to let my body relax to conserve oxygen. Spearfishing became a kind of underwater meditation. In the spring I swam through the strings of fish eggs and schools of mulet, saupe, and barracuda and settled on the bottom of the sea. The biosphere revealed its layers to me: the bottom feeders like rouget or labres, the lone rockfish or sar, the rocks nipped clean of vegetation by schools of saupe. On the edges of clouds of anchovies, I'd find other fish in open water: foot-long tuna-shaped chincard or mackerels or striped pelamides. I was like the plastic diver in an aquarium, patiently observing the abundance around me. I'd hold my breath for a minute or two, going deeper, staying longer, till the mysteries of the deep began to reveal themselves to me.

Chapter 32

Demolition

THE MOST PUZZLING FEATURE of our apartment was a half-partition wall that divided the front room into living and dining areas. The wall was about three inches thick with white molding around an opening the size of a pair of double doors. During the filming of HHI, Bart explained that the whole building had once been offices. The partition was likely a provisional office divider, something to provide privacy but maintain a communal work space. But it arbitrarily closed off the living room, making it feel cramped.

"It would be no problem to take out this wall," Bart told us. "It's not load-bearing."

The wall's appearance seemed to support his opinion. It was only three inches thick. If it was indeed just an office partition, it was likely a recent enough renovation that the materials would be mostly wood and plaster, easy to dismantle in an afternoon. But for some reason we kept putting it off.

"I wonder if knocking down the wall is even necessary," I said to Rixa.

We had set up our TV and furniture so that the living room side of the partition created a comfortable nook. A steamer trunk sat under the window and the oriental rug that Thierry gave us fit neatly between the TV and couch. It was closed off enough from the kitchen to feel like another room but we didn't have to open doors to get from one side to the next. I liked that we could have a meal in the kitchen/dining area with adults and the kids could watch a movie on the other side. After all the renovations and then House Hunters, it would be nice to relax for a while, not to immediately throw ourselves into another project. Couldn't we just leave everything the way it was?

"It cuts off the room and blocks the light. Plus we can't fit the hide-a-bed without moving the TV," Rixa said.

I tried to imagine the space without the dividing wall. We would have to reconfigure everything, maybe put the couch in the middle of the room and the TV on the opposite wall.

"Just mount the TV on the wall between the windows," she said.

"But then it wouldn't be directed at the couch."

"Get a swivel arm. You can put it out of the way when you're not using it."

I was reluctant. Knocking down another wall signified an overwhelming commitment to more hours of work. I wanted to spend at least part of our sabbatical year not doing renovations.

"We'll have another HelpXer for the next three weeks."

"Fine," I said. "But I still don't think it's necessary."

Phillippe the HelpXer was supposed to arrive later that afternoon. Our experience with Jean and Adilah now filled me with dread. Rixa tried to reassure me by showing me his HelpX profile. He had already accumulated two years of happy recommendations from people all over Europe. "Warm and sunny personality" one host said. "Good fun to have around." "Honest and trustworthy," others said. But I had seen positive profiles before—Jean and Adilah had such glowing recommendations, I was sure the problems were our own. I tried to look for reviews that gave me a better sense of his character. One reviewer described his work as professional, noting that "fast and slapdash" was not his style. Did this mean that he was a slow worker? Too much of a perfectionist?

I would find out soon enough. After a late arrival, a jovial Phillippe buzzed up from downstairs. It was evening, the kids already asleep in the attic. He carried a grey backpack and shouldered an army bag almost as big as he was. His white-and-grey beard continued untrimmed partway down his neck. The clothes he wore—baggy jeans turned up at the ankles and a collarless long-sleeved Henley shirt with yellow suspenders—made him look like a slight circus performer. He wore a flat cap and spectacles with a plastic strap.

"Hello it is so nice to meet you!" Phillippe said. I found it much easier to understand him in person; on the phone he had a soft voice that had become softer still from so many years of cigarette smoking. He continued speaking in English for a while till he realized that French was our lingua franca at home and that he'd be much more comfortable en français. We showed him to his room and helped him with his things.

"Oh, la classe!" he said when he saw the room. He loved the renovations and didn't mind sleeping in a loft. It was a school night and the kids were already asleep so we were free to talk about the upcoming work, to speculate and plan. "We want to take down this wall," we said.

Phillippe rapped his knuckles on the wall and pushed his slight frame against it. "There's going to be a lot of dust." The wall wasn't hollow, he said, so that meant it was likely full of dirt, especially if that's what we found in the back bathroom. My hopes of an easy demolition were starting to vanish. We told him of our plan which had solidified over the past couple weeks: we would demolish the wall, then wire Ethernet and electric in the remaining plaster beam down to where we would put the TV and other electronics. Did he think this was possible?

"No problem!" Phillippe smiled and held both hands in a thumbs-up. When did we want to get started? It was an expression we'd soon get used to.

Chapter 33

Deeper

THE FIRST TIME USING MY BUOY, I found a body. I had seen people using buoys before and I knew that they were required by law but spearfishers in the areas I fished rarely used them. Boats weren't allowed along the cap or the jetty leading out to the lighthouse. Since the purpose of the buoys was to alert boats to their presence, I figured this made them superfluous. France had many laws, some that people followed and others that people routinely disregarded. It was often hard to know which ones to take seriously. My own rule of thumb was to follow the behavior of others around me.

"You really should get a buoy." I bumped into the same spearfisher along the jetty. The dorades had started to move and he showed me a string of them as proof. I told him I didn't think buoys were necessary since hardly anyone I saw used them. He explained: it's for your own safety. Just because you are in a no-boating zone didn't mean they wouldn't motor in anyway. And what did I do with my stuff while I was fishing?

I told him I stashed it in the rocks.

"You haven't had anything stolen?"

"Not yet."

"You're lucky, then." He continued to try to impress on me the importance of a buoy. He also disabused me of some of my misconceptions. I thought it would be cumbersome to fish with a little inflatable dinghy attached to you. No, no, he said—you just pulled it along till you found a good place to fish. Then you weighed it down and you could fish all around.

As evidence, he showed me a square 1 kg lead weight, typical for a weight belt, attached to a fluorescent orange line. After that, you attached your ac-croche-poissons and a dry bag with all your stuff to it. That way you weren't lugging all the fish around with you—"conger food" he called it. Lie in the wrong spot on the sea floor and a conger eel would chomp the fish right off your dandy accroche-poissons.

I remembered a couple weeks ago when I felt a tug on my belt and looked down to see the rouget I had just caught gone. At the time I had thought it had snagged on a rock. Or that I had somehow lost it earlier. I hadn't realized I'd been providing resident congers with free meals.

Still I resisted. It just seemed like so much to haul around. I already had the wetsuit and the weight belt and fins. Plus there was the added ex-pense of the thing.

"Get a guitar case," he said. "One that you can carry like a backpack. A cheap one, used. Everything will fit, believe me."

But it wasn't until I was out fishing near the lighthouse that I finally made the decision to get a buoy. The dorades had indeed started moving. Down about forty feet, schools of a hundred or more would pass by, going about the same speed. Catching them in a school was so much easier than when they were alone and behaved more like sar. After the first couple fish passed me, giving me wide berth, the rest followed, closer and closer till I just had to wait for the largest one to pass my sight line. A quick trip topside and I waited for the next school to come by.

A small boat approached me.

"Please discharge your spear."

The two guys were standing. Little tricolore flags waved on the boat's bow. They had a megaphone or something. They waved me over.

They first wanted to know what I was catching. I showed them my accroche-poissons: a couple dorades and a sar. "Where is your buoy?"

I told them I didn't have one.

"You know it's a fifty-euro fine if you don't have a buoy."

So sorry, I didn't know. I thought I only needed it in areas where boats were allowed. I apologized and told them that I would get one immediately.

So now I had a little pancake-shaped buoy with a red-and-white flag on top. It looked like a fluorescent orange UFO. At first I found it cumber-some. I had to haul the thing with me and it kept me to a certain area before I moved elsewhere. The first dive to place the buoy was like announcing my presence: hello, I'm here to catch some fish! After a while, though, it granted me more freedom. I was more willing to venture deeper, further from shore, taking me into open water.

Which was how I found the body.

Right by Rauba Capeu where Johnny and I had fished in the fall, an enormous rock channeled fish through a v-shaped opening where the rock met the rising shore. I'd fished the area many times, waiting for schools of mulet, barracuda, or dorades. I'd caught octopus there, and once, a chapon. But I'd rarely ventured out much beyond this rock. The sheer drop-off on one side made it difficult to lie in wait for unsuspecting fish. I was worried to be so far out where boats would commonly pass by. This time, I placed my buoy at the top of the rock just before it dropped off on all sides.

I had never caught fish here before. On the rock I felt exposed without cover. The visibility so far away from shore made it so that any fish—large sar or the occasional rockfish—dove down the cliff face out of reach. The most plentiful fish were tiny castagnoles, huge schools that floated like a nimbus crown around the great peak. I had just started noticing the chinchard, mackerel, and larger pélamides that often circled these clouds in the open water. I dove down the cliff face and then pushed out into the deep blue.

Fishing in the open without any landmarks could be disorienting, a little like an astronaut floating out into space. You were suspended, alone, and every direction was filled with emptiness as far as you could see. Light was the only indicator: go up, and the blue gradually lightened till you were back in the Mediterranean sun; go down and the blue darkened till you either hit the bottom or light extinguished completely, like descending into the blackness of a cave.

So I pushed off, about fifty feet down, leaving the security of the rock behind. The water was colder, the temperature of a mountain lake. The air inside my lungs constricted, giving me an artificial sense of comfort. Down here all the air I'd packed inside my body didn't feel like it was ready to explode to get out.

I glided out into the dark. The cloud of castagnoles was far above me. About thirty feet in front of me, a figure started to emerge.

The world's oceans have long been keepers of humanity's secrets. Governments and private diving companies continue to find wrecks from hundreds of years ago on the sea floor with the aid of sonar and GPS.

Mysteries like Malaysia airlines flight MH370 may remain concealed in the deep forever. 80 percent of our planet is covered in water and yet we've explored less than 5 percent of it. Places like the Mariana trench are the last unknown terrestrial spaces on Earth.

At first I thought the body must be one of these mysteries. A concrete-shoed loan shark who lost it all to his debtors. Nice still had a mafia, still had gambling, drug trafficking, and prostitution. Since Charlie Hebdo, soldiers in camouflaged flak jackets wielding HK416s clomped through the streets of Old Nice in combat boots. The emerging figure could be the end result of any number of conflicts brought about during the night while my children slept in their attic beds.

I drifted closer. The figure looked like it was covered in a shawl, then dipped in wax, a body bag that sucked close to the skin from the pressure. The color was grayish-white, with a thin layer of algae. What looked like arms were brought together in the middle, like a straitjacket or hands clasped in silent prayer.

I shot up to the surface. I could no longer see the algae-covered head, the whole body swallowed by the blackness of the sea. I contemplated swimming back to shore for help. Give the peacekeepers carrying machine guns something to do. But what would I tell them? I found a body floating about sixty feet down. It looked like it was somehow attached to the sea floor. Would a body even be floating that deep? If it was recently dead the weight of the water would push it deeper till it hit rock bottom and lay down. But if it was older, decomposition would fill the body with gases causing it to float again. Weighted by its feet, it could indeed resemble what I'd seen: a body swinging like from an upside-down noose.

But first I needed solid proof. I hovered on the surface for a while breathing deep from my diaphragm: in, out, in, out. Then one long push to get rid of all the CO_2. I'd be diving down blind and I'd need my lungs full of air to find the body again.

I dove. About thirty feet down the whitish head emerged from the dark. This time I aimed for it like a base-jumper zeroing in on his landing. I reached out my gloved hand till the body filled my line of sight. Contact.

It was solid. No buoyancy. The body had to be a statue of some sort. I dove down further till I was face to face with it and I reached out to touch the concrete surface. The details of the statue were oversimplified, basic.

The round head, the shawl: geometric shapes like a giant pawn from a chessboard. And again the hands, brought together in prayer. Now I knew.

What was a statue of the Virgin Mary doing in sixty feet of water?

It would take internet research and some conversations with locals to figure out what I had found: a statue commissioned in 1968 and sculpted by Alfred Galtieroti, an artist known for his work at Nice's annual carnaval. Sometimes priests performed underwater marriages here, or pilgrims left boats of candles floating on the surface to mark their visit. Among spearfishers, the spot was called "la vièrge," a rich fishing area known for bigger game fish such as pélamides, sérioles, and liches. Most people who visited la vièrge came with some prior knowledge of its existence. But I just assumed that what I had first seen was a cadaver swinging in the current by its concrete shoes, a menacing reminder of what I'd soon learn, that the sea could be dangerous, claiming those who were unwilling to follow the rules.

Chapter 34

HelpX Saves Lives

SO WE TOOK DOWN THE WALL. In a strange reversal, I now found myself in the position of the muscle. I was Jad the Jackhammer while Phillippe was the cautionary one. The wall was, as he had suspected, full of dirt. Old timbers crosshatched the wall which supported it while they were forming it. The timbers also provided leverage so we weren't always hammering out tiny chunks but pulling down large sections. The concrete would adhere along a timber and I'd try to remove as much of it as I could without it disintegrating in a billow of dust.

Phillippe chipped a line in the plaster along the ceiling beam to provide a clean break while I smashed and grunted and pushed. In my haste to demolish the wall I neglected to consider the floor.

The wall must have been added before the current level of flooring. I had expected the wall to break off evenly at the floor but instead when I pushed on the wood frame it acted like a lever lifting up a two-inch layer of concrete around it. When the last vestiges of the wall tumbled down and we had put the remaining gravel in bags and swept and cleaned and vacuumed the rest, the result was a jacked up floor on one side of the old wall that would not flatten or go back to the way it was. In my He-Man haste, I was ready to start just breaking up the floor till it leveled out but thankfully Phillippe stopped me.

"If you start lifting up the floor you're going to lift it up further along."

"But we need to get it flat."

"Leave it for now. When you're ready to do the floor, no problem. We'll take off the strips of flooring to see where it's flat. You've got a level, right?"

"Not one big enough."

"A flat board will work. Then we'll use concrete and self-leveling compound over the gap. You may have had to do this anyway, you know. I don't think that the floor was level with the other side of the wall."

Phillippe spent the next several minutes looking at the four-inch-wide hole in our floor, measuring and calculating how much wire and conduit he'd need for the ceiling beam. I packed up bags of gravel and took them to the depot. Phillippe's demeanor, like everything I knew about him so far, seemed unconcerned and carefree. A big hole in the floor? No big deal. It would take a little longer but it was something we would've likely had to do anyway. His attitude alleviated stress. No need for the bourgeois concerns that governed most of our lives.

Over the weeks, we learned more about Phillippe's story. He used to run a successful kitchen installation business in Ireland. Before the 2008 market crash, he could barely keep up with demand, his coffers full of over-inflated euros. But when the crash came, his business disappeared in a matter of months. New clients canceled their orders. The few jobs that he did get changed as well. Gone were the kitchens with ten-burner stoves and acres of polished granite. "The bigger and fancier the kitchen, the less people use it to actually cook," he said. He coordinated every detail of the kitchen, down to the trim work or consultations about appliances. But soon he was back in France, unemployed, and squeezed broke from the recession. He was able to find some work as a certified electrician, but the years of having his own business made it difficult for him to operate as someone else's employee. Then, one day, he stumbled on HelpX. "HelpX saved my life," Phillippe told us. "It's been the perfect thing: meet people, travel. I don't need much and I just work my way into a household's daily routine."

He started to live fairly austerely, minimizing his possessions, a true décroissant. "If I didn't smoke, I wouldn't spend any money," he told me. And I believed him. His clothes, he explained, were mostly castoffs from people he had helped over the years. His food and lodging were taken care of. Even his phone and laptop were gifts from previous HelpX hosts, the most essential tools for plotting his peripatetic course around the world.

So far, it seemed to be working.

191

The effect of having to live with so many different people had some tangible effects on Phillippe. A man of conviction and strong opinions, Phillippe had to keep more to himself, not to make waves. His last hosts were vegetarian, so he became vegetarian. With us, he calmly endured our kids and our sometimes un-French culinary habits. After a couple days, he enjoyed the smaller meals at lunch and was ready to eat a big meal by 5:30. Kids in bed by 7:30? No problem! Not once did he question our choices or insinuate that we were abnormal. He had seen so much difference, from Ireland to Spain, Greece, and Italy, that he was sure that whatever he learned was merely one of the many valid approaches to living in the world. Each different situation was an opportunity to grow. An only child, now Phillippe could learn what it was like to be in a family of six. There is a lot of noise! You have no privacy! Wonderful!

And his work didn't disappoint. He was beyond methodical. Each morning, he would get up, usually after the kids had already gone to school, brew his "petit café" and don his flat cap, put on his baggy trousers with the cuffs rolled up, snap his yellow ruler suspenders and go to work. Each step of the project required careful planning and preparation. He picked up the electrical conduit he needed, drilled the holes, measured the conduit, cut it, and then installed it in preparation for the electrical and Ethernet cables that he would string through. He worked only in the morning unless he felt he was under hours. And after the first day of demolition and cleaning, he worked mostly by himself. I'd hole up in the attic to write and I'd hear Phillippe humming or whistling as he cut cable or measured with the occasional phrase escaping him as he talked over some problem or challenge. Our only hard deadline was in three weeks when an American HelpX couple was coming to scrape and repaint our attic. Over the next couple weeks, he installed the electrical and Ethernet cable in a conduit that he hid inside the plaster beam that ran down the middle of our ceiling and into the wall between our front two windows. He plastered up the beam so it looked like it had always been there.

Why was Phillippe's stay so harmonious and Jean and Adilah's so full of discord? Besides their experience with us, Jean and Adilah had always sought out people mostly like themselves: retirees or couples living in country homes without any children or grandchildren. In their free time, they enjoyed hiking or taking long walks in the open air, away from people. These two characteristics: preferring the country to the city and spending time with people more like themselves accounted for much of the tension they felt living in our home. The experience was a letdown. Unlike other projects where Jean stood bare-chested over a newly-erected garage, our renovation never made it onto his profile. No photos of gleaming tile or stainless-steel light fixtures. Their absence implied an experience he'd sooner forget.

We were sad to see Phillippe go. On one of his last nights, we gathered at our long table to play a game of Carcassonne, a multiplayer board game that involved creating chateaux and roads using a series of tiles that gradually shaped a medieval world. The rules were easy enough for my children and Phillippe enjoyed the added socialization after a day of solitary work or wandering the streets of Nice. I asked him, why did he contact us? Surely a cramped apartment with four kids couldn't have been his first choice.

"I guess I wanted to see what it was like living with a large family."

We divvied up the game pieces and Dio laid his first tile. We had played the game together for so many nights now that the opening moves had become routine. So had Phillippe's teasing banter and his moments of pondering after one of the kids made an aggressive move to take over one of his chateaux. The game sometimes required people to work together, a mutually-beneficial result that would disadvantage the players who didn't share. If the player was constantly only looking out for themselves, it was unlikely that they'd be able to finish any bigger chateaux and roads.

"Any news from the hotel in Cassis?"

"I'm going to Italy," he said. "The hotel was full till the summer." Phillippe depended on HelpX to chart his future. Three weeks with us was shorter than he liked to stay. Usually he preferred to stay a month at least but we had already promised our home to the American couple HelpXers who had contacted us to scrape and paint the attic.

"Is it a good situation?"

"I've never really liked Italy," he said. His last experience in Italy was the only time in three years he'd felt abused as a HelpXer. He had worked on an organic farm that originally had asked him for help wiring a series of greenhouses before winter. Workdays became longer and the stress increased till he abandoned the project, risking a bad review from the host. Other experiences in Italy made him feel the same way; he felt treated more like an unpaid general contractor and less like someone entering into a mutually-beneficial exchange.

I told him I hoped that his time here had felt like a mutually-beneficial exchange.

I always worried that we didn't have much to offer him in terms of entertainment. After our kids were in bed, both Rixa and I generally worked or read, not exactly the social activities that he craved. Sometimes at night he would come out of his room with a cup of coffee and sit at our table and sip thoughtfully and I knew exactly what he wanted: someone to talk to. I would fold up my computer and we'd talk about politics or the environment or new technologies that had the possibility of changing the world. He'd been reading about the Solar Impulse 2, a completely energy-neutral aircraft that had recently started circumnavigating the globe. Every day he followed its progress as it traversed Asia during its maiden voyage. When the plane stopped in Japan to wait for more favorable weather conditions, Phillippe was frustrated and despondent. A trip around the globe could prove that we no longer needed fossil fuels, that we could transition to more sustainable energy sources that would be less expensive and more efficient.

"2015 is the year," Phillippe told me. The Solar Impulse 2 was proof. For Phillippe, 2015 was when everything would start to change. Conventional money would disappear. Wars would grind to a halt. Governments would be replaced by concerned citizens working to better their own communities. Sometimes I would try to check his optimism. All money gone? But for him, money wasn't important—exchange was. Most everything could be shared, worked out through barter according to his needs. His décroissant way of life would inspire others to do the same. All the technologies existed now to effect the kind of change he was looking for.

The day Phillippe left, he got up early with us to see the kids off to school. We told them that he wouldn't be home when they got back for lunch. The kids opted for some American hugs rather than the typical French *bise* and they wished him luck. "If you're ever in town again, look us up," I told him.

The last people who stayed with us were from Oklahoma, a young couple who had been backpacking through Europe the past several months. They fit the profile of a lot of the HelpXers: young, wanting to travel cheaply, and with more basic skills to offer like painting or childcare.

Something about them reminded us of ourselves ten or fifteen years ago. Michele was a curly-haired brunette with a broad smile of the perfect white American teeth that were so often the envy of the French. Connor also had darker hair and had been growing a scraggly beard the last couple months. He was a soccer aficionado, an extrovert who liked playing board games and telling stories. Our kids took to them immediately.

What had their experiences with hosts been like so far? They had done painting, worked in vineyards, and twice were receptionists. The only negative experience they had was working for a hostel in Ireland. The host hadn't done his taxes for the past three years and the Irish tax man had come knocking during their stay. Michele was an accountant and when it quickly became obvious that the host was unwilling to do his taxes or incapable or both, she stepped in to straighten out his finances. But even the mounting pressure of an impending deadline and the added work and stress for them was worth it. A learning experience, something that they could sock away for later to help them with their own life decisions.

Which seemed to be exactly why they were here.

When I first met the hitchhiker who told me about HelpX, I was struck by how this program could enable a traveler to experience different environments in ways that were often unavailable to tourists. It also provided enough essentials and security that a HelpXer could extend their stay past conventional vacations. People could actively suspend their lives, hold off on decisions that they had been needing to make for some time, and travel with very little money set aside for contingencies. Before traveling to Europe, the hitchhiker had been a professional diver who contracted with oil companies to fix or repair underwater rigs. It sounded glamorous to me—a professional diver!—but he quickly downplayed its allure. He had got his certification through the army but it was long, relentless, and boring work, an occupation he felt like he'd ended up in almost accidentally. It paid well but he didn't have an education beyond his certification and he didn't want to do it long-term. But then that stop-gap job looked to expand to fill maybe even his whole life. When he heard about HelpX, he set up a few exchanges and then bought his first ticket to Europe and hadn't left since.

Michele and Connor were in a similar situation, though their planning was more deliberate. Connor had started law school a couple years ago and then dropped out. The jobs that he saw lining themselves up in his future were not what he wanted. He liked people, liked making things, liked business. Michele was fascinated by food and for her the trip to Europe was a culinary pilgrimage, complemented by an *actual* pilgrimage they made through basque country in Spain and southwestern France. What were they going to do when they got home? They didn't really know. But they had a commitment to a mutual destiny. They'd figure it out together.

HelpX also exposed Michele and Connor to different ways of living that they hadn't considered before. Our own model of buying a property abroad and renting it when we weren't there especially appealed to them. Perhaps they could take advantage of the collapse of the Euro and the flagging Greek economy to buy a bed and breakfast or a restaurant/hotel? They were newlyweds and didn't have kids. That traditional careers hadn't yet materialized wasn't a problem. Their families were supportive and they could live at home till they found out what they wanted to do. Maybe they would try to bring something of what they had learned this past year to enhance the culture of Norman, Oklahoma in some way. It was a town they loved, with good schools and a university. They could open a Greek restaurant. Start a student-exchange program. Become landlords like us.

For now, they would live with us, eat meals with our four children, come play pick-up soccer with my local group. During the morning, our apartment was abuzz with work. Connor would be mixing leveling compound or sanding away sheetrock mud. I holed myself up in the back bedroom, facing the wall, to write. Above me, I could hear scraping and whistling: Michele in the attic. Sometimes she sang along with her iPod while she painted and I would keep tempo by tapping my fingers on the computer keys. In the evenings after the kids' teeth were brushed and everyone's pajamas were on, we'd get out board games like Carcassonne and Quirkle, "Jeux de société" the French call them: games of society. Our children laughed at Connor's exaggerated attempts to speak French and coached him on what to do with his tiles. For a couple weeks, we had been thrown together, both parties providing something that the other party lacked. At the end, the attic was painted, the floor leveled, the wall sanded and smoothed. Each a permanent reminder of the ways we had all changed.

Chapter 35

La Haine

AFTER THE CHARLIE HEBDO SHOOTING, family and friends would write me to communicate their solidarity with France. On Facebook, people tricolored themselves, superimposing the French flag over their profile pictures. Everyone became Charlie. In Nice, "Je Suis Charlie" banners appeared on prominent public surfaces. What was an attack on the free press? We were all implicated in what had happened.

Our daily walk to school changed. Our children still bounded down the stairs too noisily, opened the door and raced or fought their way up the Rue Rosetti to the school but now instead of accompanying them by hand to their classroom, watching them hang their jackets on their designated hooks and dutifully saying bonjour to their teachers, we brought them up to the closed green gates of the school, the fleur-de-lis-tipped pickets standing accusatorily in the air, and waited for the school to open. The heightened emergency status of *vigipirate* prohibited anyone from entering public buildings. But the result at our school was ironically less safe. Instead of parents bringing children in directly, spreading people over the whole footprint of the school, they were concentrated at the entrance gates, a mob of parents and children who would make easy targets for any terrorist bent on doing harm to the most vulnerable segments of the population.

How long would the vigipirate last?

At the time, it seemed temporary. In a couple weeks, a month, maybe more, François Hollande would loosen the restrictions that vigipirate imposed on its citizens. People had come together, intent on keeping alive the ideals of liberté, fraternité, and égalité. In Old Nice especially, the patrols of machine-gun-toting peacekeepers seemed unnecessary. The police who rented my car often boasted of their luck—imagine a few weeks' paid work in the south of France! We were one, united in the values of freedom and equality. Children of Muslim parents in their hijabs and punk-rocker parents with their green Mohawks deserved equal attention in the school system, equal rights under our law. Vigipirate added tension to an otherwise benign and welcoming environment. All of us were victims, all of us Charlie, but unlike the terrorists who mowed down a cadre of journalists and artists to make a political point, we would not hate or fear those who were different from us, for what we didn't understand.

Later on in 2015, France would experience the deadliest attack on its soil since WWII. The attack would be coordinated and vicious, targeting specific venues that the terrorists felt best represented western values: a French-German friendly soccer match in preparation for the Euro Cup, cafés and bars in St. Dénis, and the Bataclan music hall. Of all the venues, the Bataclan was perhaps the most symbolic. Long a venue for rock concerts, the Bataclan was also home for pro-Israel activities, making it target for Palestinian protesters and extremist groups. Over the years, the Bataclan had endured bomb threats and demonstrations and then on Friday the 13th of November, 2015, a mass shooting that brought a violent halt to a concert featuring the group The Eagles of Death Metal.

Vous n'aurez pas ma haine. You will not have my hate.

Those are the words that journalist Antoine Leiris wrote in response to the shootings. His wife Hélène was killed in the attack along with eighty-eight other people. Leiris wrote the words first in an open letter to the killers, a Facebook post that gained instant notoriety in the media and prompted Leiris to write a book by the same name. In the letter, Leiris says,

"Friday night you stole an exceptional life, the love of my life and the mother of my son but you will not have my hate. I do not know who you are and I don't want to know.

"So I will not give you the satisfaction of my hate. You wanted it, yearned for it, but to respond to your hate with mine would be to submit to the same ignorance that defines you. You want me to be afraid, that I look at my fellow citizens suspiciously, that I sacrifice my liberty for a feeling of security.

"Of course I am devastated by my loss, I give you that little victory, but it will be short-lived. I know that Hélène will be with us every day and that we will find each other again in that paradise of free spirits that you will never know.

"There are only two of us—my son and I—but we are stronger than all the armies of the world. And I don't have the time to dedicate to you; I have to get Melvil who just woke up from his nap. He's barely 17 months old and he will eat his little snack and then we'll go play like we do every day and all his life he will be an affront to you by being happy and free.

"Because no, you won't have his hate either."

The letter doesn't translate well, starting with the crucial word: *haine*. La haine is hatred and rage combined, a deep-seated feeling of loathing and disgust.

In the 90s, Matthieu Kassovitz produced and directed a film titled *La Haine*, about the Paris banlieu that defined a generation of French youth. The film follows three French hooligans: one Jew, one Algerian, one black North African. They comically disrupt every environment they encounter, from their neighborhood shops to a haute couture party in central Paris. They don't belong. They're targeted by the police. Everywhere they encounter la haine, that gut feeling that most of the world despises them and would rather that they just disappear. But while many felt the film was critical of the banlieu, the *branleurs* without a future, I saw the film as hopeful. Here were three men from different backgrounds who found themselves in the same dead-end situation, and that produced a common identity that they were willing to defend with their lives. In their desperation, distinctions of black and white, Jew and Muslim broke down. If anything, the film was a plea to acknowledge the humanity of all French citizens, regardless of their heritage. La haine was the force pushing these men to the margins but it also brought them together. Their solidarity was proof that French society shouldn't discriminate against them. Humanity could transcend hate.

I've often felt more faith in France for overcoming issues of racism than in the US. Colonialism produced similar problems but France didn't have the same legacy of slavery. Today, French cities aren't as rigidly segregated, not as heavily policed. Violent crime is minimal in comparison to the US. But adopting French customs and social mores has proven difficult for huge segments of France's population. Granted, the social programs available to them would make marginalized groups in the US jealous. Here, the state subsidizes healthcare and shelter in ways that many French think are overdone or extreme. But the higher echelons of French commerce and French government have proven more difficult for marginal groups to penetrate. Where is the French Obama? *Le Monde* asked after the 2008 election. American individualism ensured that at least some of its minority citizens were able to overcome barriers that in France seemed insurmountable. But those individual stories are the exception, not the norm. Obamas do exist, but they are anecdotes that often create false hope and then offer scapegoats for people looking to disenfranchise the ethnic groups that they belong to.

Between terror attacks, there was a brief loosening of vigipirate. Soon, the schools would open their doors again, if only for the école maternelle, the kindergarten ages from 3–5. It was easier logistically since their school sat behind the elementary school and it was difficult to get everyone to sit calmly and wait while all the teachers showed up. Opening the gates was like giving back a gift we thought was lost. Parents walked up, said bonjour to the attendant and entered, hesitantly at first, then with vigor as they mounted the steps holding their children's hands. We followed the path along the hedgerows and heard the elementary kids playing soccer in the adjacent cours. We crossed the threshold to the school. Children hung up their coats, wandered into classrooms and sat on tiny stools. Fabienne, Inga's teacher, said, she's finally going potty now. I thought she'd get a urinary infection for a while! And we said, yes, she can be stubborn that way. We said goodbye. At the top of the stairs, a mother wearing a purple hijab and knee-length boots helped her daughter navigate the steps. She smiled, relieved. This is so much better, she said. I agreed. Those last few moments, ushering our children into the sanctuary of the school, seemed a fitting antidote to la haine.

Chapter 36

Homeless

A COUPLE WEEKS AFTER Michele and Connor left, we received a phone call.

"It's Phillippe. I was wondering if you might be in need of my services again. If you had anything, it would really help me out."

Rixa and I talked about it. It had been gratifying not to have visitors. Guests had been in our tiny apartment for the past three months. We could finish the rest of the work ourselves. But then Rixa reminded me what Phillippe could still do, putting more lights and outlets in the attic and also fixing some of Jad's botched work. Unlike last time, we wouldn't have any firm exit date. We did, however, have school vacations coming up and it would be nice to rent our apartment during that time. We called him back. He could be there the next day.

Italy looked like it had taken its toll. Phillippe's clothes were disheveled and his packs were worn and dirty. His explanations about Italy were vague. It hadn't worked out, whatever it was, and he was grateful to be back.

I intuited that Phillippe was homeless. Not HelpX homeless, but homeless homeless, one of the panhandlers we'd see under the arcades leading to the Promenade or sleeping in the tiny rock caves on Rauba Capeu. A couple weeks ago, our neighbor Sam thought she had seen Phillippe wandering around near the train station. We told her she must be mistaken. Phillippe was in Italy.

Italy.

The path to homelessness is rarely simple, nor is there really a home-less type with a familiar story. In the US, homelessness can be brought about by loss of employment, by lack of loved ones who are in a position to care for them, by mental illness, or by bankruptcy due to medical bills. Phillippe made me realize a contributing cause: independence and pride. It could be exhausting to be always on the recipient end of charity, not to have anything to give in return for the basic human necessities of food and shelter. Phillippe had said that HelpX saved his life. I was beginning to un-derstand what he meant.

I tried to piece together what I knew of Phillippe. In our earlier board-game-playing binges, my children would often ask Phillippe personal questions—what was his family like? Did he ever get married? Why did he smoke so much?—questions I would never dare ask but that he seemed to welcome from my kids. In between placing tiles for Carcassonne or rounds of the matching game Dobble, he opened up about his life. He was an intel-ligent and precocious child, but rebellious. He left home as an adolescent, never finishing school, and he was estranged from his parents who were both now dead. He had never married but he did say, somewhat wistfully, that he had wanted to once but she wouldn't have him. No kids. As for smoking, he had started young and just never found a way to stop.

So, no family, no attachments. His closest friends seemed to be other HelpXers, people who now formed an online support group via Facebook.

Gaps in his story started to emerge. "If I were better organized," he told me, "I would try to line up jobs in advance." This was during the week or so of searching for another HelpX gig before supposedly heading off to Italy. What it implied, and what his behavior over the next few weeks confirmed, was that the happy jaunts from one job to the next, his HelpX lifestyle where all his basic needs were met by hosts all around the world, was often punctuated by periods of inactivity. Sometimes exchanges just didn't match up. They needed someone for summer and he was available NOW. What did he do when he wasn't working?

Many words for homelessness exist in France: *sans abri, sans domicile fixe,* or the more recent, most PC term *sans domicile stable.* Sans abri, lit-erally meaning "without shelter," has endured the most among the three, although it implies a higher level of desperation—no shelter at all?—than the other two terms. Sans domicile fixe, or "without a permanent home" has become common enough that it devolved into the tidy acronym "sdf."

In conversation, in newscasts trying to raise awareness, or in euphemistic fashion, people use "sdf" as a shorthand to describe the panhandlers or people stretched out on sleeping bags or on dismantled cardboard boxes that became more and more ubiquitous as the weather warmed up. Our neighbors in Old Nice were generally sympathetic to sdfs, but sometimes the business owners, the restaurateurs, and increasingly moneyed foreigners used the term the way generations before said *clochard* or "bum." The Old Town was full of sdfs, these people told us, shaking their heads. Why couldn't we be more like Monaco? The mayor Estrosi really needed to do something.

Sans domicile stable conveyed a more inclusive connotation: these were the people who didn't have a stable home. They might have shelter, might even have fixed address, but it was changeable, mutable, depending on their shifting circumstances.

Like Phillippe.

It wasn't difficult to imagine Phillippe surviving on the streets while he waited for HelpX opportunities to line up as the weather improved. If anyone saw Phillippe outside the confines of our apartment: worn, oversized jeans; unkempt beard, cracked hiking boots with rusted eyelets, they might naturally assume that he was homeless. What would be more difficult to imagine, and what we kept coming back to the longer he stayed with us and became a part of our quotidian lives, was that we would accept him into our home so readily. Other expats were often incredulous.

"You're not worried about him around the kids?"

"Why don't you just hire the work out?"

"I don't think I could handle anyone in my space like that."

Often these observations were borne of a misunderstanding of our financial circumstances. As part-time academics, we were unlikely homeowners, especially for a property in the south of France. Other expat homeowners we met were often in different stages of their lives, with high-earning careers or inherited wealth behind them. During the spring, I met one of them at the Associated Writing Programs conference in Boston: Anne Giardini, the daughter of the beloved late Pulitzer-prize-winning Canadian author, Carol Shields.

"You should really visit our home in Burgundy," she said.

We were at dinner. I had chosen the place, a high-end French restaurant called Le Mistral in Boston's South End. I was the panel organizer and

I had invited several other prominent Canadian writers to join: both Genni Gunn and Aritha van Herk, women who had been writing for years, who, like me, were interested in Shields, her work, and creative legacy. Aritha had been a friend of Shields before Shields died of complications of breast cancer in 2003.

"We'd love to," I said.

As we discussed details—when could we come? During your May school vacation? Perfect since we'll just be opening the house up—I couldn't help but feel like a poseur. During the conference, I was staying in a rooming house that catered to lower-wage workers or the unemployed, people down on their luck who couldn't afford Boston's lofty rents or home prices. Sans domicile stable. For fifty bucks a night I had a bed, a hook for my coat, and a shared dormitory-style bathroom. Yet here I was eating at a Michelin-starred restaurant with world-renowned authors. Anne herself was something else, not only an accomplished author but the president of the Canadian subsidiary of a Fortune-500 company. Anne was keenly interested in our story of a large family moving to France. Carol Shields and her husband Don Shields, the Dean of Engineering at a Canadian university, had bought a small village house in Burgundy. Her parents' story, as Anne told me years later, had some resemblances to mine. During a brief stint working for the Canadian government, in 1970, Don, Saskatchewan-born and unilingual, had been sent to learn French on the French islands of St. Pierre and Miquelon, off the coast of Newfoundland. Carol and their five children, twelve years old and younger, went with him. By the end of that summer Don was a Francophile. Summers and sabbaticals in France followed. In the late 80s, constrained as I was by academic salaries and the costs of raising a large family, they had managed to buy a stone cottage in the remote Jura region of France, one of a row of low houses connected to each other for company and for heat. A few years later, they moved up-market, buying the house in Burgundy. At about the same time, Shields's novel *The Stone Diaries* won the Pulitzer Prize for fiction and Shields's children sometimes jokingly called the Burgundy house the "Château Pulitzer." The house became a refuge for all of them as they raised their own families. We absolutely *must* come to visit, we must, we must! Anne said, implying that her home might speak to our experience. Our lives were intertwined now, grafted together through common interest: a passion for France, the appreciation of family, and a deep and abiding love for her late mother.

After the conference, I flew back to Nice. Electrical supplies crowded our front entryway in preparation for Phillippe's arrival. Over the next few weeks, Phillippe would methodically renovate the rest of our apartment, starting with rewiring the attic. This ancient space with its exposed stone wall and original timbered ceiling had always been dark, owing to the absence of good lighting. Now that Connor and Michele had repainted it, the space was much brighter but it still lacked the luminosity to make it feel like anything more than a glorified cave. So Phillippe crawled into the storage space and installed a light fixture, then worked his way back to the main room. Because of the wall separating the storage from the living space, he was able to install most of the other lighting and outlets without using the plastic exterior channels that are so common in French renovations of older spaces. We would now have light for the living area, light for the storage space, even light in Inga's tiny closet-bedroom: light where none existed before.

Chapter 37

Mystery Girl

IN THE SPRING, MANY Mediterranean fish species spawn, creating long strings of eggs that fill the Baie des Anges. Every time I fished, I navigated through these giant translucent tentacles. If I looked closely, I could sometimes see the fledgling fish starting to develop in their own tiny membrane casing. The water was warming up. After school now, we resumed our habit of changing and going to the beach. I was spending so much time in the water, I felt like I was growing gills.

Every day that the temperatures were high enough and the sun was out, our family trekked with bags of arm floaties and snorkeling equipment and snacks through the sun bathers past the private beach till we found a spot on the easternmost corner of Castel. We repeated the activity so many times that each child had developed her own routine. Zari liked to jump off the rocks, counting with her fingers—1, 2, 3—before hopping into the chilly water with one hand plugging her nose. Dio walked among the plastic debris that had washed up, looking for busted fishing lures, decapitated dolls, or bottle caps. Inga decided to follow her father and don a mask and snorkel and Zari's fins. The fins were laughably over-sized, but we cinched them up so that they only occasionally fell off. Every time she saw a fish she talked through her snorkel, a high hollow sound like the underwater communications of a whale. Our youngest Ivy bobbed in the water with her orange arm floaties and shorty wetsuit like a multicolored cork.

Often I would join my children, then head out with my wetsuit on little solo dives to practice holding my breath. The area was rich in marine life as well as in junk from human activity. I could spend more than three minutes under the water now, plenty of time to assess pollution on the sea floor or chase schools of saupe. Sometimes I would pick out plastic bottles or submerged shoes and bring them topside to throw them away, my own undersea Boy Scout cleanup. And sometimes, I found treasures of my own.

The first time I found anything worth keeping was while I was spearfishing on the other side of the rocks underneath the imposing Monument aux Morts war memorial. Something white flowed with the current like an unfurled flag. I picked it up and brought it to the surface. It was an OGC Nice Handball t-shirt with logos from local sponsors and the coats-of-arms of several cities: Nice; the Ville d'Isola, the town where we'd been skiing just a couple months previous; and St. Étienne de Tinée. I took it home and laundered it and now wore it on occasion to give me some local clout.

I found other clothes on the sea floor that always miraculously fit: a pair of Levis 501s, multi-colored board shorts, a cable-knit wool sweater. Once I bumped into a friend of mine on the way to the beach and I said, "Everything I'm wearing right now I found on the bottom of the sea." He said, "You're really into this, aren't you?" I've found goggles, snorkel masks, a watch, several wallets, a pair of Ray-Bans, and enough fishing lures to fill a tackle box.

On a normal after-school afternoon, my kids splashed in the shallows while I took a brisk swim out to the edge of the rocks. A few days earlier I had seen a magnificent mérou, proof that France's anti-fishing laws were working. It was guarding the passage between the rocks and the open sea, about sixty feet deep. I purged my lungs and gulped some extra oxygen before diving down. It was there again: its russet body peppered with white and yellow, its fins ringed with light blue. It fled into a hole and I skirted the rocks. Striped sar fled before my bright body. Whiskered rouget fanned out on the sea floor, darting away and then coming to rest again.

I skimmed the sand till they gave way to pebbles, then rocks, all the contours mottled and natural. Now a black line bisected the coral-encrusted rocks: a baton like a billy club attached to a square silver casing. I grasped the foam handle and ascended to the surface.

It was a GoPro camera.

I had seen videos online from GoPros before but besides my short stint filming with House Hunters, I had limited personal experience with them. What most impressed me about the device was its compactness. It was about the size of a box of matches with two buttons and a square protuberance for the lens. The plastic housing kept the camera sealed and protected from the pressure of being under fifty feet of water. It looked small and solid, an electronic marvel like a tiny brick.

I beached myself and pushed myself backwards up the rocks by my fins. "Look what I found," I said.

My children and Rixa crowded around. "Do you think it works?"

I pressed the front button and a slit of red light began flashing. Almost out of batteries. It recorded a couple seconds then automatically shut off. "We'll have to recharge it."

I kept thinking that someone around us would see me waving the camera on a selfie stick and approach me, relieved—*you found it! I thought we'd never get it back!* But nobody came. I packed the camera home and read up online how to charge it. A standard USB charger, same size as our Nikon DSLR. Done. In a few minutes, I had enough battery power to get the thing operational.

It was a GoPro Hero 4, top of the line. With the selfie stick and the waterproof housing, it would cost around $600. It was the kind of expensive toy that I would never buy for myself but that I could find plenty of ways to use. We could film our children learning to swim, or document some of my deeper dives. But then I felt the sting of guilt: this expensive toy belonged to someone else, not me. As I pressed the buttons on the camera and watched the tiny icons flash to life, I started on the path to finding its rightful owner.

I opened the oldest video first: an Asian woman in her twenties, the GoPro's wide angle lens keeping her oval face and the eaves of her tiny apartment in focus. She was on the top floor. Only the middle meter or so of the apartment was tall enough to stand up in. The rest of it swooped to either side with a bed tucked in the corner and a kitchenette wedged next to a dormer window. The camera swung around. The woman wore earbuds while she swiped at her smartphone with her free hand. She panned past a low, square table to a flat-screen TV and a window looking out into the dark.

The next video caught the mystery woman from the side. In profile, she was maybe older than I originally thought. Her hair was the color of straw on top with a darker layer underneath. Impossibly large white-framed sunglasses perched on her head. The image shifted to terra-cotta hexagonal tiles set into descending stairs. She took a tentative step, then another. The image panned back to her profile, her face never shifting from the rectangular smart phone gripped in her other hand. She pursed her lips for a kiss.

Now we were at the front door, opening to full Mediterranean sun. The video properties were time stamped at Tuesday afternoon, 1:30 p.m., just two days before I found the GoPro at the bottom of the sea. She was in the Port neighborhood on the other side of the chateau. She walked along the Port, past the multi-million-dollar yachts and the dock for the Corsica ferry. She passed the jetty of concrete blocks leading out to the lighthouse. Now she rounded the cornice. She turned the camera to look down at the rocks.

They were the same rocks where I went spearfishing that day, at that very time, down to the minute. I recognized the two guys sitting on a flat rock behind where I glided into the water. One was bald and wrinkled like the head of a turtle. White sunblock lined his nose. The other guy was hairy with a beard, burned as dark bronze as the first despite the hair. I looked for evidence of my spearfishing. But from the angle, rocks blocked the view. No snorkel or disturbance revealed my presence. Maybe I was further out, beyond the frame, holding my breath and waiting for a hapless dorade.

The next three videos chronicled her walk to the beach, the descent down the stairs, lying out on her beach towel, listening to music. Almost every shot was of herself watching her projection onto her smart phone. She had used the GoPro merely to document her quotidian activities: this is me getting up, this is me leaving my apartment, this is me walking to the beach. She chronicled her life like the Lumière brothers who thought that moving pictures would be a passing fad as people ran out of subjects to record.

The next few videos were more interesting for how they began to construct the narrative behind how the GoPro ended up on the bottom of the sea. It was Tuesday evening now, back at the apartment. Mystery Girl decided she wanted a better view. First, a shot of her face. Then the camera panned to an open window that grew until it filled the frame. The frame shook and tilted to show sloping orange roof tiles. Her feet clacked as she stepped out. One hand balanced on the spine of the roof and the other kept the GoPro aloft to show her descent. Soon we were at the final dormer before the roof dropped over a hundred feet to the street. The Port was lit up, the white yachts bathed in light from streetlamps. One false step could send her flying off the roof and down to the street below.

So Mystery Girl didn't always value her personal safety. It was a Go-Pro after all, a device designed for thrill seekers. The next videos were of Castel Plage again, this time at our favorite spot: the easternmost section next to the rocks. She waded in and plopped the GoPro under water. When it surfaced, it tilted up to the old terrace where two French men sat in cheap collapsible chairs. Then one of them waved.

Finally, our first dialogue. Mystery Girl flirted with the two men on the terrace. They looked about her age, early to mid-20s, bronze from many afternoons like this one, sitting shirtless in sunglasses, fleecing naïve tourists. One had a shaved head and a short goatee. The other was wiry, with a flat-billed Bulls cap turned backwards. They mumbled in French to each other.

"What is he saying?" Mystery Girl asked. Her voice was playful, inflected with Australian diphthongs.

Shaved head laughed. "He says you have a nice ass."

"Aww, merci!" The girl said.

The next videos set up the GoPro's demise: here was the girl swimming on a rubber raft, here were the boys jumping off the rocks, here was the girl trying to film the guys swimming. The frame was shaky while the girl swam and then it stopped, evened out, became one fluid shot of deep water. A green rock emerged from the blue till it filled the frame. The camera bumped on the rock, flipped around, and landed with the lens facing up.

And then came the most beautiful shot of Mystery Girl's videos: a long static shot of a faraway sun, filtered through about fifty feet of water. Two-inch-long black castagnoles flitted in front of the frame, probably drawn to the GoPro's shiny casing, the blinking red recording light. It was calm, serene, like an aquarium screen saver. After about fifteen minutes of footage, the camera shut off.

I watched these last videos over and over again looking for clues that might help me to locate Mystery Girl. Part of me felt like I was reconstructing a crime. The guys were hitting on her. They came there regularly, probably lured her in like so many other unsuspecting young women on solo vacations. When they were swimming, it was hard to discern exactly what was happening. Most of the video showed the underside of a plastic dinghy that they used for floatation and then the occasional shot of either Mystery

Girl or the bald guy's thrashing limbs. The girl said, "I'm only here three days" and the guy said, "We all happy in Nice. You stay with us. You are so much happy!" At one point, the guy wrapped his arm around her waist. Were they fooling around? The halter top she was wearing was gone.

Maybe she was fighting him off.

Finding the girl became more urgent. I canvassed the hive mind of the Internet. Facebook. Close family and friends. I didn't reveal my concerns about what may have happened to Mystery Girl, except to Rixa who told me that I was overreacting. "They're just swimming," she said.

"She's half naked."

"Lots of women take their tops off in France."

"Don't you think it's weird that nobody dives down to get the GoPro? You'd think they'd try to help her find it if she dropped it."

"It was probably too deep. Most people can't dive down that far."

But something about the video still didn't sit well with me. Friends started posting suggestions on Facebook for how to contact her. If she downloaded any video, you could find a digital signature. Maybe Google face recognition? My brother Kent told me about a guy in NY who had his phone stolen and then someone started uploading content to his iCloud. He tracked the phone to China to a guy who had bought the phone from an online vendor. They entered into correspondence. They arranged to meet. Meanwhile the story of their contact went viral and when he came over to China people recognized him on the plane. A crowd showed up at the airport. He got a bouquet of flowers on television and millions of followers on Twitter. "Maybe that could be you?" Kent said.

No, my story was more sinister. There could be confidentiality issues, identities to be protected. I could be witness to a crime. I almost expected someone to show up on my doorstep, demanding the footage. They'd been waiting for someone to retrieve the GoPro on its selfie stick from the bottom of the sea, watching the spot from noon to night, and now they had tracked me to my home. "You don't know what you have," they'd say.

My friend Damien who runs a vacation rental business suggested trying to find the apartment online. I knew the approximate address. I told him that the woman looked Chinese but sounded like she was from Australia. "Try Airbnb," he said. "It's really popular with Anglophones." I checked, using the map view to see if any rentals showed up. The apartment was quite distinct with its dormers and sloping roofline, easy to recognize if

I had a few photos. A couple clicks and I found it: a one-bedroom rooftop studio in the Port neighborhood.

I clicked on the apartment and a list of recent renters showed up. Each left glowing commentary: *perfect location! Charly was so accommodating. Make sure you pack light as there are a lot of stairs.* The most recent one had a dime-sized icon of a blonde Chinese woman. The site listed her first name as Chen from Shanghai. *The room was amazing,* she said. *Nice view and super clean love it.*

Hunh. Mystery Girl was no longer a mystery.

I phoned the owner Charly and explained about the GoPro. He was confused at first: was I a friend of Chen's? How did I come by it again? Eventually he understood but he was stupefied by how easily I found the apartment and was able to track her down. "You're very nice to be doing this," he said. She had already returned to Shanghai but he would email her with my contact information and let her know what I had found.

"What a coincidence she was from Shanghai," Kent told me. The day before I found the GoPro, we had been talking about China, a country that he studies extensively as a Political Science professor. The college where I teach has a summer program in Shanghai and a colleague of mine had recently posted enviable photos of the food and culture: a Buddhist temple with a peaked roof, basted meat kebabs, space-age-looking skyscrapers, and a multinational pick-up Ultimate Frisbee team.

But Kent was dismissive. "Westerners love Shanghai but it drives me crazy." So materialistic. Very consumer-driven. A feeling of superiority to the rest of China. He also cited personal experiences: the teenaged girls who tried to sell themselves like door-to-door salespeople, the selfish reciprocity. In Kent's mind, it was a city with too much new money, full of people who cared only about Prada, smart phones, and sports cars.

Like the Chinese version of the Côte d'Azur.

"She probably won't even care if she lost it," he said. "I wouldn't be surprised if she hasn't bought another one by now."

And yet I was still apprehensive about Mystery Girl, wondering after her well-being. The ambiguity surrounding the GoPro's loss had created a narrative that was difficult to dismiss. *Mystery Girl was in trouble!* Sure, she seemed a little daft and materialistic, but I wasn't willing to condemn her for her choices. In my brother's mind, the GoPro merely confirmed his impression of privileged young people from Shanghai. Go ahead and keep it, he told me. Don't give it a second thought.

I still half-expected an email from Mystery Girl. I had watched her videos when no one else had; sat in front of my computer and thought about who she was. I wanted to understand her, to show her: here was someone different, a father with four kids who dove among the rocks to clean up trash from the bottom of the sea. I was trying to return something—not just the GoPro, but her belief in men who only wanted the best for her. But no email came.

After a few days, friends asked: whatever happened to Mystery Girl? You ever hear from her? When I told them, no, they speculated about why. Maybe the Airbnb guy never emailed her. I followed up and he said that he had. Maybe she was traveling again? Possible. She might not know where I should send it. Or, maybe something did happen in the footage that I had found, something that she would prefer to forget.

Rixa has since made a compilation of the videos, constructed to show Mystery Girl's 3-day trip to the Côte d'Azur and the GoPro's eventual demise. Zari narrates the movie: *They swam in the clear blue sea. They splashed and played and then they swam some more. Until. . .dun dun dun! . . .Mystery Girl dropped her camera. It fell to the sea floor, bounced off a rock, and landed facing the sun.*

I have given up on Mystery Girl. Her comments on Airbnb have diffused the power of my narrative. She wasn't assaulted, didn't experience humiliation or aggression. She's alive and well, giving five stars to her experience. Best location ever! The story becomes an oddity, a joke. At the end of the video compilation, my daughter says, *The fish swam by, minding their own business, until one day, my Papa dove down. . .and found a camera!*

The last image in the compilation is my own, the first of many since then, after I hauled the GoPro to shore with the batteries running out. I sit on the beach with the sun at my back, casting a shadow. I hold the GoPro triumphant with discovery, like my children searching the rocks for a severed doll's head, a watch strap, half of a gauzy net. My shadow arms rise. Clear water laps at my flippered feet. I have tried to learn about Mystery Girl, have wasted countless hours reaching across our time zones, across the digital landscape, to break down the barriers of our difference. I want to ask her: are you OK? Would you like me to send you what you have lost? Please let me render you this service. But instead I have this box with its silver buttons, a red flashing light announcing that I'm behind the camera now.

Chapter 38

A Perfect Fit

WORK FOR PHILLIPPE STARTED drying up. Some mornings, Phillippe would stay in bed till our kids came home for lunch. Once, even lunch-time spats and an animated game of Dobble neglected to wake him. We kept thinking at some point he'd wander out, smile, and get his petit café as per usual. But nothing. After the kids were back in school, Rixa and I started to worry. What if Phillippe was dead? He had no living relatives, no people we knew to contact. A lifetime smoker, Phillippe could easily have had a heart attack during the night. Just as I was about to knock or go in his room, we heard the telltale rustle of activity.

"We were just about to check on you," I said.

"Oh, Netflix you know. Ever watch *Broadchurch*? After the first episode I couldn't stop."

Phillippe had almost finished the lighting in the upstairs hallway and we were scrambling for other jobs he could do. This time we wanted to make sure that he had another HelpX position waiting for him but so far nothing had turned up. Our only hard deadline was the first week in May when we were renting out the apartment during school vacation. I had continued to correspond with Anne Giardini about visiting the Shields' family house in Burgundy and the week's worth of rent would help pay for our trip. But the apartment now was essentially done. We only had a couple days of work to stretch over the next few weeks.

"That place in Cassis turn out?"

"They still want me for the summer. I don't know why—I could do the work for them now but I guess they want to wait till high season. I think I found a place in Spain, though. I love Spain. The corrida! Brutal practice. But the people are so friendly."

A few days later he came with the news: he'd be wiring a barn on a goat farm. Then they had cherries to pick the end of May and who knows what going into the summer? Plus they were hiring two other HelpXers, Phillippe's preferred way of working. It always made the job more pleasant if others were around doing the same thing.

So it was settled. Phillippe would need to leave April 11th to get there for sure by the 14th. It was up in the hills, basque country, and he might have to hitchhike for part of it. Phillippe's departure this time felt more perfunctory. We engaged in rituals of exchange near the end: we took him out to eat at Sam and Vincent's restaurant Chez Palmyre and promised to be in touch. Phillippe also gave me an unexpected gift: a pair of Levi's. Phillippe folded the jeans and then held them in his hands like he was gauging their weight. His spectacles dangled from his neck and he wore his English flat cap and his ruler suspenders. "These should fit you," he said. The jeans were brand new, slim, very different from the baggy jeans Phillippe wore every day. "I couldn't," I said. But he explained: someone had given them to him as a gift and they were too long. Not his style. Really. More room in his pack! Finally I acquiesced. And he was right. The jeans fit perfectly.

It wasn't the last time that we would see Phillippe.

In order to rent our apartment, we needed to have air conditioning, even though we personally never used it. Buildings in the Old Town generally stayed cool due to their relative proximity and abundance of shade. Out on the Promenade, the weather could be hot and dry but the nearby Old Town could be five or more degrees cooler. Transom windows took advantage of this, pulling the cold air into buildings and then wafting it up through interior courtyards or "puits de lumière." If we opened our windows in the morning, we'd feel the cold air suck up through the stairwell and into our apartment. If we closed the windows before the afternoon sun was out in full force, the cool air remained bottled inside, very slowly warming till we could open our windows again at night.

The air conditioning was for potential renters. Every property manager we talked to emphasized its importance. Even if we never used it, we had to have air conditioners to advertise it. Fail to do this and we'd miss out on over half the market.

I turned again to Leboncoin. It was May and people were renovating, installing "climatisation reversible": permanent heating/AC units that often made portable AC units obsolete. When I found someone getting rid of one of these giant toasters-on-wheels, I phoned him up.

I took the tram to Liberation and tested the unit before rolling it into an elevator and out onto the street. The man I bought it from couldn't see me till nine and I knew if I took our car that I wouldn't be able to find a parking spot when I got back. So I wheeled the unit along the street, carried it downstairs, and up to the platform for the tram.

On the way home, I saw Phillippe.

I was just passing the train station when Phillippe marched past the late-night Carrefour grocery. It was ten p.m. I wanted to shout from the tram: Phillippe! What are you doing here? I was only about thirty feet away and if I'd been able to open a window, I was sure he would have heard me. But instead we zoomed past. He'd left our apartment more than two weeks ago, supposedly this time for Spain.

When I got home, I told Rixa.

"Why did he tell us that he had to leave?" Rixa asked.

"Maybe he did. Maybe it didn't work out. Like Italy."

"He might've realized we didn't have enough work for him to do."

"Still, we could have helped him out."

"He doesn't want charity. He wants another HelpX gig."

A few weeks earlier, in the midst of renovations, Rixa had called her mother DeAnn extolling the virtues of the HelpX program and working with Phillippe in particular. We couldn't have done the work without him and we felt that we had mutually complemented each other's lives. "Do you think Phillippe would be interested in coming to the US?" she asked. Yes. Definitely. In all his HelpX travels we were his first North American hosts and he talked frequently about how much he wanted to visit both the US and Canada. He had heard that you could hitchhike on boats from west-coast port cities, gaining free passage across the Atlantic. Why pay for plane tickets when you could travel by boat for free? It sounded unlikely to me but with Phillippe you never knew.

"The only problem for him would be getting there," we said.

"Oh, if he'd be willing to come, I'd pay his way," DeAnn said.

217

Now, we decided to call it in. DeAnn had so many projects to finish, she would have enough work for at least a couple months. She wanted wainscoting in the music room, a full bathroom remodel. They still hadn't installed a deck since they built the house over twenty years ago. It would be nice not to have their back sliding door opening to a ten-foot drop to the ground. We told her to make a detailed list of the projects and then contact Phillippe to see if he was interested.

He was.

For a while it looked like it might not happen; getting a passport was the big hurdle, mostly because he didn't have a permanent address. DeAnn bought him the ticket anyway. Up till she picked him up, she still wasn't absolutely sure that Phillippe would be there. But Phillippe wandered off the plane in Minneapolis and into my in-laws' lives as nonchalantly as he had into ours. Long after he finished the renovations on her home, after we'd also finished our apartment and rented it and moved back to the states and then come back to France again, we'd check his progress; from Minnesota, he went to Montreal and from Montreal he went to Mexico, and from Mexico finally to Spain, each stop another testament to his adaptability. Where was home for Phillippe? Wherever anyone recognized his skills, saw him as a person of value with something to give.

Chapter 39

Abandoned

AFTER OUR SPATE OF renovations, we invited Bart to come see our progress. We still had some small touches left. We hadn't installed a railing on the loft. Rixa wanted to put curtains upstairs and bars over the attic window so you couldn't fall out. Then there were the little things to make it perfect: a new latch for the bathroom, changing the light fixtures in the kitchen, installing a lock on the storage space. But thanks to Phillippe most of the work was done.

On the way up our stairs, Bart told me that several of the buildings in our neighborhood used to be family homes. "The second floor was the 'étage noble.'" We had just passed the abandoned second-floor apartment in our building. He noted the higher ceilings. It's where aristocrats would have their reception rooms. From the looks of the stairwell, it was all likely renovated in the forties or fifties. "This was probably one residence," he said, "with some kind of commerce downstairs."

"A mattress maker." I told him about the Jean Gilletta photo of our street from the 1880s.

"Et voilà," he said.

I tried to imagine our four-apartment building as one narrow, luxurious home. It was first built in the late 1300s, a time when the population from the fortified chateau was expanding to the new city beneath its walls. But the buildings as we knew them today were of the baroque era, in the late 1600s. Around that time, Jean-Baptiste Lascaris de Castellar bought the ensemble of buildings that would make his aristocratic palace in 1657.

Unlike most of the buildings in Old Nice, the Palais Lascaris has an ornate façade with stone balconies and carved faces. This prompted some of the décor of the neighboring homes, resulting in much smaller stone balconies with ironwork railings. Our building at 18 Rue Droite is without such flourishes and instead resembles the vast majority of buildings in Old Nice: four floors, flat cement façade, wood shutters open over windows of the same size during the day and then closed at night. If any decorative flourishes had existed, they would likely have been removed during the last major renovation. Could our building have once looked like one of these Baroque palaces?

Bart walked into our living room and said, "Oh wow. I told you opening up the wall would give you more space." He craned his neck to follow the beam running down the center of the room. It was like it had always been there. The room felt expansive. In the afternoon the sun slanted through the big front windows, filling the space with light. "Congratulations, guys. I knew you would get it done."

We offered Bart something to drink and sat and talked about Old Nice and how property values had stabilized. Uncertainty was keeping interest rates low but that was causing people to jump into the market who had been on the sidelines before. Rates would soon start going back up. The challenge now was finding a property at the right price. He was looking as well—he and his wife were expecting their first child and he wanted to buy before the market took off. They'd probably have to get something like ours that needed renovation. Had we found out who owned the apartment beneath us?

Not yet, but we wanted to.

As the year wore on, the abandoned apartment below us became more and more of a curiosity. Once, right after we moved in, Rixa saw three men enter the apartment at three o'clock in the morning. We were still jet-lagged and the visit spooked her. Who were they and what were they doing in the abandoned apartment so late? After a while they left, clomping down the stairs, laughing, tossing insults back and forth. A few minutes later, another couple guys came in, the same lean one with a ponytail leading the way. They were noisy, seemingly unaware that others lived in the building. Worst of all, they left the door to the street open and weekend revelers crouched on our front steps, their chatter reverberating down the hall and up the staircase. The next week we changed the locks and installed a magnetic closure that couldn't be forced from the outside. But since then, nobody had come or gone from the apartment.

Right away, we wanted to find out who owned it.

"It's the young communists," our neighbor Sam told me. "They used to have offices till about the time we moved in."

"Does it still belong to them?"

Sam shrugged. "They pay their taxes. You could try asking the syndic."

The syndic was its own kind of impenetrable French bureaucracy. For most apartment buildings in France, a syndicate manages the property and acts as a mediator and tax collector. They convene annual meetings, arrange for cleaning and maintenance services. Everything that happens to the building must go through the syndic, sometimes making even small changes like installing a bike rack or repairing a leaky drain, take months.

The syndic said, we have no idea how to get in touch with the owners.

I was incredulous—surely they should at least have an address where they received bills or other material? No, they said, everything was electronic. A bank automatically deposited the money every month. Good luck finding them.

Bart said that there should be a record if the owners were paying taxes. I didn't have to go to the syndic but could go straight to the town hall. "It's public information," he said. "It's a little extra legwork but you should be able to find out. You might even be able to get it all on the internet. The cadastral website."

I told Bart that I'd look into it. Now, as we came to the end of our renovations, the abandoned apartment started to take on more significance. It would likely be inexpensive, especially if it was in disrepair. Plus we wanted to have some say in what happened to it, in who our neighbors might be or what it could become.

The government cadastral site that Bart directed me to contained information about every parcel in France. But the site was difficult to use, with little explanation about what to do once you'd located a parcel of interest. Finally I figured it out: if you marked the parcel with a dot and then pressed print, you could see a preview as a PDF that would let you know which local government agency processed its taxes. And on the PDF was an email address that you could query.

My first emails were very straightforward. I wanted the ownership information about our parcel, s'il vous plait. I had dealt with French government agencies before and I was expecting a long wait, but a day later, I got an email from someone named Sebastien Men with the contact information of all the properties in the parcel attached. The only problem? None of them were for our building.

Thus began a largely frustrating correspondence. I knew from past experience not to get exasperated with French bureaucracy, to always be congenial and polite even when I wasn't getting results. Flippant emails would only mean that Mr. Men would dismiss me more quickly. I queried about other nearby parcels all along the street, one after the other. This time the return emails took longer. Next, I explained more clearly in my email that I was looking for the parcel that corresponded with 18 Rue Droite. Would he mind finding whichever parcel housed this address? No response. I queried again. Then again. Finally, a week later, he emailed saying that he had already sent me everything. He could no longer help me.

I wasn't about to give up. I had the address for the Centre des Impots Foncier et Cadastre so one afternoon, I queued up outside the building during lunch. I was prepared for a long wait. But when the doors opened, everyone filed into line for property taxes while the hallway to the cadastral office was clear and wide. I was uncharacteristically nervous when I arrived; I had, after all, corresponded with Sebastien Men for a couple weeks and he had told me that he'd given me everything that he had. And yet, I couldn't help feeling like the guy was putting in bare minimal effort. His actions showed someone who wasn't used to thinking past exactly what was asked of him. Send me a document of a particular parcel? Sure! But look through the parcels to find what corresponded to a street address, even if my demand was couched in the most careful pleading French? Sorry, can't help you. Luckily, I didn't meet Sebastien Men right away. Instead, an eager receptionist took my request. He was short and lanky with curly hair and glasses. I explained my dilemma: I had looked through every parcel in the area and still couldn't find our street address.

"Sometimes the street address isn't on the parcel," he said.

"Really?"

"It's a problem we've had for a while, especially in Old Nice."

"But you receive taxes from these properties."

"From the parcels, yes. That doesn't mean that we know the street address."

Incredible. They were receiving taxes and didn't really know where they were coming from. "So how do I find the apartment? "

"What size is it?"

I told him, same size as ours. Then we looked through the parcels till we found a building full of apartments that size. Parcel 91.

"Sometimes the parcel actually contains several buildings. The address for the parcel is on the other side but that doesn't mean your building isn't there. Even though this says Rue Droite, you're probably on Rue de la Croix."

He printed out the information for the parcel. Most of it was in a table, like a mini spreadsheet with names and addresses on a couple pages. "What floor is the apartment on?"

"The second."

He flipped through the pages. "Looks like the PCF owns it."

"The PCF?"

"The Communist Party of France."

He handed me the papers and smiled. The PCF! Sam was right. Next to the PCF's name was an address in the nearby Port neighborhood: 6 Rue Balatchano, just a block away from the first apartment we looked at for HHI.

"Is there anything else I can help you with?"

I was stunned to finally have the information I needed—information that would have just as easily been communicated to me via email. Mr. Men had done his job but not very well. If the receptionist hadn't been more forthcoming, I would never have put everything together on my own. "I corresponded with an employee about this. I was wondering if he is here?"

"Yes, of course."

The young man walked to a nearby room that looked a lot like a computer lab at a university: desktop after desktop in regimented rows with flat-screen monitors. A small, neurotic-looking guy with dark curly hair and wireframe glasses glanced my direction when the young man pointed to me. Mr. Men didn't look up from his computer and he mouthed "putain"—a French curse word meaning "whore." He clicked away on the mouse, entered something into the computer and the white screen reflected off his spectacles. Of course. He would make me wait. I probably seemed menacing standing there near the doorway. Five minutes later, he pushed away from the computer and got up to meet me.

Mr. Men was diminutive in stature. He wore a green polo shirt and jeans. "Mr. Men," I began. "Sorry to bother you but I just wanted to meet you after corresponding for so long. I'm Mr. Freeze, the Canadian who was inquiring about the abandoned apartment last month."

"I gave you everything I had." Mr. Men brought his hands up in front of him like he had just touched a hot stove.

"I know that, Mr. Men."

Mr. Men eased up a little. "Did you find what you wanted then?"

"Your colleague has been very helpful. I didn't realize that the street address didn't always correspond with the cadastral address."

"Yes, that can be confusing."

"Do you mind if I ask you a few questions?"

"Go ahead."

"Is it very common that apartments are abandoned like that?"

"It happens all the time."

"Why is that?"

"People have too much money."

"Really?"

"They could care less. They have an apartment and just hold on to it and have a fund that pays the taxes."

"That seems very unusual."

"That's the way it is. Now if you'll excuse me."

"Certainly. Thank you so much. It was a pleasure meeting you."

Sebastien Men shrugged his shoulders and let his hands slap his jeans. "You're welcome."

The whole conversation was rapid-fire, without hesitation. I had information that I wanted and he would give me what he knew only if asked directly. Mr. Men wasn't the kind of guy to sit gossiping at the water cooler.

I've thought about this conversation over and over again since it happened. I wrote everything down in detail, Mr. Men and his curt responses. His brusqueness bespoke a resentment of the "people who have too much money" who were sitting on properties in Old Nice and not doing anything about it. He was also likely from a different caste, the largely Muslim immigrant population that has irked right-wing French purists trying to define a centuries-old line of who is French and who isn't. His statement confirmed what I've found out since then: Old Nice is a hotbed for abandoned properties. The most famous is the ornate building at the east end of the Cours Saleya, a belle-époque-era building where Matisse once lived that guards the last entrance to the sea. Like Matisse's old residence, many buildings in Nice remain abandoned, owned by Niçois families who, rather than try to divide them piecemeal between the various relatives who can stake a claim to them, leave them empty with a fund set up to pay the taxes indefinitely. Like many things in France, it's much easier to maintain the status quo than to go through the hassle of changing it. But the ridiculousness of empty properties in a town where affordable government housing is bursting at the seams and with a significant homeless population was an irony not lost on me or Mr. Men.

It's hard not to make comparisons to the US after my experience trying to track down the owner of this property. In France, it is notoriously difficult to find abandoned properties and even more difficult to purchase one. In the US, prime real estate like apartments in Old Nice would have been scooped up long ago and turned into luxury residences with security and underground parking. I have a sister-in-law who lives in the overheated market of Palo Alto and has been dismayed by long lines of people wanting to rent or buy the same place and multiple cash offers far beyond the asking price. This has never happened here, even as properties in nearby Villefranche or Cap Ferrat have become the most expensive for sale in the world. Several reasons account for the slower upward creep of prices. It is illegal, for one, to make an offer beyond the asking price. So if you have an apartment that a realtor underprices, surprise! You got a deal.

I'm not sure if I would want France to adopt a more market-driven system where cash is king. While it would certainly improve the property values in Old Nice, making it even more exclusive, it would also push many of the regular people, the boutique and shop owners, the artists and artisans, far from the city center. Anyone who was left would soon be here only for show, a gentrified Monaco-like Disneyland.

Now I was about to approach the Communist Party of France to find out about their abandoned property. I only hoped that they saw in me some of the values that they held dear and not as some moneyed opportunist. We were broke after all. But I had to see my inquiry to its conclusion. The abandoned apartment signified future possibility—perhaps we could sell our apartment and then buy this one to renovate next? I had a name and an address, enough information to endure any French suspicion and distrust. I would come like Jean de Florette and hope that the PCF didn't dam the spring to irrigate my fields.

Chapter 40

Lost in Old Nice

WE STARTED TO USE the GoPro. At first, I was intoxicated by its versatility and ease of use. Long a social media lurker, I finally posted my first videos on Facebook: this was me snorkeling in our inlet. This was me diving down fifty feet to see a mérou. This was me approaching a school of barracuda. This was me finding a neon mask on the sea floor. To avoid long videos that we would never watch, Rixa started editing them, collecting the best shots into short montages around a particular theme: Freezes at the beach, hiking on the Côte d'Azur, fun at the splash pad. It was also the first time that I'd inadvertently induced what I had felt so many times watching the Facebook representations of other peoples' lives: voyeuristic envy. Here are some of the comments that people have posted:

I love living vicariously through ur family! What great experiences you guys are having!!!

Quite a cute crew.

So jealous!

Love watching your adventures.

Looks like so much fun! Jealous of your international lives!

AMAZING!!!! Hiking a mountain with the Mediterranean RIGHT there! Sigh. . . .

None of our videos reached much of audience, racking up a hundred or so likes and garnering just the occasional comments, but what surprised me about them most was who watched them. Among the close friends and family were sometimes friends from high school to whom I hadn't talked in over twenty years or people who I had met at conferences or readings, people I really didn't know at all and who didn't know me.

I started to wonder if my posts were doing more harm than good.

I have a writer friend who swears by Facebook, who relies on it to promote his work and build up a following who will buy his books and invite him to readings. Other writers use it as a platform for activism, dialogue, or support. But while Facebook enables these kinds of activities, making them effective and efficient, it also elicits negative behaviors of envy, spite, greed, and depression. It also poses a conundrum for many writers I know, writers like me who publish in tiny magazines and have never, in today's parlance, "gone viral." Writers are by nature a reclusive bunch, more willing to sit in their rooms or closets than network with a group of people. But Facebook gives us the impression that we *should* be engaged in the latter kind of behavior. Our culture puts a premium on it. And if we ever want anyone to take us by the hand out of our writer closets, we had better be prepared to start building a social media presence.

So, I posted. And posted again.

After finding the GoPro, I was posting more regularly than I ever had before. The videos seemed to create buzz—finally some original content!—different from the occasional re-posting of an incendiary news story or link to an article about higher education. It also felt more natural than the occasional humble-brag about publication in some obscure magazine (sorry obscure magazines!), actions that still fill me with remorse and dread. People found the videos funny, amazing—you found a GoPro on the bottom of the sea?—and their reactions confirmed what I'd felt while filming them: it was all mildly entertaining.

I didn't give much thought to the kind of media presence I was creating. Without a context, the videos seem devoid of any social consciousness. They are simply videos of a family enjoying their time in France, offensive only in their innocence. One of my colleagues from where I teach refuses to invite people she works with to join her social network. She doesn't need people speculating about how her social and professional lives might be perceived in conflict with each other. One less headache. How would my dean and colleagues read my videos of octopi changing colors or my children diving off rocks or riding their scooters through mist clouds on the miroir d'eau? Hmm. Sabbaticals must be a lot of hard work.

With the GoPro now, we'd become accidental players in the fiction of our privilege. Who else has the time and money to take a family of six to France every year? My posts are lopsidedly France-heavy and rarely include anything about our day-to-day activities in the states. It never occurs to us to bring along our GoPro for Sunday afternoon hikes at an Indiana state park or swimming at our local pool. But transfer those same activities to the limestone cliffs and coves of the south of France? Now you've got a narrative guaranteed to induce envy back home.

It's hard to know what the tangible effects of our posting will have over time. I remember once when I was about ten, going over to my cousins' house to watch a slide show about my aunt and uncle's recent trip to Mexico. Slides were a way of preserving or memorializing an event specifically for an audience. Several of my aunts and uncles and cousins from different families were there, crowded on the floor of my grandparents' living room. My uncle erected a projector screen and we dimmed the lights. My aunt clicked through the carriage of slides, each movement sounding like an old cash register without the ding—chug-a-chunk!—while she narrated what we saw on the screen: buying trinkets at the market, an expanse of empty blue beach, stone ruins of a jungle temple. Soon the children were bored, bombarded by photos of the same things over and over again. We memorized my uncle's khaki shorts, his Crocodile Dundee hat, my aunt's flowered blouse. But on the way home my parents talked in the car: why didn't they ever go on a trip? A sudden lack in their lives that hadn't been there before.

Now, with Facebook, that lack is on constant display. Every selfie, every Mediterranean montage of surf and sun is a permanent reminder that we were once or are now in the south of France. We've replaced slideshows and postcards with the stronger combination of image and video. Each posting potentially creates a hole in someone else's life.

Rixa insists that her scrupulous editing and kid-narrated voice-overs are simply to consolidate our digital files. Why take hours of footage if you're never going to watch it again? Each video becomes a mini-narrative for our children, to mark the passage of some event or series of events in their childhood. The viewing and reviewing of the videos are like moving picture albums. They reinforce their significance, becoming touchstones for memory and family solidarity. We watch them alone or together as a way of memorializing the past. In this light, France becomes the backdrop for their childhood, proving that moments of significance occur more frequently in Nice than anywhere else in the world. But once the audience extends beyond ourselves, even this is on display. Our narrative becomes not just a family in Nice but a family enamored with this place where they live, that sees it as more notable and exceptional than the American Midwest, a conclusion that makes me cringe.

But we didn't post all of our activities on Facebook. In Nice, not every day is a fair weather day. James Baldwin famously said when criticized by his African American peers for living in the south of France, "It rains here too." April is sometimes cold and stormy. Waves batter the coast and wind picks up. Sheets rip from our clothesline and end up in wet matted heaps in front of the Palais Lascaris. On overcast days it can be difficult to find kid-friendly activities if we're cooped up in the apartment. Drawing or reading aren't always adequate for our physically active kids. So one day I proposed a game, a way for us to enjoy our neighborhood and also teach them more self-reliance and independence.

I took Zari and Dio outside with two blindfolds. I tied the blindfolds around their heads and told them—no peeking!—that I'd maneuver them into some obscure corner of Old Nice and after that it was up to them to find their way back home.

Old Nice is notoriously confusing for visitors and residents alike. Its impenetrable streets and alleyways differ substantially from the flat square grid of our Midwestern hometown. I took Zari and Dio around corners and through small squares and rotated them till they lost all sense of direction. Then I removed their blindfolds.

We were in an alleyway near the Bar des Oiseaux, not far from Johnny's old apartment. It was quiet—no tourists—and far enough from home that I knew they wouldn't immediately know where to go. Zari and Dio looked at each other and started to laugh. They were lost!

I imagine what it must have been like in this moment, surrounded by the familiar pastel-colored buildings with their vented shutters and peeling paint, the gum-splotched black pavement with the tiny troughs on the sides to carry water away. Near our house they would race match cars down the troughs next to French youth leaning on their Vespas. But here? They didn't recognize the garbage depot with its green-topped bins crammed into a white-tiled room. They didn't recognize the windows with their barred grills or the local businesses. Where in Old Nice could they be?

Dio started off first, choosing a route that sent us back behind the Cathedral St. Réparate and past a tiny cabinet maker who cut the plywood for our attic hatch with his radial saw. A couple more turns and they were lost again, near the Porte Fausse but further away from our apartment than when we had started.

"This is so hard!" Zari said.

Soon, though, they recognized the Rue de la Parolière, a street that runs parallel to the tram all the way to the Place Garibaldi. But it still took them almost till we reached the Place Centrale to know where they were going enough to lead us confidently back home.

So I did it again. And again.

Each time, the kids removed the blindfolds with a sense of wonder. We had lived here almost a year and they thought that they knew this place—they really did—but here they were just steps from where they ate and slept and played and fought every day and they could be in another city for all they knew.

The last place I tried was the landing of a staircase in haut Vieux Nice, up behind the Place St. François on the way to Segurane. It was familiar territory for me, not far from the shortcut I'd take every time I wanted to fish over in the Port, but it was an area that we had never visited as a family. When I removed the blindfolds this time, Dio said, "Are you sure this is Old Nice?"

I likely would have forgotten about this game, just one more way to pass a boring afternoon, had not my children reminded me of it recently. We had gone home to the states, come back to France for three months, gone back again, and come back for six. Unlike other events during our stay, we had no physical record, no recorded video or photos, no lost-in-Old-Nice selfies or even journal entries to mark the game. Just the indelible impression it had left in their six and eight-year-old memories.

We started playing like we had nearly two years ago. I blindfolded and rotated them so that they were adequately disoriented. Then I led them up and down streets, winding around till we were in a *place* I was sure that they had never seen, just behind the ancient Sénat. It wasn't far from an apartment I had looked at with a realtor once, a *place* where I had imagined my children playing, sitting on an ancient oval water trough that sat off to one side. I removed the blindfolds and witnessed once again that look of wonder.

But the look was short lived.

One turn, then another. We know where we are. This is the Rue Droite.

OK, I thought. I'd try something a little further away. It was true that the *place* really had only one entrance and exit and after that they were in familiar territory. I'd try haut Vieux Nice again, or maybe one of the tiny *ruelles* behind St. Réparate. But each time my kids would turn once and then exclaim that they knew exactly where we were.

"Why don't you find someplace harder?" Zari asked.

"I'm trying—you guys know it too well now."

It was late and we needed to head home but Zari wouldn't budge. "I'm not going till you find a better place."

And then she started to cry.

I asked what was wrong. It took time to extract something concrete from her. She didn't know exactly why she was upset. This wasn't like two years ago where she felt totally lost and couldn't find her way home. This led to a conversation about what it meant to grow up, how things change, and how that feeling of being lost would soon be just a childhood memory. But it was a good memory, wasn't it? One of the best, a memory that would survive on its own without being canonized in Facebook or digitally reproduced and stored in some vault of cloud-based servers. We held each other while she cried. It was good to grow up too, to be ten now and responsible, to know where she was and how to get home. I loved her more with the passage of time but I cherished the memory of her too, a time when she was truly lost and turned to me with an open palm to lead the way back.

Chapter 41

For Sale

VISITING THE PORT NEIGHBORHOOD always feels like an exercise in what could've been. From the very beginning we had considered the Port as one of the neighborhoods to move our family. The taxi driver had chided us on not choosing to move there. We had looked at an apartment in the Port for House Hunters International. This was the neighborhood to live in if you wanted an authentic Niçois experience and not be choked by the glut of tourists crowding the Old Town. At some point the PCF must have felt this as well; according to the tax records from the Centre Cadastre, they'd been in the Port since 2008.

Rue Balatchano was a quiet dead-end street with cars parked perpendicular to the sidewalk. The PCF office was the only address. Flat concrete framed two glass-fronted doors with windows on either side. If the scrolling metal *volet* had been closed, it would've looked like the entrance to a garage or a closed shop front. I buzzed in. Tables piled with tracts and copies of the PCF newspaper and posters of past and present protests or conferences filled the walls. One office door listed open: the PCF secretary Cécile Dumas.

I rapped lightly on the pebbled glass and presented myself. Bonjour! I was a writer and academic who lived at 18 Rue Droite. I was interested in the apartment just underneath us, the old Jeunes Communistes office. Cécile listened, nodding her head. She was short with a round face. While I explained, she smiled—such a surprise!—and before I could finish she said, "What a coincidence that you're here. We just had a meeting today and the 18 Rue Droite property came up. We're in the process of getting it ready to sell."

"Really?" I was excited at first—wasn't this why I was here to begin with? The coincidence was serendipitous. But we were in no position to purchase it. Buying and renovating our apartment had cleaned us out and now we were using every tactic we could think of—renting our car out through Drivy, buying discount bruised vegetables, spearfishing for food, even salvaging cribs or books or clothes from the garbage depot and selling them on Leboncoin—to avoid plunging further into debt. I worried that I had misrepresented myself. I was a writer, yes, but a broke writer who duct-taped his shoes and wore the same pants every day and who found his clothes on the bottom of the sea.

"We just have a little problem of the title for the property. A lawyer is working on it. I don't know when we'll be ready to sell but I don't suspect it'll be for the next several months."

"Oh good," I said, "because we're broke right now and couldn't afford it anyway. Could you let me know how it progresses?"

She said she would. We exchanged cards. I was going to do business with the Communist Party of France.

At home, I discussed the meeting with Rixa. The abandoned apartment would be coming up for sale. Would we even feasibly be able to do anything about it if it did? She had a better sense of the precariousness of our finances. We were under water as it was just trying to finish up the renovations in our own apartment. The plunge of the Euro had eased the tightness of our budget somewhat but we were still losing money. We would need years to recover, not months. Then maybe we could look at it. And what about Sam and Vincent?

I had forgotten about our neighbors. They would likely never have sought out this information on their own but they had lived with this abandoned apartment above them and wondered about its status longer than we had. Plus we had become friends. Their son Jessie was in the same class as Inga. We had play dates together and went on hikes on the weekends. To hide this information from them would seem like a petty betrayal. So we invited them over for dinner to talk about it.

Cooking for Sam and Vincent is always somewhat stressful even though they reassure us that it's such a relief not to have to cook again.

Their restaurant Chez Palmyre has become one of the most sought-after culinary experiences in Old Nice. Vincent regularly receives accolades for his work, from the local newspaper *Le Nice Matin* to further-flung periodicals like *The New York Times*. His restaurant is always full, even in the leaner winter months. He opens only during the week and never the weekends. His menu changes with the seasons and he uses local ingredients from within a few-mile radius of Old Nice. Their success has also altered their lives in significant ways. Their vacations have become more elaborate. Last year they bought a new car and a parking spot on Ségurane. They dress their son Jessie in designer clothes, wool blazers and Bellamy shoes and Hermès scarves. Plus Sam and Vincent are beautiful themselves. Both are tall and lithe, tanned, and coiffed. When they showed up for dinner at our apartment two floors up from theirs, Sam was dressed in a pencil skirt and leggings. She had done her makeup and her perfume wafted through the apartment like a freshly crushed rose. Our kids surrounded Jessie and soon they were playing soccer in the hallway and rushing to the attic to make Legos and watch a movie.

I was in a t-shirt and board shorts. Rixa wore a tank top and a bohemian cotton skirt.

"I dress up whenever we're invited somewhere," Sam said, "even if it's just upstairs."

With the kids in the back, the front rooms were now miraculously silent, leaving the adults to talk. Vincent was interested in Rixa's bread, a no-knead bread she had started making to save money from buying baguettes every day. It was dense with a hard crust and it had a complex yeasty flavor that he'd love to try out. But he'd have to double his hours if he wanted to produce enough for the restaurant.

Then I dropped the news. I had tracked down the owners of the second-floor apartment. I told them everything, how the PCF was planning on getting it ready to sell. Did they think that they would they be interested?

"This is incredible," Vincent said. "Of course we would be interested. But aren't you guys interested as well?"

"I don't think we could afford it right now."

"What about if we split it?"

"That would make it easier."

We got to talking. My palm leaf would not go unrewarded. Neither of us needed all that extra space and it would make it more affordable if we found a way to work together. Suddenly more possibilities emerged: we could divide up the apartment, creating two floor-through duplexes. Alternatively, we could take the front half and use it for a large kitchen/ living area and then dedicate the top half to bedrooms and a family room. Sam and Vincent wanted a large master bedroom/bath suite. Both halves of the apartment had 14-foot ceilings, enough space to make mezzanines large enough to be their own floors. It was something that could make our snug little apartments feel positively palatial.

We called the kids back in and crowded around for dinner. Rixa cut into her signature loaves of bread, still steaming from the oven, and passed around slices to eat with our salad. Together, we thought. In the communist spirit of the PCF, we would find a way not to allow contracts and capital and differences to divide us.

Chapter 42

The Château Pulitzer

IT WAS MAY, OUR LAST *vacances scolaires* before we would be traveling back to the Midwest and resuming our lives temporarily in the US. I had maintained contact with Anne Giardini, and arranged to stay at Carol Shields's home in Burgundy. It had taken longer than we thought it would to get there, and traveling up North had sent us back two months in the weather. Where Nice now was sunny and beach-worthy, Burgundy was cool and rainy. We found the town of La Roche Vineuse easily enough and phoned the sometime-caretaker François who opened the gates and led us in to a courtyard of tiny gravel next to the slate-roofed stone house.

Our children took to the place as though it were their own. The massive front door with its metal stays and thick slabs of oak opened to an entryway with a staircase. Our children rushed in and climbed the stairs, already laying claim to their sleeping arrangements. They could each have their own room if they wanted to but out of habit Dio and Zari chose to sleep together. Our cozy apartment had made it unnatural to be apart. François disappeared for a while to check that the heat was working and then met us downstairs in the dining room where he laid out our keys.

"If you're free later on, do your kids want to come over and swim?"

We said yes, certainly, but the conditions weren't anything like what we'd come to expect for swimming back home. The sky was overcast and drizzly. He explained: he had four children. They would love some friends to play with. He gave us the address and phone number and told us to come by that afternoon.

The Shields house was more than we could've asked for a week-long vacation. Anne had told me to feel free to use anything we found, just put it back in its proper location afterward and top up what we ate from the pantry. The limestone village home had carved lintels and high, shuttered windows. The property with its garage and outbuildings was surrounded by a ten-foot-high stone fence. I imagined Carol's protagonist in the Putlizer-winning *The Stone Diaries* being drawn to this place, although the limestone from her book was mined from a quarry on the other side of the world. After months of living in our tiny apartment, we now found ourselves in a home with a living room, dining room, a kitchen, four bedrooms, sisal rugs, an ensuite bathroom, and closets bigger than the attic where our children slept and played. What a place. It was also in town, only a few blocks from a bakery but the nearby creek and bike path out to the country made it feel more rural, like we half expected to turn a corner and see a herd of goats being led to pasture. But swimming? Once our kids caught whiff of the invitation, they were already digging through their suitcases. After a quick lunch we were back in the car, following Google Maps to François's home in nearby Bussières.

"I think that the Shields family wants to sell it."

We were in François's home, a caretaker's house on the property of Château Bussières from whence the town derived its name. François's state-ment was borne from comparison: where the Château Pulitzer exuded the faded charm of a French village home, Château Bussières was a nineteenth century belle-époque pleasure palace with tasteful modern amenities. The pool, for example, wasn't some outdoor kiddie above-ground pool but a marble-tiled lap pool in an all-glass pool house that overlooked the valley. I wasn't sure if the various members of the Shields family were really intent on selling their house or if François was saying, in a kind of veiled way, look at what kind of place they *could* be living in, the luxury! François was an architect by trade, a designer who was responsible for the pool house and the sleek modern renovations of his adjacent caretaker's house. He gave us a whirlwind tour through the living room, the kitchen, then upstairs to the bedrooms and bathrooms. Along the way, we met his four children in random succession: Lilly, a daughter, in rollerblades; Marcel and Adam, two boys on the staircase; and reclusive Sophie, a teenager who ducked into her room shortly after meeting us.

"Elle est un peu sauvage," François said.

Ah, we said, no problem. The apology was for her shyness, to account for her sudden disappearance. Unlike the other three children, she would not be joining us in the pool. She would not backflip into the water or teach our daughter how to properly dive. *Sauvage* in French meant wild in the way that animals recoiled from human presence, burrowed away into their secret places.

"Nos enfants ne sont pas très sauvage," I said. "But they *are* wild." François laughed. I'd been saving the joke for someone bilingual who was aware of the almost opposite connotations of the two expressions. Compared to Sophie, our kids were a screaming snarling mess of hair and teeth and nails. Inga's knees and shins were scraped from wrestling out on the gravel driveway. Dio had a potato-shaped bruise on his stomach from an accident with a makeshift bow and arrow. Zari's waist-length hair, thick as straw, had proven the perfect nesting ground for ants. Now they were fighting over the fountain that sent a curtain of water into the pool. They kicked through it, dunking themselves, punching into the water with a pugilist's intensity.

"Come over anytime," François told us. "My kids leave tomorrow to go to their mother's but I'll be here."

After the visit, Rixa and I wondered about the almost brusque way he paraded us around his home. He wanted to know: how did we come to know the Shields family? Several of the Shields children were very successful and they visited every summer. Some, however, couldn't afford or did not make time to come. The conversation revealed speculation about where we were on the spectrum. Four children in France didn't mean middle-class minivan suburbia like it did in the rural Midwest. But here we were, with our banged-up Opel and our children in their second-hand clothes and skinned knees. Perhaps François had been looking to connect with one of the Shields's more well-to-do friends. He saw in us an opportunity to try to forge relationships with his children, to provide them with some international exchange. Or he could have been, as we thought later, a man who simply wanted to entertain his children on the last day of vacation with their father.

"Our parents are separated," the youngest daughter told us before we left them, still swimming in the pool. She stated it matter-of-factly, no sorrow or regret, no martyr, woe-is-me indulgence. Just our parents lived in two different places: one in Paris, one in Burgundy, two spheres in their solar system rotating in concentric circles around their lives.

We left Château de Bussières tired and refreshed. The Shields home was much more to our liking, with the accumulated games, toys, DVDs, sports equipment, bikes, books, and crafts of a home used to the presence of children. In the main dining room was a rustic farm table, varnished planks with cracks the width of a penny surrounded by straw-backed chairs with seating for eight. The floors were terra-cotta tile from the 80s, practically indestructible. Every shelf or cupboard or armoire revealed evidence of years and years of family lore and love. This was where Carol came with Don to decompress, to enjoy the countryside, to read and relax and sightsee and practice French. This was where Carol's grown children walked, to the bakery up Rue de Linde, baguettes tucked under their arms. This was the bike path where her grandchildren teetered unsure, observing the flooding from the nearby Le Fil river. This was where they played epic games of Risk, Kamchatka and Alaska piled high with star-shaped plastic armies, locked in the treaty that finally ended in a genocide of green, red dice rolled a thousand times in attack after attack. This was where they watched *Annie*, and *The Princess Bride*, and, at night, when their parents were asleep, *Fast Times at Ridgemount High*, their fingers still greasy from popcorn they had half-successfully popped in the big metal colander—and why didn't mom just bring one of the hot-air poppers from Canada? This was where they caught Burgundy snails, rounded them up in a big red bucket after an unusually damp June rainstorm, and wondered if the French called this dinner. This was where they cycled along the *voie vere* past the grape vines and horse-studded pastures and perched villages toward Macon. This was where they played Monopoly on the jute rug in their pajamas, or Scrabble on the round table in the living room. This was where, year after year, three generations of Shields argued and laughed and wrestled and laughed and loved and laughed and whacked badminton birdies and played *petanque* with multicolored plastic *boules*.

I thought back to what François said: I think they want to sell it. Who was they? One child, two? The ones who came regularly or the ones who never came? Carol had loved this house Anne had told me, and her death, a terrible one, meant there would be memories associated with convalescence and pain. There was also the question of legacy: what would Carol have wanted? Since she divided it up among all five, she must have wanted some perpetuation or continuance of what she had imagined for her immediate family. Now that her children had children of their own, it could also be the place for the gathering of other generations. But Carol was always practically minded, a realist. Even after winning the Pulitzer for *The Stone Diaries* in 1993, she never had delusions of grandeur. "A book has a shelf life of about four months," she told an interviewer not long before her death. "Most of the Pulitzer winners I've never heard of." Even though she was originally from the US, there was something refreshingly Canadian about Carol's candid humility. She was not the kind of author who was afraid of her own mortality or the disappearance of her name over time. Writing was a job she enjoyed for many years. Now it was done, so what? She couldn't control whether or not her work endured. Holding on to the Château Pulitzer, even though it was a place she loved, would be sentimental if it outlived its purpose.

Most of the week I wondered about Carol and this place that housed her summer dreams. Carol came early in her career to France and like me, developed a lifelong love for the country. During the week, I read two of her novels, early novels that till now I hadn't read: *Small Ceremonies* and *The Box Garden*. Each reading was beset with irony. *Small Ceremonies* was about a biographer who steals a plot from an author while she is on sabbatical living in the author's house. And here I was now staying in Carol's home and reading her books and writing on the double desk where she worked every day. I felt like I was reading myself into her novel.

My own small ceremonies included periods of nosing around similar to the biographer, opening cupboards and drawers. It was hard to know what belonged to Carol. So much of the home had been taken over, supplanted by her children and grandchildren. I found drawers full of old VHS tapes. I found a pile of padded envelopes from publishers asking her to review the enclosed book, please. In an armoire in the attached gite apartment, hung two pantsuits, one a pink plaid with pearl-like appliqué. I took it off the hangar and tried on one of the sleeves, much too small. It was horrible for me to be doing this, too invasive; and what if the clothes were actually a daughter's or daughter in law's or belonged to Don's now French partner? Would I be able to conceal my embarrassment even as she read these words? But I couldn't help myself. Never had I been so overwhelmed by the need to know someone as I wanted to know Carol Shields. The first night, my kids tucked in bed and snoring after a long day on the road, I sat up with Carol's library, the most complete portrait I could find of her. Most of the books were from the 70s to the 90s, hardbacks or paperbacks with a preponderance of Canadian authors. And when I opened them, I was delighted to find something that made me feel more connected to Carol than all the stone solidity of her house.

Her handwriting.

I had to check online first (thank you, internet!) but the illegible scribbles were definitely hers. Some words took time to decode. Having equally messy handwriting, I felt an immediate closeness to her. Perhaps there were similar elements of our characters that pinched our r's to slits or flattened our t's. Her annotations followed a predictable pattern. Often she underlined, then put a checkmark or a star in the margin. Occasionally she wrote down the side, turning the book so she had room for a full sentence. Then, at the end of the book, always a few catch phrases to help her remember the book's contents, along with page numbers to find the place.

Carol's study was curiously open to the rest of the chateau. Instead of a locking door, a molded archway joined the study to the living room. From the sturdy double desk, a wall of books faced me. To the right was a stone hearth and a round game table with four chairs. Next, an entertainment center, two square couches, and a coffee table. The TV wasn't entirely visible from here, the archway cutting off my line of sight. But I could see the table and chairs, the edge of one of the couches. Behind the desk was an artificial fireplace, a heater I imagined Carol using on the occasional cold May night in lieu of turning on the more expensive central boiler heat. To her left was a long window with a view of the courtyard and the garage. If her grandchildren were playing volleyball or getting out bikes, or surreptitiously meeting French boys they met in town, she would know. It was an office that served multiple purposes, a place to be slightly apart, to peripherally engage in all the chateau's activities.

In the mornings, I wrote at the double desk while my children played and explored their surroundings. From the window I could see the kids tossing plastic multi-colored boules. Rixa toweled off a portable slide they found in the garage and Ivy climbed and descended it over and over again like she was a perpetual energy machine or a video GIF stuck on repeat. Inga found a red Huffy bike with wheels the size of dinner plates. She wheeled it around the courtyard or mounted it and pushed it along with both feet.

I wondered how our children's lives would have developed here, had we chosen a home in the lush Burgundy countryside rather than a tiny apartment in a city center. Soon the other children found bikes their size.

They brought them out into the overcast courtyard. They squeezed brake calipers and felt for air in the tires. The bikes would soon become a daily routine, little trips up to a bike path fronting Le Fil river. We'd follow it down to the local park where my children would school a couple locals in a game of pickup soccer. Inga would teeter on her bike while we held the seat and she got up enough speed for us to let go. Soon she was riding confidently, attached to this machine that enabled her to go faster and farther than she had ever gone before. Speed and independence eclipsed every tumble or scraped knee. She got up, checked her bruises and cuts, then whizzed off again, blood streaking down her toddler legs. This could be a good place, I thought, with the space and open air and tempo to allow our family to find its own way, not forced into the confines of our apartment where we were always stumbling over each other.

I read Carol Shields's *The Box Garden* next, a companion book to *Small Ceremonies*. *The Box Garden* follows Charleen Forrest through her life's challenges and disappointments. She's a failed poet who edits a botany journal. Her husband has left her and she's searching for love. Here, I thought, was a novel that didn't so eerily parallel our own experience, the ghost of Carol present not only in the bones of this place but in the words I was reading every day.

Then the plot of *The Box Garden* started to accelerate.

Most of the novel dealt with the mystery of correspondence. A long-time contributor to the botany journal who identifies himself as Brother Adam, writes extensively to Charleen about the nature of ordinary lawn grass. The correspondence takes a desperate turn when Charleen's son is abducted by a well-meaning friend to reunite him with his estranged father. Suddenly, her son is gone and she needs to find him. His absence is somehow tangled up with Brother Adam's letters.

As a parent of four children, I've often felt a lurch of fear that one of my children is missing. Once, on a typically sun-drenched afternoon in Nice, I took all four kids to the miroir d'eau near the Place Masséna. I found a bench where I leaned their scooters and I sat to watch them splash about in the fountains. The fountains cycled through a number of routines, sometimes gushing fifty feet into the air and other times sending up little squirts like shots from a water gun. Ivy and Inga always stayed relatively close, but Dio and Zari liked to wander further away. Today they raced through the film of water in between fountain blasts and lay out on the black paving stones and let the water tumble over them. But after a half an hour, I realized that I couldn't find Zari.

The miroir d'eau is more or less enclosed with a gate that's open during the day on either end. But it's a large area, large as a city block, with a constant stream of residents and tourists passing by on the Promenade du Paillon. Zari has long braided blond hair and a fair complexion, usually easy to spot among the more olive-skinned and multi-ethnic southern French. But I couldn't see her anywhere. Probably a hundred kids, maybe more, splashed among the fountains. Parents pushed strollers or took photos. The ecstatic screams of wet children masked any abnormal sounds. My daughter could have struggled with some unknown assailant and I wouldn't have heard a thing.

I gathered the rest of the children together. We needed to find Zari and go home. "But we just got here!" Dio said. I handed towels to the kids and they put on their sandals. Three park police strolled in front of the fountains. My girl was gone. I approached them to ask what to do next and tried to keep the panic out of my voice.

Just before I opened my mouth to explain, Zari came running up.

"Where were you?"

She had been playing behind the benches, collecting leaves to press in a book, crouched and out of sight. I was relieved and held her to me. The experience was the most acute of all my where-are-my-children moments but never had a child not turned up. So I empathized with Charleen and her abducted son. There was no worse feeling than finding yourself without your child and believing that you were somehow responsible.

The next day, Rixa got an urgent message from her mother.

"Lance is missing."

Lance was Rixa's cousin, a young father of two who was just finishing his PhD in microbiology at Howard University. He was last seen at a bank machine where he withdrew some cash. He was on his way to pick up his regalia for graduation but he never showed up. He'd been missing three days. His wife had their second baby a little over a week ago.

The disappearance eerily echoed Charleen's son's abduction in *The Box Garden*. I was reading moments of tragedy into existence, like Carol's books were somehow impacting my present reality. We were sitting in the living room after putting the kids to bed. We had thought: why not watch a movie? But then Rixa's mother had messaged us and Rixa phoned her and now both of us cradled phones to our ears.

"Did he own a gun?" I asked.

Rixa's mother paused, surely not liking the implication of my question. "It really could be anything," she said.

She filled us in on some of the details that news stories hadn't caught. My laptop was open and we scrolled through press releases while Rixa's mom described a fight with mental illness. One photo showed Lance with long curly hair and an untrimmed beard, such a different look from the last time we saw him five years ago. He was a newlywed then, waiting for the birth of his first child. He wore glasses. He had just started his PhD program and they were brimming with optimism, a couple not unlike ourselves at the beginning of our studies. Now he looked like a homeless person or a theatre major getting ready to play Jesus.

"He left without his cell phone," DeAnn said.

One news outlet showed a short video of his wife pleading for his return. "We love you," she said, tearing up. "Please come home." She looked into the camera as though she were speaking directly to him. They distributed his image along with a reward poster to anyone who might recognize him or know his whereabouts. It was a bizarre disappearance that had local law enforcement stumped.

"I hope they find him," Rixa said.

The next day, we decided to visit the Château de Pierreclos. The area around Carol's home was rich in privately owned châteaux, each one with a public section that you could visit for a fee. Sometimes individual châteaux would provide unique entertainment to set themselves apart from others: an evening son et lumière, hedge mazes, guides dressed in period costumes. Pierreclos had an armor room with medieval weapons and chain mail that you could try on. We got to the château in the morning and took the obligatory guided tour. Vineyards and formal gardens surrounded the two château towers. In between lectures about regional history and medieval cooking, we took turns entertaining the kids outside. When we finally ended up in the armory, we were thrilled to have something more for the kids to do.

"Go ahead," the guide said. "Try it on."

Our kids started tentatively at first. All the helmets and shields and chain mail and weapons lay on a huge oak table. Dio reached for the handle of a mace and the spiked ball nearly hit the ground when it rolled off. Zari grabbed a broadsword and Inga a short sword. We draped chain mail over their skinny bodies and positioned loose helmets on their heads for pictures. Wearing the armor and wielding weapons, the kids were emboldened, powerful. It wasn't long before Dio let loose a *Braveheart*-worthy battle cry and swung his mace in the air.

"Attention, attention!" I said. Careful, careful! Part of me wondered if this was really all OK. These weren't plastic replicas but real armor and swords. The edges were dulled but they were solid metal. Dio's mace could still bludgeon an enemy if swung with the right strength and intent. But the guide smiled and laughed—everything fine here!—while our children parried and lunged. Only Ivy was having none of it.

"Inga coupé." She folded her arms and made a face. As far as we could tell, she was afraid that someone would cut her. She kept saying méchants— bad guys? Our kids had transformed into the siblings of her nightmares. "It's OK," we told Ivy. "Just pretend. They're not going to hurt you." But she refused to come back into the room while our children channeled their inner savages. Even at two, she understood what we adults were ignoring: that even the most well-intentioned and loving creatures can change in an instant when given a tool of harm.

They eventually found Lance.

Like *The Box Garden*, the ending was almost too serendipitous, a letdown. Carol spoke of her own disdain for the abduction and forced resolution in the novel, saying that it was at the behest of an editor who complained that not enough happened in *Small Ceremonies*. One can almost hear the echoes of these conversations in her last book, my favorite, *Unless*, a book that I read for the first time several years ago in Nice. The book inadvertently led me to this moment, staying in The Château Pultizer. My love for *Unless* led to the conference presentation, which led to me meeting Anne, which led to the invitation to come here.

In *Unless*, the narrator Reta Winters meets an overbearing editor who tries to get her to alter the plot of her most recent book. The editor interrupts the story, an unwelcome male presence in a drama that doesn't concern him: a daughter who has decided to become homeless after witnessing

246

the self-immolation of a Muslim woman. He's thrown into a world that he can't understand. Shields artfully weaves the narrative around him, despite him, to a conclusion that gives Reta and her daughter a chance to voice their discontent with a world that still so frequently marginalizes women.

Now, it was the last day of our trip. We had cleaned Carol's dishes and silverware and put sheets in the washing machine. We had swept and wiped up toothpaste splatters and packed our Opel Zafira Disneyland with our bags and leftover provisions. The house would be empty for the next couple weeks, plenty of time for François to look through and make sure everything was in order. Before we left we checked our email and read that Lance was found safe at the Brunswick Family campground, only about sixty miles from home. Over the next several days we would learn more details of his story, how he hadn't finished all the requirements to graduate and found himself suddenly unable to deal with the looming possibility of his failure. He had to escape. Later, I would think how moments of crisis can creep up on you, how our choices set events in motion that leave us feeling trapped. But for now, we would buckle Ivy into her car seat and drive out the gates and past the Burgundy châteaux through the lush rainy hills back home to Nice, to the sea, to where this chapter of our own story was also coming to its close.

Chapter 43

The PCF

I STARTED TO STOP BY the PCF office on my regular walks. The Rue Balatchano was just a block from the Port near the Boulevard Carnot and the Basse Corniche heading to Villefranche and Monaco. I often passed by there on the way from dropping the car off around Coco Beach, one of the largest free on-street parking areas in Nice. Cécile always greeted me warmly and updated me on the PCF's progress for getting the apartment offices on Rue Droite ready to sell.

"We have cleared the hurdle of papers but now we have to get a complete *estimation*."

The first appraisal came in with a recommendation to empty and clean the apartment. When the offices moved, they left all the old furniture, filing cabinets, and mess accumulated from over 30 years of being the departmental headquarters for the PCF youth organization. According to Cécile, everything was still there: an apartment full of junk. The appraiser wouldn't put his final recommendations forward till he had seen the apartment completely unencumbered. That way, he could take measurements and better see what the apartment could be, what kind of work needed to be done.

Once, a guy in his thirties sat in Cécile's office when I stopped by to say hello.

"Monsieur Freeze! You must talk to my colleague here. He practically lived at the Jeunes Communistes office."

The man had black curly hair and a scrabble of an unkempt beard that continued partway down his neck. He wore a white t-shirt and loose jeans and he was a little heavy around the middle. "If you only knew all the *betises* I did there," he said. He put his hand on the side of his face and shook his head.

"Can you tell me a little what it's like inside?"

"A mess. You must be brave if you want that place."

I wondered what kinds of activities could make buying it so daunting. I imagined all-night parties, drugged-up marathons reading Marx and planning communist coups. It was primarily a youth organization, a place for social rebels and iconoclasts. It could have been anything.

I still couldn't get many specifics from the man, nor from Cécile. She had been there a couple times. It was two apartments: one for the front offices and the other with a low-lit room and toilet. The back didn't have any windows and the front had a small mezzanine. But neither went beyond generalities for its condition. It was dirty. The floors were cracking. There was junk everywhere. I wanted to know: what kind of junk? Were the cracks structural? How tall was the mezzanine?

"You just have to see it," the man said.

At home, I'd make various attempts at discerning the layout of the rooms and their contents. I tried jimmying the locks. I fiddled with the windows on the internal staircase. One window was missing with only bars separating it from the outside. Now that I had a GoPro, I could use it to try to capture the interior. I extended the selfie stick out to maximum length. But when I poked the GoPro through the bars, the footage revealed that I was in some sort of false ceiling. A wall divided the opening, showing that the apartments were indeed separate. The back windows were painted yellow like the rest of the interior stairwell but a fist-sized hole punctured one of the panes. I pushed the GoPro carefully through the hole and then panned from side to side, hoping to take in the front rooms. The shutters were closed, making the footage dim, but I could make out walls, lots of walls, and maybe a filing cabinet? Most of the footage was shaky, like the uncut video from *The Blair Witch Project*. Whatever could be in there?

We didn't have to wait long. One day, we heard the metallic scrape of a door swinging open. I stepped out onto our landing and peered down. Two women were talking in entryway of the apartment, saying "Oh la la," and gesturing wildly. Finally. I went down and introduced myself. I'd no longer need to speculate about the abandoned apartment and its contents.

Chapter 44

Caught

I NEVER COULD BRING MYSELF to take the GoPro with me spearfishing.

I didn't know exactly why. I had watched countless videos of others spearfishing, waiting while the *chasseur* lay on the bottom of the sea, and anticipating the moment when a dorade or a barracuda would enter his line of vision. I learned how to minimize my movement and hide among the rocks from watching these videos. I learned how to let the fish come to me, to wait for it to turn and offer its flesh up. And while I was catching more fish now, paying back the cost of my gear many times over, I couldn't bring myself to film any of my exploits. Each time my spear shot through a fish, I still felt a mix of regret, pain, and elation. I had caught food that we could eat and each catch signified hours diving deeper, holding my breath longer, to better understand how each fish species behaved. I had learned the underwater terrain from Castel out to the lighthouse. I knew each submerged rock. I knew where fish often congregated or passed by in schools, swimming against the current. I took pride in these skills but I felt part of my life force leave me when I'd drive my spear into a fish's head to keep it from suffering. And my trips into deeper water brought me into contact with bigger fish, into terrain I'd never experienced before. I was pushing my physical limits.

"Why don't you ever go with anyone?" Mourad asked. I was at the butcher's, talking about spearfishing. I had just caught a good-sized loup and I had described how the predatory fish approached me, wondering if I was food or foe.

"I usually go in the afternoon while the kids are at school," I said.

"You know should really bring someone along. With a buddy if you go under or something happens they can pull you out. By yourself you're playing roulette."

"I try not to push too much when I'm by myself." But the opposite was probably true. And now that the weather was warming up and the fish were moving, I was taking more risks than ever. A couple weeks ago, for my birthday, Rixa bought me the last piece of my spearfishing gear, a dive knife that I now strapped to my leg. The knife was primarily for safety, in case I ever got caught on anything on the bottom of the sea. But subconsciously I think the knife made me bold, more willing to go to places I hadn't dared try before.

That week, when I went to fish la vièrge, two buoys bobbed on either side of the great rock where I'd often prostrate myself à l'agachon in wait for unsuspecting prey. A net wound down and around the rock between the buoys, cutting off the channel where fish would often swim. This was a fishing area but it was supposed to be closed to boats, meaning that whoever had placed the net had done it illegally. I swam out to the first buoy. The net descended into the depths till it was a tiny ribbon. I held my breath and dove.

I followed along the net, noting the trapped fish and octopi. I knew these prizes were off-limits. Anything in a fisher's net was his, not mine. Finally I got to where the net crossed the channel. It was at its deepest point. Bunches of net clumped around trapped fish. In the middle, a Moray eel snapped its jaws when I passed.

I'd seen Moral eels before, called *murènes*. Last month I caught one in the inlet. It was about 50 cms long, the width of a zucchini. Yellow spots decorated its sides. Even after I speared it, its mouth snapped at me then locked onto to the spear as though it could break it in half. This murène was larger, bigger than anything I'd ever speared before. Its long body coiled through scrunched netting.

I surfaced and blew the water out of my snorkel. I wanted to release this fish. It was mid-afternoon when the murène likely slept. It wasn't moving—could it be dead? If so I could take it home and cook it up. Boats weren't allowed in this area anyway. I purged my lungs of CO2 and dove again.

This time, I hovered in front of the murène. My lungs were full of air, plenty of time to see my decision through. I reached my spear up to the immobile murène and poked it. The murène whipped its head around, writhing in the net. With my free hand, I tried to untangle him while avoiding the murène's snapping jaws. But pulling the net drew me closer to it. In a second, I realized my mistake.

My fin was caught.

Over time, a diver's fins become like a lost appendage, evolution in reverse, making us more like our orca-like forbears. On land, fins are awkward, impossible to use for our usual bipedal maneuvers. But in the sea, they moved me through the water as economically as possible. As soon as I dove, I felt a lightness and grace, a freedom of movement like a dancer released from the constraints of gravity. But I had forgotten the terrestrial laws of physics. I wasn't standing on firm ground but suspended in water. Any reaction had an equal and opposite reaction. As I pulled, I didn't remain stationary but instead moved closer while my fin was quickly tangling in the net.

A moment of panic. I thought, this is how divers die. My obituary would read: father of four loses his life caught in a fisher's net. Every success would be reduced to this one moment of stupidity. But no! My fins were removable! How daft could I be? I slipped the caught fin off and kicked, one-footed to the surface.

I had to get my fin back but needed to find some way to mitigate the risk. The net was deep, in about fifty feet of water. The eerie vièrge with her concrete shoes didn't have to be my fate. This time, I dove down and pulled at the net from above, keeping my limbs as far away from it as possible. Gratefully it budged. I took my time kicking while I tugged the net with my fin and the murène to the surface.

This time, success. But now the net was hopelessly entangled. The murène chomped on a knot. It thrashed anytime I brushed against it. Calm, I thought. I needed to be calm. Slow, deliberate movements. I unsheathed my dive knife. I sliced through the netting, pulling on the fin. The murène thrashed, wriggling free. The net twanged and relaxed like an enormous elastic till it fell back to the sea floor. I put my knife back in its sheath and bent over to slide the fin onto my naked foot.

Next time, I'd be more careful.

Next time I would steer away from any submerged netting.

Next time I wouldn't try something so dangerous without a companion by my side.

But as the months became weeks became days before our departure, the lure of the sea would yet again negate even my most basic common sense.

Chapter 45

Life as Good as This

ONE OF THE FIRST TOURIST guidebooks mentioning Nice is Scottish author Tobias Smollett's *Travels through France and Italy*. Smollett took the journey not to write a guidebook, but to seek warmer climes for his failing health. By 1766 when *Travels* was first published, Nice had already gained some renown as a winter tourist destination for the British. At the time, Nice wasn't French, but instead existed as one of the jewels in the crown of the Duke of Savoy. The culture was distinct from its immediate neighbors: France, to the west, starting on the other side of the Var river, site of present-day Villeneuve-Loubet; and Monaco, the city state buffer with the declining Republic of Genoa.

Smollett was immediately taken with this sleepy seaside village nestled against the rock of the chateau and he stayed a good part of the year. While many of his observations are monetary, about the price of meat and accommodations and furnishings, some extend to the character of the Niçois people and their habits that he both admired and despised. "The artisans of Nice are very lazy, very needy, very awkward, and void of all ingenuity," he wrote. "The price of their labour is very near as high as at London or Paris. Rather than work for moderate profit, arising from constant employment, which would comfortably maintain them and their families, they choose to starve at home, to lounge about the ramparts, bask themselves in the sun, or play at boules in the streets from morning till night" (172).

I think about this last quote every time I'm at the beach. On occasion, while the kids are at school in the afternoon, I'll take a book to the beach to read. I carry a striped cushioned mat and will lie out with my clothes serving as a folded-up pillow. If I've given it enough forethought, I'll put my swimsuit on for an occasional dip in the sea. Otherwise, I'll remove my shirt or strip down to my underwear and hope that my sun basking and afternoon torpor doesn't end in a less-than-productive nap.

Smollett's certitude often feels like an accusatory slap when I'm confronted with the leisurely pace of life here. But as my French friends are apt to remind me, I probably wouldn't love Nice so much were I cloistered in an office during the working hours of the day. The very conditions of my presence allow that I'm free to make decisions regarding how I spend my time. The evening hours when the kids are in bed or the mornings when the rush of school suddenly leaves the apartment quiet and empty are immensely productive for me. But the afternoons when the sea beckons and the sun cuts shadows across the way often see me relinquish my duties in exchange for a couple hours of soaking up some vitamin D.

The implications of Smollett's economics are still present in Nice. I've often talked to shopkeepers or realtors or restaurateurs about growing their businesses. Wouldn't lowering their prices and building their clientele lead to larger scale and possibilities for expansion? Yes, but it would also mean more work, more time away from family, more stress. Their restaurant may only accommodate a handful of people but the alternative would mean giving up their Saturdays and hiring more workers. Sure it could improve their bottom line, but it would disturb the work-life balance that brought them to Nice in the first place. Better to lounge around, bask in the sun, play a couple rounds of boules and sip a little pastis. This place engenders principles of les décroissants. It's made for it. What's more money when life is as good as this?

One sun-loving retiree regularly greets me whenever I trek down to Castel either alone or with my family in tow. He's skinny with walnut-colored skin and almost white hair. He wears aviator sunglasses and his resting face is one that seems to be perpetually smiling, his teeth the unnatural white of dentures. Every day he sits on a beach mat right on the rocks and reads the paper. He is rarely not there and he stays out as long as the sun is shining. I've come once in the early afternoon and again with the kids after school and we'll pick up parts of earlier conversation like I had been there the whole time. We've talked politics (Macron is an opportunist, Trump a lunatic), environmentalism (why do your kids pick up trash all the time?), and fishing (you know I've lived next to the sea my whole life and never once gone diving).

I don't know his name and I don't want to; it would weirdly formalize a relationship that functions well enough without it. Once, he asked me where I was from. I told him: I'm originally from Canada. "Never say that," he said. "You are either Canadian or you are not!" Saying that I was originally from somewhere implied that I had transitioned away, that I had forgotten or was ashamed to belie my roots. He, for one, was Niçois. Forever Niçois. And like generations of Niçois before him, he had perfected the art of surviving from day-to-day without giving up a healthy chunk of leisure time. What was always striving for something but an acknowledgment of lack?

As a destination for so many career-driven, over-achieving expatriates, Nice becomes an ironic choice for them to call home. It's an expensive real estate market, one that usually excludes people like us. It's people who have amassed a lifetime of wealth and who pay cash to buy property and move here, an attitude that can put them at odds with the Niçois. Sometimes outsider presence creates tension, as politicians try to cater to this privileged demographic without listening to the locals. The most egregious of these in Old Nice is the currently-under-construction Hotel du Couvent, a five-star renovation project that could fundamentally alter the composition of our neighborhood. My sun-loving friend has lived his whole life in Old Nice and he barely recognizes the exclusive neighborhood it has become.

When he was growing up, he explained to me, the Hotel du Couvent was an actual functioning convent and his apartment overlooked their gardens. Every day, the nuns would come out and dig and plant and weed their vegetables, the only glimpse anyone would ever have of them. "One of the nuns was allowed to come outside," he said. "And she had to buy everything for the rest of them." The convent has since closed down. In the 80s, the gardens became a boulodrome and a small concrete soccer field. But now the stone convent has degraded, chinks in the stones gradually sprouting weeds, the windows gone black.

The new hotel plans include a full renovation of the convent but also construction of several floors on top of the already existing structure. This means that the buildings across the street will suffer with a blocked view and a loss of privacy. Most of all it means a change in the clientele and nature of the quarter. Will the adjacent low-income housing disappear? What about the drug dealers who hang out near the Snug? Gentrification isn't as swift in France as it is in the US and I worry that the change will lead to tension and not progress. What kind of client would want to stay in a five-star hotel in the middle of the Old Town if not the tourist hung up on a romanticized vision of French village life? All it would take would be a few muggings, a flag-waving protest, or a megaphone from one of the apartments across the street for the hotel to realize that they had made a gross miscalculation. We don't want you here. And yet, those tourists would likely come to experience exactly the life that we were pushing to protect.

As immigrants, we are constantly aware of this conundrum. We have invested in this community, have endowed it with the power to transform our future selves. We want the quarter to retain its bohemian charm, to remain affordable to the artists, restaurateurs, and musicians who call it home. But our very presence threatens the quarter's identity. We are different, and we have brought with us ideas and values that could entice others like us to come here. The Niçois have reason to be afraid of Jean de Florette.

Then why do we feel so at home?

This is where I tell you: our plan worked out. We finished the apartment. Every doorknob and latch, every caulked baseboard and installed fixture attested to our apartment's completion. Done. And in the process, we secured renters for the following year before we'd return to this place, re-enroll our children in the public schools where they'd find their old friends and catch up the six months they'd missed. To rent the apartment, I found myself in the position of Old Nice booster. I relayed all the cultural amenities and proximity to the sea. This could be their ideal haven. Why would they want to stay anywhere else? Still, before renting it a family wanted more specifics. How was the community with bi-racial families? "I'm black," she wrote to me. "My husband is white." So I told her what I had seen: our community of Old Nice was full of biracial families, of people from different social, ethnic, and religious backgrounds. If there was any community in the south of France that would welcome a bi-racial American family, this would be it. She said thank you and rented our apartment.

I had the chance to meet the Browns later on the following year. They decided that they wanted to extend their time in Nice so they rented another apartment after our arrival. Their son was in Dio's class in school and they quickly became friends. At his birthday party, we talked about their experience so far. "We're actually looking for an apartment now," she said. "We want to move here permanently." Not only that, in the interim, as they tried to alter their employment situations and work out logistics, they decided that they would move from the Boston suburbs to a more affordable city center, like Baltimore or Philadelphia, places with public French immersion charter schools. They needed to downsize. Experience over money. Vive les décroissants.

Something about the Browns' interactions with people, their time living in this place, made them want to change their lives. They may have come here with idealistic expectations, no doubt buoyed by my own enthusiastic endorsement, but that idealism led to a willingness to try a less consumer-driven way of living. People may come here wanting what they see advertised—the cobblestone streets and pastel colors and trompe l'oeil paintings—but those romanticized images aren't diminished but complemented by their interactions with the environment. In some ways, Old Nice has come to exemplify inclusion. The leisurely pace of life and the willingness to experience other cultures—these are the values at its bohemian heart. It's no wonder that Old Nice is the political and social center of left-leaning institutions like the PCF. Due to its high retiree population, Nice is often considered a conservative city. The youth and artistic vibrancy of Old Nice differs from the neighborhoods like Cimiez or Mont Boron. Old Nice could accommodate a five-star hotel as long as it's also willing to accommodate immigrants, lower-income housing, and the LGBTQ community. I can think of no better location to explore the idiosyncrasies of race, culture, and income distribution than this place.

Our own experiences with compromise are ongoing. I finally got to see the inside of the PCF apartment. The two women to whom I introduced myself were both PCF employees, members of the party who wanted to disentangle themselves from the abandoned apartment in our building that had so long been a drag on their finances. Now, they clicked photos and wrote in notebooks as they surveyed the apartment and its contents. Their plan was this: in a month, a mover would come by and haul everything away to the dump. Anything reusable or of intellectual or monetary value would go with the current PCF Youth president. All the rest? Refuse. After that, a real estate appraiser would come by to make a full estimate and disclosure. By then they should have a price, a rough idea of how much the apartment would cost and if we could divide it among two different parties.

I didn't entirely know what to expect when I entered the old PCF Youth offices. Cécile had said that there was "rien" inside, meaning no dedicated bedrooms or kitchen/bathrooms. It wasn't habitable. But "rien" was far from what I saw. Newspapers, old books, toppled filing cabinets, and stained futons filled the space. Melamine desks with PCs from the 90s sat against walls covered with posters and old protest placards: *Violence faites aux femmes assez! Quelle connerie la guerre. Une femme n'est pas une marchandise.* Photos of Fidel Castro and Che Guevarra competed with shelves overflowing with boxes of documents and spray-painted PCF stencils. It was definitely not "rien" inside but instead a surfeit of stuff.

The two women seemed exasperated or embarrassed by the disarray. They saw hours of cleaning, money draining out of their communist coffers to pay for movers and disposal, an electrician for the faulty wiring. But we were ecstatic. The rooms, although arbitrarily divided up, had features like original tomettes and moldings. The ceilings were fifteen feet high. A mezzanine already existed in the main room, perfect for an over-the-kitchen study. The back section was a little more disappointing. Besides sheetrocking over all the windows, the PCF had installed a false ceiling, making it cramped, spare, and nondescript, like some underground Soviet interrogation room. A huge painted red hammer-and sickle filled one wall and the other looked like it was caked in dried human vomit, giving me an idea of the kind of "betises" that the PCF youth may have been up to.

Outside, I thanked the women for letting us see the apartment. I told her about my book. "I've been wondering what's down there for the past year," I said. I also wanted to know—did she have an idea of its history? Why the PCF youth moved there in the first place? She would ask around, she said. We exchanged contact information. As soon as the estimation came in, they would let us know.

Although all my interactions with the PCF thus far had be amicable, giving me every indication that the PCF was willing to sell, our neighbors Sam and Vincent were suspicious.

"I talked to them too," Sam said. "It seemed like they were hiding something. Holding back." She described a conversation she had with Cécile where she seemed to want to put some distance between them. "I'll call you," Cécile had told her. Sam was sensitive to the subtext. What she was *really* saying was not to bother her again. Was this before or after the PCF cleaned out the apartment? I asked. It was before. So I doubted her conclusion. They were waiting for information that they couldn't give us yet. We would know soon enough.

Putting it off also avoided the more complicated conversations that we'd need to have once the PCF was ready to sell. Dividing up the property would create some logistical headaches. We would need to hire a lawyer to divide it and re-issue the paperwork, a process that could take months. The syndic would then need to vote on how to divide the co-op payments. The syndic and the city both had to approve the division. In other words, more work.

But for now, everyone was willing. We could reach a compromise. The magic ingredients of time and exposure would eventually result in its division which was resolution enough. Till then, we could plan and wait.

Chapter 46

Surfacing

I WANTED TO GO SPEARFISHING one last time before the end of the summer and our return to the states. I was at the height of my ability, diving deeper and more effortlessly than ever before. I no longer had to pinch my nose and blow air to equalize my ears and instead dove directly to the bottom of the sea, my body regulating itself. But the weather the last few days had been windy, the currents strong. My favorite fishing spots from Castel to the vièrge were milky and rough. But the pier out to the lighthouse looked passable. I gathered up my gear. Now I had a reusable Carrefour bag that I filled with my orange pancake buoy, my wetsuit, my gloves and neoprene socks. My diving fins jackknifed out at odd angles. In my corded backpack, I carried my weights, my mask, the waterproof bag, and my diving knife. I still held my speargun out in the open like a walking stick or a baton, the top protected by a cork. I alternated arms every block or so, heading out to the Cours, then the Promenade, then up around Rauba Capeu to the Port. A walkway led along the parking lot down the rocks to the lighthouse. Here, square blocks of concrete shored up the pier. Some barely protruded from the sea, providing flat platforms for laying out my equipment and getting in and out of the water with ease. Today the current pushed along perpendicular to them, sending waves cresting over top. But I'd been out in similar weather and the sea looked clear enough.

A Corsica ferry was approaching, a boat the size of a cruise ship. The boats used to scare me—concerns about getting sucked into the engines or churned about in its wake—but I'd endured countless ferry dockings and departures by now. Other than the constant low buzz of the engine noise, the experience was fairly benign.

So I got in.

It was warm—too warm—even in my shorty wetsuit, and I'd need to dive deep to cool off. I started out at the point where various species of fish occupied different depths. Near the shore, schools of mulet and saupe nipped at vegetation on the rocks. Further down, sar, labres, and dorades zipped around the square blocks or into holes, out of sight. Where the rocks met the sand, rougets and mabres swam in large schools. I set my buoy and armed my spear then expelled all the CO_2 from my lungs and dove for some chasse à l'agachon. With all the traffic I'd been seeing, I was sure to get at least something to bring home, one last dorade to share with my children, even if the conditions weren't optimal.

A rock partially shielded me from view. A few undesirable labres swam nearby, submarine-like, their fins clapped to their sides. Then I saw the tell-tale wobbling cross of a dorade coming my way.

Once seemingly unobtainable, dorades had become the most common fish I'd catch. They had started traveling in huge schools since about May now, always on the move. Alone, dorades were *mefiant*, easily scared. But in a school, they followed robotically behind the pilot fish, often unaware that I was hiding in the dark. Down about sixty feet now, I waited for the largest dorade to come into view. They were close, but not close enough. If I ventured from my hiding spot, they would detect the movement and steer the school away from me. I had to wait.

And wait.

The school was thinning and the dorades were getting larger. I zeroed in on one that looked like it would pass right by me. It turned its head just slightly, offering up its meaty torso as a target. I fired.

The spear nicked its dorsal fin. It swam away to a rock while the rest of the school scattered. I should have re-armed my spear and tracked it down. But I'd been holding my breath for two minutes now and the fish had swum even deeper. Who knew if I'd even be able to find him again? I cursed my bad luck and kicked up to the surface.

The Corsica Ferry was before me, just coming into the mouth of the Port. People lined the decks with their arms resting on railings. I would be some kind of sideshow for them—welcome to Nice!—evidence that Nice was a city that accommodated all sorts of different activities. I kept fishing, noting the clouds of turbulence in the water, the occasional bit of seaweed or algae churned up as the ferry turned into place. I always hoped in vain that the incoming ferry would also send schools of liches or pelamides my way, larger fish that I rarely saw except on occasion out at la vièrge. Seeing these fish was always breathtaking, a reminder that the sea could support life forms as large as my own. But all the fish today seemed unusually skittish. Plus I was having more and more difficulty remaining stationary on the sea floor.

The currents were too strong.

I surfaced again. The waves were much larger than the cloudy wake from the ferry. In a half an hour, the sea had changed constitution so drastically that I felt like I'd been plunged back into a winter storm. The direction had shifted. No longer did the current hit the pier indirectly. Now waves crashed against the flat rocks, foaming the water up to the lighthouse. All around me, the sea crested and broke. I felt like a surfer waiting for a wave. No problem. Sometimes a change in the currents resulted in more fruitful fishing. Once I was caught in a small afternoon squall and suddenly there were octopi and cuttlefish where there had been none before.

So I dove. And dove again.

Still no fish. I was starting to get pushed around under water, the currents sweeping down into the rocks. Usually this didn't affect fishing much as long as I didn't force myself unnaturally against the current or make any sudden moves. Today the fish seemed to know I was there. Since the first dorades, I hadn't seen anything of size. Maybe I could get a couple rouget. The kids always liked the nice individual fish on their plate, just right for a tasty kiddie meal.

Nothing. I was getting bounced around like I was in a washing machine and the water was foaming out further, messing up my visibility and aim. I dove down one last time for my buoy and I tucked the line into my weight belt.

The rocks were covered in foam now, way too dangerous for climbing out if I didn't want to get bashed against them. I'd have to find another way.

At the beginning of the Port was a small rocky beach with a railing and stairs that led bathers into the water. If I could swim to it, I might have a chance.

I was against the current. Each kick felt like I was pushing through sand. I inched my way down the pier, my breaths coming heavy through my snorkel. One kick, two. Below me the fish were like residents in an apoca-lyptic movie, ducking into crevices or holes. When the railing at the begin-ning of the pier came into view, my legs were cramping and a slick layer of sweat mixed with sea water coated the inside of my wetsuit.

I disarmed my spear. I let the waves carry me in. I lunged forward, then stalled. The next wave sent me forward again. I would have to grab and then hold on to the railing while the water sucked me back down. I just hoped I didn't drop my speargun in the process.

No time to think. With the last swell of the wave I latched on to the ladder, flipped myself around and dug in my heels. The wave pulled at me. I felt the fullness of my terrestrial weight and almost buckled under my lactic-acid-saturated thighs. I pushed up to the next rung, then up again and again till I was on the rock. I took off my fins and moved back further to where the waves could no longer get me. I coiled the orange line of my buoy around its plastic spool.

But there was no buoy.

When the spearfisher encouraged me to get a buoy, he touted the practical nature of it, the way it could give me more freedom and flexibility. I could put all my gear in a water-tight bag, making it so that I could end up wherever I wanted to without having to always return back to the same spot to recuperate my gear. The solution seemed optimal: keep all your possessions with you like a solitary hermit crab. But now I was without my buoy and everything stashed in my waterproof bag: my sandals, my t-shirt, my keys to get back in the apartment. I examined the severed end of my lifeline to these articles. It looked like it had been cut. Had some opportunist angler broken the unwritten rule of fishing and tried to steal another angler's catch? I hadn't seen any. But where was my fluorescent buoy with its attached (and empty!) accroche-poissons and bag of gear? Someone must have seen it. I gathered together my fins and speargun and ventured further down the pier.

A police boat rounded the point navigating through the swells. I waved to them.

"Bonjour," I said. "Did you happen to see a buoy?"

"These are no conditions to be fishing. Were you fishing out here?"

I told them yes, yes I was. Then it got rough so I headed in.

"You know it's drapeau rouge today. All the beaches are closed."

"I didn't know that."

"Your buoy is over at the base nautique."

"Where's that?"

"The other side of the Port."

The guys sped off in the boat, looking pissed. I felt like a toddler being reprimanded. I had violated yet again some unwritten French rule of behavior. But they were right. "Drapeau rouge" probably wasn't the best time to go spearfishing. Rules helped ensure that I wouldn't hurt myself. It wasn't like "après-ski" boots or scarves during the winter to stave off colds, things that sometimes seemed like unnecessary precautions. Fishing during drapeau rouge put my personal safety at risk, and by association, the security and well-being of my family. Now I was here, feeling very visible in my wetsuit and snorkel, holding aloft my naked spear like some sort of truce flag.

I climbed up the rocks and then took the stairs to the Promenade. I walked carefully, avoiding any jagged edges or broken glass that could harm my bare feet. When I got to the top, the white stone gave way to black pavement and I jumped like I'd stepped on hot coals. Putting my fins back on would make walking a chore, so I pulled my gloves onto my feet like oversized toe socks. I walked down the dock and the fingers flapped with every step. Eventually I made it to the Lou Passagin ferry and I waited in line with tourists till the bohemian skipper nosed the navette into place.

"J'ai perdu ma bouée," I told him when he helped me on board. Did he know where the base nautique was? The pompiers had picked it up.

"C'est juste derrière le Port." He gestured with one hand, keeping the other on the tiller. It looked like he was waving at the Corisca ferry. All right, then. I'd just head in that direction and then ask for more help.

A retired couple of tourists were the only others on the boat. They wore hiking boots and backpacks and carried ski-pole-like walking sticks in each hand. Americans. I chatted with the skipper in French, waiting to hear if the Americans would comment on my garb, the diving gloves on my feet. But the only thing that impressed me was their silence. I was in a port town by the sea, after all. What was more normal than a guy in a wetsuit? My behavior was no more bizarre than dogs eating their kibble at restaurants or having to pay to use public bathrooms.

The skipper dropped us off and I flapped my gloved feet up the stairs and across the blacktop to the lines of cars driving up to the ferry. At the gate, a yellow-vested woman stood with three similarly dressed men. What have we here? they said. Hey Jacques Cousteau, what can we do for you? I told them about my buoy, and that I needed to get to the base nautique.

"You were out spearfishing in this?"

"You must be brave."

"Or *tarré*."

"We have to finish loading but then you can go through."

"Where was the base nautique exactly?" I asked.

"Just over there, behind the Port." I still had no idea where exactly "behind the Port" was. Wasn't all of this behind the Port? I knew this area well and couldn't think of anything that I would describe as a base nautique. There was the stone yacht club and the newly-renovated La Reserve restaurant and then the beginning of the coves and rocks of Coco Beach, nothing that would qualify as a nautical base.

Now one of the guys was arguing with the woman. He had the black curly hair and accent of a North African, probably Algerian or Tunisian. He was saying how much he admired women but that they shouldn't be seeking employment that was more prestigious than their male partner's. The woman found this ridiculous. Now he was saying that he loved women—I mean he had two kids, how could he not?—somehow equating his ability to produce biological children with respecting a woman's right to pursue whatever employment suited her.

"Attends," he said, when he felt her anger rising. "You see great men in the world and every time there is a great woman behind him. But she is behind. She understands it is her place to be his support."

"Tu vas trop loin là," I said. You go too far. I couldn't help myself. Me, this outsider baking in the Mediterranean sun with his speargun and diving mask and snorkel on his head and neoprene gloves on his feet felt that this man's opinions were sexist and informed by culture not biology.

"You must forgive my friend," one of the guys said. "It's just the way he sees things."

But I couldn't stop. The woman wanted to hear what I had to say. Did they know that the most effective way to bring third world countries out of poverty was to grant more rights and autonomy to women? So many examples existed today of the inverse of what he was talking about. Take Hillary Clinton for example.

The guy started to laugh. He waggled a finger at me. "Hillary Clinton is not a woman."

"Not a woman?" I wanted to know what he meant. But now there was movement at the Ferry. Gates were closing, the big yellow boat was gliding away from the dock. The man shrugged off my protests and then waved me through. I could go on to the base nautique now. The woman who had been engaged in the heated discussion said "bravo" and wished me a good day.

What did he mean about Hillary Clinton not being a woman? Was it because she accepted her husband's dalliances? A kind of cuckolding that somehow negated her sex? Or was it something about her invisibility, a loss of sexual attractiveness brought about by the combination of age, education, fiscal and political power that emasculated the men around her? So bizarre. Our conversation showed me how difficult it can be to change or even moderately understand the cultural forces that shape our experience of relationships and gender. And we weren't exempt. My own marriage and current situation highlighted my accomplishments and diminished my spouse's, yet she was the one who has always had the most intellectual and fiscal promise. While I graduated from high school and college with better than average grades, a passable ACT, and an eclectic mix of extracurricular and service experience, she was one of two women in the US her year who achieved a perfect score on her SATs. She was a violin performance major and could've gone on to a career as a violinist if she so wished. She has perfect pitch, complete financial independence at age eighteen, enabled through multiple scholarship offers and grants. Then graduate school with prestigious fellowships, offers to edit and publish her dissertation.

And then? We decided to have children. She continued to publish and work part time in academia, but her resume had gaping holes, one every two years for the past eight that corresponded to our children's births. Meanwhile, I had secured a job at a selective small liberal arts college, the Holy Grail for many writers with an MFA or PhD in creative writing, published three books, and gotten tenure. My visibility was greater than ever while Rixa was slipping into a supporting role. And even though I told her over and over that I'd be willing to be the primary care giver and let her pursue her professional goals, we had young children at home. Ivy was still nursing. For Rixa, pursuing her career didn't make sense till all the kids were in school.

And now, here we were, in France, living out some romanticized expatriate dream for which I was largely responsible. While my wife picked up the kids from school and took care of Ivy, I wrote in my room, worked on home renovations, or went spearfishing. When I asked Rixa what the most significant challenges of our year were, most came down to childcare. During the year, Ivy had difficulty sleeping and she would often wake up in the middle of the night to nurse. Sometimes she'd scream so much that she'd make herself puke. During renovations it was even worse; Rixa would have to cram in the back bedroom with the tub skirt crowding the bed amid dust, endless dust, coating every surface. Even as progressive academics we had somehow not avoided certain cultural traditions of our genders. The woman is behind. So as I walked to the base nautique, my gloved feet slapping the pavement, I felt like a hypocrite.

A muscular guy in a black speedo greeted me at the entrance. The base nautique looked temporary, a series of squat tented structures and one trailer formed an L with a dock protruding out into the Port. I explained: I had lost my buoy while spearfishing and a police boat told me to come here to get it. Had he seen anything like that?

"You're lucky to be alive. We found that buoy almost an hour ago. Those police you met were searching for your body."

"Sorry, it must have broken off sometime while I was swimming to try to get back to shore."

Mr. Baywatch had some papers for me to sign, a description of the buoy's contents to fill out. It was all just protocol, he said, something they had to do whenever they recovered lost items. He started to explain: usually when a buoy floated in the open like that, they expected the worst. It came into the mouth of the Port, blown and tossed by the sea. He was admonishing me again, asking why I was out on a day like today.

"I'm going back to the states soon and I wanted to get a last spearfishing trip in."

"You're from the US?"

Canadian, but that's where I lived now.

He was surprised. In all his years working with the sapeur pompiers, he'd never met a North American spearfisher. Just not something we usually came over here to do. But then, we weren't here for a two-week vacation but had planned to partially raise our children here. Then it all came out, a summary of our whole plan. We bought an apartment so that we'd have a permanent address and we could put our children back in French public school. This way, our kids would have at least three-seven months in Nice during their formative language-acquisition years. Our ideal, and what we hoped to achieve, was a six-months on, six-months off contract with the current institution where I taught, thus enabling us to split our time between France and the US and secure true bilingualism for our children.

"Won't that be difficult for your kids?"

Not really, I explained. It took care of many of the hurdles that itinerant families had to cope with: making new friends, following a different curriculum, integrating into a new environment. With our plan, our kids would find themselves back with their old friends, renewing acquaintances and returning to places that were already familiar to them. While I recounted the benefits of raising bilingual children and living in two cultures, Mr. Baywatch nodded and smiled.

"Sounds like a good plan."

"It is."

"As long as you don't screw it up."

The dinghy full of divers motored in to the dock and they hopped out, one after the other. I recognized them as the crew that directed me over to the base nautique. These were my potential saviors, the guys who churned through rough seas looking for evidence of an asphyxiated spearfisher submerged in the water. I could've been anywhere: stuck on the bottom with a bit of rope caught around my ankle or floating near the top after hitting my head on a rock. I could sense relief but also resentment. This was the fool they'd been looking for all this time?

Mr. Baywatch helped the guys off the boat and returned with my buoy and waterproof sack. Everything was as it should have been: my keys, my cork, my crappy t-shirt and sandals. My reusable shopping bag for my wetsuit and weights. I picked through my belongings and changed into my clothes while the men unloaded their gear. When I left, Mr. Baywatch shook my hand. "Good luck with your plan," he said.

I had to hustle during my walk of shame. I was coming home an hour later than usual and Rixa would be worried. The whole ordeal had cost me time but even more, it had cost me pride. While I touted the benefits of buying a home in Old Nice and living here on and off the next several years, I also felt the sting of Mr. Baywatch and the rest of the sapeur pompier team's disapproval. I had put our good plan at risk. Why would I do something so stupid when there was so much at stake? I was a father with four young children and a spouse whom I adored. We lived in Nice, France and

wfordsville, Indiana. Every time I recounted these facts to people, I was
.....azed at how well they were received, how they didn't doubt that someone like me could live in both these places at once. "It must be nice to be
rich," a truck driver in Crawfordsville told me. And I thought, an academic
in the humanities, rich? But I was rich, rich in the sense that I was able to do
what I set about doing. Rich because I lived in a world that validated an experience like my own. Rich because the world assumed that I must be rich,
a person with an education and four children dividing his time between
the US and the south of France. The only other people I knew of with such
large families who came year after year were people like Angelina Jolie and
Brad Pitt. Living out our plan had suddenly thrown us into a privileged
demographic, rocketing past the doctors and lawyers and investment bankers and dot-commers who earned multiple times what I could ever hope to
earn, who could afford homes here and in the US if only they had the time
to enjoy it. But one look at our kids' threadbare hand-me-downs or our bat-
tered car or my glue-gunned sandals and people would question. Was this
guy for real? Why if we were so loaded did we dress like the working poor?

These assumptions compounded the shame I felt when confronted
with the lived realities of other large immigrant families in France. Before
we left, we visited the prefecture once again, this time to renew our one-
year visitor visas for us and our children. Since we would be returning
regularly for more than the legal three-month tourist visa, it made sense
to continue our residency here, to eventually work our way to the coveted
carte de sejour, the French equivalent to a Green Card. And then afterward,
who knew? Maybe we'd even become fully vested members of the 5ème
République. Our treatment again was the same. We waited in line with the
Tunisians, the Senegalese, the Moroccans, and Malgache. We wore shorts
and summer dresses while Muslim women perspired in their hijabs and
abayas. A woman and her husband in front of us were told, you don't have
the right document. You need a *timbre fiscal*. You'll have to come back. The
man began arguing with the woman at the desk behind the plate glass. I
felt shame when a security guard escorted them away and we approached
the desk next with our smiling child and were given a number and told,
right this way please. I wanted to say: take us! We are undeserving! But
our papers were in order and we had waited three hours in line for this
moment. Those few brief conversations and stamps and ceremony were
the beginning of a trajectory, a path toward citizenship that would open a

world of possibility for our young family. For us, France signified a richness in education and culture, opportunities for our children down the road. But for the couple being led away, it signified survival, access to the basic necessities of life.

When I got home with a bag dripping from my wetsuit and my super-glued sandals and my shirt that I found on the bottom of the sea, Rixa was sitting in a chair, getting her hair done by Kahina, the Muslim woman who had approached Rixa about meeting for English conversation. They had struck up a relationship over the past couple months. She talked to Rixa in English and Rixa talked to her in French while our children played together at the coulée verte. Now her four kids and our four kids were crowded in the attic watching *Le Château Ambulant*, a Miyazaki film while Kahina turned my wife's hair into a steampunk wonder.

"I was about to call the police," Rixa said.

"Sorry, I lost my buoy. The saupeurs-pompiers picked it up. I had to walk to the other side of the Port to get it."

Kahina's fingers wove and teased, like a bird building a nest. She was a hair dresser by trade, even though she concealed her own hair with a hijab whenever I was around. Kahina crimped, pinned, and curled my wife's hair into ringlets.

"Every time you leave, I prepare for the worst," Rixa said.

While I was off spearfishing, Rixa had invited someone into our home. It was something we'd become accustomed to. This year, we'd had visits from friends and family and months of HelpXers. Besides the people who lived with us, we had also invited friends for birthday parties and get-togethers for any number of reasons. At Ivy's birthday party we counted six nationalities: Irish, East Indian, Dutch, French, Turkish, Canadian, and American. I'd been a part of all of these groups, dutifully helping in their genesis and developing friendships. But I'd also been partially underwater, living the meditative seclusion that a writer seeks, holding my breath, waiting to surface.

What would our apartment, our French dive signify? When we visited Carol Shields's house, we found a guest book going back several years where visitors would express their thanks for being invited to stay. I thought, this is what the Château Pulitzer meant to Carol Shields: a place to share freely with others, so they could know the beauty and happiness that she felt there with her family. James Baldwin, who like us chose the sunny south of France, used his home in St. Paul de Vence to welcome marginalized others.

I'm particularly drawn to these two examples as I think of how to configure our place in the world: one, as a place for family and friends that builds collective memory; the other as a haven for people unlike ourselves. Already nooks, furniture, even the pictures on the walls have accumulated meaning for our young family. A red starfish and a green sea turtle, each formed from colored sea glass that my children found after raking through pebbles with their tiny hands, now decorate a glimmering attic space, made bright by Phillippe's LEDs and Michele's careful layers of white paint. Johnny's painting of colonial-era boats with the words "Boys on Tour" that I first saw in his apartment now hangs in our living room. Our mahogany Throne of Peace has held our children's young bodies as they tied on their shoes. Imperfections: a crack in the ceiling plaster, a dime-sized welt in a stair tread, the lines outside our windows stretched from drying laundry: all attest to the presence of children, the passage of time. In a corner of our attic, directly above the narrow hallway, a two-foot-wide platform now served as Ivy's bed, a place where she'd finally sleep so soundly that each morning we'd have to crawl into bed to shake her awake.

We'd mark events and seasons, altering our cuisine Américaine to accommodate others. I'd startle Kahina here cooking dinner and then serving her and Rixa before the rest, a man knowing it was his place to be behind. It's where I'd see in a couple years' time, Rixa's career finally realized, the bottling up of potential energy finally boiling over, sending her to Greece, Russia, the UK, the Netherlands, and all around the US to educate health professionals about breech birth.

More important still were the talismans of childhood socked and stored away in the apartment and rediscovered every year: a blue butterfly preserved in an ebony-and-glass case, a wooden sailboat with toothpick-sized masts and rigging, a glowing yo-yo that lit up when you threw it. And the detritus treasures my children amassed and couldn't part with: a hard plastic doll's head rolled smooth as it purled through the waves, a silver worm-shaped fishing lure with its basket of hooks, a brass sauropod dinosaur knocked loose from its keychain and found among the rocks.

Baldwin said "I am a stranger everywhere." On the St. Paul de Vence website, I'd find a video of Baldwin walking around the streets of Old Nice not far from our apartment while children rolled balls or strolled beside him, wondering who was this black man with his manners and accent? We'd be similarly visible, the eternal strangers, cast into a role that we didn't yet understand. Our apartment could never answer the question of our own or others' difference, but it would be alive with our striving. We renovated our apartment and transformed a dive into a haven, a place for Jad, Phillippe, Jean and Adilah, Connor and Michele, Kahina, my parents, my brother, all those people who we have met and who we have yet to meet: anyone who we can accommodate, anyone who needs a place to stay. Our apartment belongs to all of us.

And now, dear reader, it belongs to you.

Acknowledgments

I'M GRATEFUL TO SO MANY FOR INFLUENCING and advising me on this book. I thank my colleagues at Wabash College for their support in the book's early stages. For Marc Hudson and Warren Rosenberg who encouraged us to first take the plunge, for my brother Kent Freeze who deciphered Flyertalk and found the ticket that led to this adventure. For Bart, realtor extraordinaire. For all the friends and neighbors who welcomed us to Nice, for Sam and Vincent, Cass and Fabrice and Ash and Allie, for Damien and Rindra and Tiernan and Gosia, for Jérémy Guedj and Phillippe Ribot at Cavigal Football. For Mourad and Laurent for all the fishing advice. For Johnny Gent, an artistic collaborator, and for all the books and writers who whether they knew it or not helped me get the words down. A special thanks to Anne Giardini and the Carol Shields family, for House Hunters International, and Pam Houston and the Mont Blanc seminars for giving me a boost when I needed it most.

I'd also like to thank my editor Gregory Wolfe and Slant Books and for all the editors at the literary journals and magazines where portions of this book have appeared, for Steve Charles at *Wabash Magazine* and Sarah Strickley at *Miracle Monocle*, and Jill Patterson at *Iron Horse Literary Review*.

And finally, my thanks to you, for picking up this book and thumbing through its pages, for letting me invite you into my home.

This book was set in Arno Pro, designed by the American typographer, Robert Slimbach, for Adobe Systems. Named for the river that runs through Florence, Italy, Arno Pro is a contemporary adaptation of type styles that flourished at the height of the Renaissance Humanist movement.

This book was designed by Shannon Carter, Ian Creeger, and Gregory Wolfe. It was published in hardcover, paperback, and electronic formats by Wipf and Stock Publishers, Eugene, Oregon.